"*Jesus Speaking* encourages
it to your life. Each devotic
minutes to read. It's the per

—Chris Broussard
Founder/President, The K.I.N.G. Movement
NBA analyst and sports broadcaster

"I had the privilege of working with Mike Lutz in ministry for a couple of years, during which time I came to appreciate his simple, straightforward walk with the Lord. In *Jesus Speaking*, Mike mines from the very words of the Savior the encouraging principles you'll need to face life every day. This book will freshen up your spiritual walk."

—Skip Heitzig
Pastor of Calvary Church, Albuquerque, New Mexico
Author of The Bible from 30,000 Feet

"Mike serves up fresh-brewed wisdom and encouragement through thought-provoking daily devotions, reminding us of the sufficiency of Jesus and His grace."

—Miles McPherson
Founder and Senior Pastor of the Rock Church, San Diego, California
Former NFL defensive back, author, and motivational speaker

"It is my deep conviction that through the Bible, God tells us both who He is and how He is. *Jesus Speaking* is a compelling devotional that focuses on the words and teachings of Jesus Christ, the *who* and *how*. I pray that all who read this book will find a deeper relationship with God, prepare themselves for the challenges of this world by studying the Bible, and enjoy the blessings of following Jesus!"

—James Mead
Guitarist for Kutless

"In this beautiful devotional, Mike Lutz allows readers to first experience the magnificent, all-powerful words of Christ and then offers thoughtful meditations on those words. You will undoubtedly be blessed as you read!"

—Ginny Owens
Dove Award-winning singer and songwriter

"*Jesus Speaking* is greatly needed in our world today. It is simple, gospel centered, and theologically sound. My friend Mike takes the words straight from Scripture, and that is always relevant! There's no extra fluff. It's straight from the Bible and straight to the point!"

—*Shane Pruitt*
National Next Gen Evangelism Director, North American Mission Board (NAMB)
Author of 9 Common Lies Christians Believe

"At a time when a million things are clamoring for our attention and dedication, it has never been more important to listen to the words of Jesus. His words are a guiding lighthouse in the middle of life's storms. I am grateful Mike Lutz is reminding us of the New Testament's 'red letters,' which are as relevant today as when Jesus first spoke them two thousand years ago."

—*Samuel Rodriguez*
New Season Lead Pastor, NHCLC President, author of You Are Next!
Executive Producer, Breakthrough

"For those of us who believe Jesus was the very Word of God, His words must be held in the highest of regard. Mike Lutz has beautifully expounded on one statement of Jesus for each day of the year, providing powerful insights. Mike's thoughts show respect for the validity of all Scripture and the sovereignty of our great God. Prepare to be encouraged, and challenged, with the words spoken by our Savior!"

–*Aaron Shust*
Christian recording artist
Dove Awards Songwriter of the Year, 2007

"How can there be a better devotional than one that points you to the words Jesus actually said? I highly recommend this book if you are looking for some solid spiritual sustenance to start or end your day. Thanks, Mike!"

—*Holly Star*
Recording artist and worship Leader

JESUS
SPEAKING
Daily Encouragement from His Words

MIKE LUTZ

CONTENTS

PREFACE

How spectacular it must have been to walk alongside the Savior, to hang on His every word, to marvel at His every miracle, and to witness His every public conversation. How wonderful it must have been to hear the gently spoken words of healing to hurting souls. How amazing it must have been to see the marvelous light of God radiating from His eyes as words of truth were spoken like never before. How thought-provoking it must have been to listen to His authoritative commands.

The words of Jesus have been wonderfully impactful for millions and have brought life to countless more. They have been water for thirsty souls and food for hungry spirits.

The Bible is filled with the precious, life-changing words of Jesus. As you read and meditate on His words, they will refresh your soul, feed your spirit, and minister to your heart. Though we cannot turn back time to hear firsthand the words of Jesus or witness His life as it unfolded, we can still hear Jesus speaking.

May these daily devotions, taken from the words of Jesus, not only give you a sense of what it was like to hear Jesus speaking during His earthly ministry, but also encourage, refresh, and instruct you each day as you hear Jesus speaking to you.

JANUARY

Christ, Our Role Model

"Why did you seek Me? Did you not know that I must be about My Father's business?" (Luke 2:49 NKJV)

We need role models today as never before, and there is no more magnificent role model than that of Jesus Christ. He is the embodiment of perfection and the visible portrait of God. Even from boyhood He was the paragon of behavior and the quintessential standard for living. From our first encounter with adolescent Jesus in the Bible, He had a clear understanding of His heavenly calling and a focused single-mindedness to fulfill His earthly mission. From adolescence to adulthood, Jesus always purposed to be about His Father's business (see Matthew 6:33; Luke 22:42).

Jesus had a uniquely specific mission and an explicitly tailored calling on His life. And because we were created in the image of God, we, too, have a unique mission and calling specific to our own lives. Our mission and calling highlight our individual gifts and are tailored to our particular talents and personality. Yet despite the diversity of gifts and the variety of personalities in the world, we can still look to Jesus as our role model and serve God with the same focused single-mindedness to be about the Father's business.

Heavenly Father, I have been created in Christ Jesus to do good works that You have prepared for me to walk in. Assist me to both understand my calling and to faithfully complete that which You have equipped me to do.

Jesus is the perfect role model, because He is perfect in every way.

Our Daily Bread

*Jesus answered, **"It is written: 'Man shall not live on bread
alone, but on every word that comes from the mouth of God.' "***
(Matthew 4:4 NIV)

Temptation is real. Just ask Jesus. He marked the beginning of His
public ministry by being baptized in the Jordan River. During this
meaningful event, God gave His approval from heaven by declaring,
"This is My beloved Son, in whom I am well pleased" (Matthew
3:17). Shortly after this event, Satan propositioned Jesus: "If You are
the Son of God, command that these stones become bread" (Matthew
4:3). Satan was not questioning Jesus's deity, but he was attempting to
persuade Jesus to *doubt* in God's provision and to *disobey* God by serving Himself. Satan used the same method against Eve in the Garden
of Eden (Genesis 3:1), and he continues to use these methods against
God's people today.

The enemy of God wants you to doubt God's authority, God's
provision, and God's affection. And the sad reality is that it often
works. Most of us have questioned God's love at one time or another.
We have questioned God's provision in our lives, and we have questioned God's timing, which means that we have questioned His
authority. Doubts like these, left unchecked and uncorrected, can
lead to selfish solutions that only *temporarily* satisfy. So the next time
you're tempted by the Enemy to doubt God, go back and feed on the
bread of God's Word.

*Father, forgive me for those times when I have doubted You, when
I have given in to disobedience, and when my doubts have led me
to seek self-serving solutions. Assist me to distinguish and dismiss the
Devil's doubting whispers.*

**Jesus declares the Word of God to be our
strength and our sustenance.**

The Truth Test

*Jesus said to him, **"Again it is written, 'You shall not put the Lord your God to the test.' "** (Matthew 4:7 ESV)*

Don't test God! It sounds simple, right? The fact of the matter is that we all have tested God at one time or another, whether knowingly or unknowingly. It is certainly correct to trust in God's promises. But when we make assumptions as to how and when God should deliver on those promises, we tread dangerously close to testing Him.

For example, we test God when we demand that He does something to prove His love, His power, or His wisdom. We test God when we say, "If God loved me, He would . . ." or "God, if You are real, then . . ." Testing God shows a lack of trust in God, in His Word, and in His sovereignty. God has given us His promises to encourage us and to reassure us; they are not for us to manipulate or strong-arm God into meeting our demands according to the conditions we've set. That is testing God, and that is sinful. Trusting God counters our tendency to test God. We must learn to trust that God will accomplish His will, His way, in His time, and for His glory.

Dear God, You have given me Your promises to comfort me and to give me hope. Your promises are not for me to exploit Your love or abuse your power. My doubts can lead to fear, and fear can lead to a lack of trust. Help me to guard against prayers like this one: "If You'll do this, then I will do that."

Jesus wants us to test less and trust Him more.

What Are You Worshiping?

Then Jesus said to him, **"Be gone, Satan! For it is written, " 'You shall worship the Lord your God and him only shall you serve.'** *" (Matthew 4:10 ESV)*

"You become like what you worship," wrote N. T. Wright. "When you gaze in awe, admiration, and wonder at something or someone, you begin to take on something of the character of the object you worship."[1] If we become like what we worship, then it stands to reason that the sole focus of our awe, admiration, and wonder should now and forever be God.

Satan demonstrates his craftiness by seeking to ever so slightly divert our attention away from God. However, it isn't by enticing us to such sizeable, recognizable sins; those would be easy to identify and, therefore, simpler to resist. Rather, Satan is far more subtle with his bait-and-switch methodology. For example, a prolonged gaze at power can lead to misplaced priorities. An unrestrained curiosity can result in improper pursuits. Innocent flirtations can lead to infatuated relationships. Subtle, slight temptations can lead us down a disorienting path that leads to misguided worship in which we no longer worship that which conforms us into the image of God. Instead, we pursue some lesser imitation or an artificial *imago Dei*.

Lord God, let nothing diminish or take the place of my awe, admiration, and wonder for You. May I never accept artificial substitutes for the true and genuine worship of You. May I forever worship You, Lord, and serve You only.

Jesus is clear that unadulterated worship begins and ends with rightly worshiping God.

Q and A

Then Jesus turned, and seeing them following, said to them, **"What do you seek?"** *(John 1:38)*

What do you seek from Jesus? This is a question that must be asked of everyone who follows Him. Are you looking at Jesus with idle curiosity? Are you looking to Jesus to meet your every need? Are you looking for Jesus to make your life easy and peaceful? Or, are you looking at Jesus with a genuine desire to grow in the knowledge of Him? When Jesus first posed this question to Andrew and John, they answered commendably. They stated they were not seeking what they could get from Jesus but were looking to learn from Him by spending time in His presence.

It is very easy to miss simple opportunities to spend time in the presence of Jesus, worshiping, learning, and growing. All too often we come to Jesus looking for Him to do something for us. How many church services have we weakened because we were seeking to get something *from* worship rather than simply seeking *to* worship? How many of our prayers have been one-sided, asking something of God yet lacking praise or exaltation? It is not wrong to ask things of God, because He tells us to do this. But we should spend more time simply seeking to grow closer to Jesus.

Jesus, Your Word tells me to set my mind and my heart to seek You (1 Chronicles 22:19), knowing that as I seek You, I will find You (1 Chronicles 28:9). May I seek You for the right reasons, may I seek You in the right way, and may I seek You "knowing that in Your presence there is fullness of joy" (Psalm 16:11).

> **With Jesus, life is fullest when He is the center of our affection and attention.**

Jacob's Ladder

"Most assuredly, I say to you, hereafter you shall see heaven open, and the angels of God ascending and descending upon the Son of Man." (John 1:51)

In a surreal conversation with Nathanael that we find in the first chapter of John, Jesus referred to what is commonly called Jacob's ladder. Jacob dreamed that angels were ascending and descending from heaven upon a ladder. When he awoke, he declared, "Surely, the Lord is in this place" (Genesis 28:16). Jesus alluded to the fact that He is the personification of Jacob's dream (see verse 51), meaning that He is humanity's point of contact between the eternal and the finite, the ladder that joins heaven and Earth, and the only bridge between God and man.

This is a beautiful picture of Jesus as our reconciliatory connection to a holy and pure God. Jesus is our bridge to the Father. Therefore, we should never feel that God is unapproachable, because in Jesus we are cleansed from all sins and free to present all our cares and concerns before God, anytime and anywhere. Nothing is too big for God to handle, and nothing is too small to bring to His attention. Jesus is all-sufficient, and because of Him we can approach God in humble assurance and confident justification.

Thank you, Lord Jesus. You are our "Jacob's Ladder." It is upon You and Your work that the angels ascend and descend to accomplish Your purposes, and it is upon You and Your redemptive work that we can meet with God.

> **Apart from Jesus, there is no other ladder to reach God.**

Untangling Our Worship

*And He said to those who sold doves, **"Take these things away! Do
not make My Father's house a house of merchandise!"***
(John 2:16)

God doesn't get angry, does He? Simply put, yes, He does. Just because
God is a God of love doesn't mean that He never gets angry. But God's
anger is not like human anger that is so often tainted by sin. When
God gets angry, He does so with an unadulterated, righteous anger.
Jesus was filled with a holy hatred for the defilement of a sacred place
of worship because it had been turned into an extortive, moneymak-
ing profit center. As a result, He reacted swiftly and decisively. The
worship of business had become more important than the business of
worship, and it negatively impacted the flock of God. This made Jesus
mad. His response was to drive out these money changers and over-
turn their tables. This cleansing was a microcosm of His larger desire
to cleanse religion of its selfish and erroneous practices and remove
worldliness from worship. God gets angry when people pervert or
prevent proper worship.

Today, we are the house of God (see 1 Corinthians 3:16), and
as such we must keep ourselves free from the defiling influences that
might pervert or prevent proper worship in our lives. We must prevent our hearts from becoming like the outer courts that Jesus acted
against, where worship became motivated by self-interest. If anything
is perverting our worship, then Jesus is saying the same to us: "Take
these things away!"

*Lord, I seek to embrace a lifestyle of pure worship that is free from
selfish desires and worldly influences. Fill me with a spirit of genuine
worship, rooted in the beauty of Your holiness.*

**Jesus cares deeply about the purity of our
worship.**

New Birth

"Most assuredly, I say to you, unless one is born again, he cannot see the kingdom of God." (John 3:3)

Nicodemus, a prominent religious leader of his day, thought that salvation meant checking all the right religious boxes: service, tradition, rituals, and liturgy. Jesus's answer was a radical departure from traditional orthodoxy, and it opened a spiritual can of worms that challenged the current religious system. Salvation, Jesus explained, was not obtained through human effort. Rather, it was a work of God, rooted in the authority of God and accomplished through the Spirit of God.

A Nicodemus's understanding of salvation is still common today. It is a type of thinking characterized by the notion that salvation depends on a person's own efforts rather than through a work of God's Spirit. However, the reality is that no amount of willpower can force it, no one is good enough to earn it, and no one is devout enough to deserve it. Obtaining and maintaining salvation are the gracious works of God, imparted through a spiritual rebirth and conceived by belief. We are saved by God's grace, and we are kept by God's grace. Everything *we* do is merely an expression of gratitude for what God already has done for us. Those works don't earn or maintain our salvation.

Heavenly Father, thank you that I can be born into Your spiritual family by simply accepting Jesus and making Him Lord of my life. As Your Spirit has given birth to my spirit, I have become part of the family of God.

> **According to Jesus, you cannot be a Christian unless you are born again.**

All or Nothing

"And as Moses lifted up the serpent in the wilderness . . ."
(John 3:14)

The Old Testament is true and relevant for your life today. Throughout the Gospels we find Jesus validating the Old Testament. He recounts some of the ancient happenings, such as Jonah's experience in the belly of the great fish (Matthew 12:40), the creation account (Mark 10:6; 13:19), the giving of the law through Moses (John 7:19), and the manna provided in the wilderness (John 6:31–51). The meaning is unmistakable: Jesus saw the Old Testament as God's Word, and He had nothing less than absolute confidence in its authority. He repeatedly endorsed its reliability and relatability to present-day living.

You cannot accept Jesus and reject the Old Testament. When it comes to the Bible, it is all or nothing. Accepting Jesus and submitting to His authority means trusting in the totality of Scripture, its inerrancy, its inspiration, and its infallibility. The Old Testament and the New Testament both exist to instruct us about God and cultivate a right relationship with Him. The entire Bible helps us see God clearly, live rightly, and worship properly. The Bible reveals our imperfect nature and provides restoration for all who apply its truths.

Thank you, Lord, for Your Word! It is the light to my every step and the fount that revives my soul. Your Word is perfect, timeless, and trustworthy. It is complete, lacking nothing, and relevant to my modern life. I seek to be attentive to its instruction, applying it to my every situation and allowing it to guide me in all my ways.

Jesus believed that every event in the Old Testament was true and trustworthy.

The Love of God

"For God so loved the world that He gave His only begotten Son, that whoever believes in Him should not perish but have everlasting life." (John 3:16)

God's love for me is astounding. He demonstrated the pinnacle of His love by giving His Son as the rescuing sacrifice to redeem not only me, but all who believe. God's love is intrinsically part of His essence; it is unconditional in nature, sacrificial in action, and infinite in magnitude. God's love for me is based on *His* character and not on anything I say, feel, or do. God's love is not simply something *He does*; it's *who He is.*

God loves me on my good days, and He loves me on my bad days. He loves me when I forsake Him, and He loves me when I follow Him. He loves me when I can feel the warmth of His love, and He loves me when I am numb to His love. There is nothing I can do to make God love me more, and there is nothing I can do to make God love me less. His love is freely given and is to be freely received.

God, Your love is a mysterious and amazing truth. I know that my shortcomings are many and my failings are frequent, but Your love for me is greater than all my slipups and sins.

God's love is perfectly revealed through Jesus's provision to redeem us to Him.

God's Love

"For God so loved the world that He gave His only begotten Son, that whoever believes in Him should not perish but have everlasting life." (John 3:16)

All the plans and purposes of God begin with His love. There would be no creation if not first for God's love for the created. There would be no cross of Christ if not first for God's love for humanity. The universe is not larger than God's love, the ocean is not deeper than God's love, and time can never exhaust God's love. His love is uncontainable, immeasurable, incomprehensible, incontrovertible, and unquenchable. God's love is for every individual, community, and country—past, present, and future. Most importantly, God's love offers eternal life to all who believe.

Jesus declaratively and authoritatively spoke of God's love, but He did more than merely speak of it as some abstract philosophy. Jesus lived out God's love, which culminated in the most loving of all historical acts: His sacrificial, atoning death on the cross. The key that unlocks the riches of God's love in our lives is belief in Jesus. Our relationship begins with belief, and our belief continues to unlock the transformative and sanctifying power of God at work in us (see Mark 11:22–23; Romans 12:1–2).

God, even with all of eternity, I still will be unable to search out the depths of Your love or comprehend the vastness of it. But I know that everything You do originates from Your love, and my faith is the pathway to unlocking and experiencing Your love in a personal and profound way.

Jesus's life was the physical embodiment of God's love.

The Centrality of Christ

"For God loved the world so much that he gave his only Son so that anyone who believes in him shall not perish but have eternal life." (John 3:16 TLB)

There is no escaping the fact that Jesus Christ was on a global mission from God. Jesus is the author and finisher of our faith. All things were made for Him and by Him, and He holds the universe together. Without Him there would be no means of salvation. He is the center of the church and the central theme of the Scriptures. He is also at the center of John 3:16, and this verse is central to the Christian faith.

You cannot think too much of Christ, but you can certainly think too little of Him. The depth of our spirituality is tied to the centrality of Jesus Christ in our lives. If we minimize the centrality of salvation in Jesus alone, then we empty the Cross of it saving power. If we minimize the centrality of Jesus in the church, then we empty the church of its power to rightly worship God and effectively love and serve others. If we minimize the centrality of Jesus in our personal lives, then we inhibit the Holy Spirit's influence and sanctifying power. To avail ourselves of the centrality of Christ in our day-to-day lives, we must keep Christ in the center of it all.

Father, I know that I have not always placed Jesus in the center of all my decisions, all my actions, and all my thoughts. May that serve as a reminder to me, today and always, of how critically important it is to keep Jesus in the center of all my plans, purposes, and pursuits.

The centrality of Jesus cannot be separated from the plans and purposes of God.

No Condemnation

"For God did not send His Son into the world to condemn the world, but that the world through Him might be saved."
(John 3:17)

All too often the unbelieving world sees God as a hotheaded, judgmental, spoilsport who is looking for ways to rain on people's parades with bolts of lightning and pillars of fire. But God is not an angry old man in the heavens, looking for ways to punish people or prohibit their fun by displaying His pyrotechnic powers. Unfortunately, some people associate the salvific work of Jesus the same way, seeing in Jesus Christ's sacrifice only condemnation and judgment. Jesus sought to dispel that misconception by stating that His mission was not one of condemnation but redemption.

Satan would like nothing more than for us to live under the guilt-ridden paralysis of condemnation, unable or unwilling to approach God for fear of being blasted because of our failings. However, when the temptation comes to recoil from God, we should hold up the truth that God is not seeking to condemn us for our imperfections but to rescue us and repair our brokenness.

Father, it's easy to feel that You want to condemn me for my failures, and it's even easier to fall into self-condemnation every time I fail and fall short. I thank You that failure is followed by forgiveness for your children who confess their sin (see 1 John1:9). Forgiveness gives us the freedom to follow Jesus, even with our imperfections.

There is "no condemnation to those who are in Christ Jesus" (Romans 8:1).

Darkness and Light

"The light has come into the world, and men loved darkness rather than light, because their deeds were evil." (John 3:19)

Darkness is the absence of light, cold is the absence of heat, evil is the absence of good, and spiritual darkness is the absence of God in our lives. The One who opened the eyes of the blind can bring anyone out of the darkness and into His marvelous light (see 1 Peter 2:9). No matter how dense the darkness, no matter how cold the heart, no matter how evil the intentions, the light of God's love and truth can shine into the darkest recesses of the human heart and light the way to fullness of life in God.

If you're walking in complete spiritual darkness today or have just wandered off the path into dimly lit spiritual shadows, the answer is to turn from the darkness and walk toward the light. If your thoughts wander in the wrong direction, if your words lean to the objectionable, and if your actions are marked by regret, the remedy is Son light. Darkness cannot drive out darkness; only light does. And only the light of God can drive out spiritual darkness. Keep your eyes fixed on Jesus and your mind set on His truth, and you will be walking in the light.

God, the desires and the pull toward darkness are real. Even though I don't always succeed in resisting the desires of the flesh and the tug toward darkness, I seek to walk in the light as You are in the light. Strengthen me today to walk in the light of Your Word, where there is no darkness or "shadow of turning" (James 1:17).

Jesus is the light that delivers us from a life of darkness.

Jesus Speaking

"If you knew the gift of God, and who it is that is saying to you, 'Give me a drink,' you would have asked him, and he would have given you living water." (John 4:10 ESV)

Hearing God's voice can be challenging in today's social media-saturated society. Endless tweets, texts, posts, updates, Snapchats, storyboards, and blogs have become time-consuming pastimes that can, at times, make it difficult to hear Jesus speaking. Add to that the emotional walls we erect to keep ourselves from becoming too vulnerable, and it is even more difficult to hear God to speak to our hearts. But God wants to cut through the hustle and bustle and our personal defenses to speak transformative truths into our lives.

For the woman at the well in Samaria, Jesus knocked down social barriers and broke through the protective emotional walls she had built. He spoke to her plainly and powerfully, and when she finally *heard* Jesus and stopped arguing with God, she was changed. If you feel as though you're having trouble hearing Jesus, then stop, look, and listen. *Stop* challenging His admonition, deflecting His directive, being defensive when He points to your problems, and allowing distractions to rule the day. *Look* to His Word. Jesus will always and only speak what aligns with the Bible, and the more time you spend in His Word, the clearer His voice will become. *Listen* by renewing your mind (see Romans 12:2) and fixing your thoughts on heavenly things (see Colossians 3:2).

"Speak, Lord, for your servant hears" was Samuel's prayer when he had trouble recognizing God's voice (1 Samuel 3:9). May it be mine as well.

Jesus will cut through the noise so we can hear Him speaking to us, but we need to let Him.

Thirsty for More

*Jesus said to her, "Everyone who drinks of this water will be
thirsty again, but whoever drinks of the water that I will give
him will never be thirsty again." (John 4:13–14 ESV)*

Are you satisfied with your life? Did you know that your satisfaction
quotient goes up or down, based on how much or how little you are
drinking from the right source? Perhaps you have gulped from the well
of work or taken a swig from the fountain of relationships. The world
offers up many choices in an attempt to satiate your thirsty soul, but
they *all* will leave you dehydrated and empty. The only source of true
spiritual hydration and fulfillment is found in what Jesus promised to
a thirsty and unfulfilled woman who was seeking to fill her buckets
with water. He promised the Holy Spirit.

We need to be aware of the fact that our thirst, that craving deep
in our souls, is spiritual in nature. The pursuits, pleasures, and possessions of this world never can satisfy the spiritual longings we were
created with. But all too often we want to drink from the wells of
this world, seeking satisfaction and purpose that can only come from
God. Our souls are thirsty for a relationship with God. So if you're
feeling spiritually dehydrated or have been drinking from worldly
fountains, then revive your soul by drinking from God's wellspring.

*Lord, am I allowing You to be my source of satisfaction? I know
that every other well always will run dry and only leave me wanting
more. But You, God, will always and forever satisfy my soul. Remind
me, Lord, when I forget that You are my satisfaction.*

**Jesus never will leave us thirsty or wanting
more.**

Real Worship

"But the hour is coming, and is now here, when the true worshipers will worship the Father in spirit and truth."
(John 4:23 ESV)

There is a right way and a wrong way to worship God. Genuine, authentic, and God-honoring worship always involves spirit and truth. We worship in *spirit* because God is spirit, and His essence is spiritual, not physical. Therefore, our worship must first and foremost be spiritual in nature (see John 4:24). Jesus gives us the essentials of real worship. Worship that takes place in spirit begins within the human spirit when our attitudes, attentions, and affections are fixed on God alone. It's when the Holy Spirit of God prompts and persuades our spirits to forsake anything that is not true to God's nature and character. God is spirit, and He is not looking for outward displays of religion but that which combines both our hearts and our heads. Anything less is holy lip service.

We worship in *truth*, because to rightly worship God, we must know Him rightly. But we cannot know Him rightly if we are not invested in studying Him through the truth revealed in His Word and in the person of Jesus Christ (see John 14:6; 17:17). Real worshipers will be lovers of the truth and consumed with rightly dividing the truth, intentionally applying it in their day-to-day lives.

God, you are worthy of all my worship. Inspire my worship to be pure and selfless. Excite my spirit to passionately pursue You without compromise. And stir my heart toward genuine, authentic, selfless, truth-centered, worship.

> **Real worship will exalt Jesus and lead to greater intimacy with God.**

God's Work

"My food is to do the will of him who sent me and to accomplish his work." (John 4:34 ESV)

Work can bring to mind a begrudging reality of unavoidable responsibilities, a sweat-of-the-brow mentality that at times feels like a never-ending hamster wheel. However, the work of God should not produce the same emotions. This doesn't mean that we never get tired, frustrated, or even need a vacation when we're doing the Lord's work. But when we work the right way and for the right reasons, the work of the Lord should be nourishment to the soul.

When it comes to accomplishing God's work joyfully and fruitfully, we are most effective when God is most glorified. The primary (but not exclusive) expression of our service to God should be accomplished using the gifts He has given us. It's then that our work will be most aligned with His will for us. God has purposely given us gifts (see 1 Corinthians 12, 14; Romans 12) to use to accomplish the work He has called us to do, for His glory and for the benefit of others (see Ephesians 2:10; 1 Peter 4:10). When we serve in this way, God's work will be more sustaining than draining.

Doing God's work is what nourished Jesus and energized His soul. And when we see God's work in the same way, we will receive similar refreshment.

God, thank you for equipping me with gifts to serve You. May I approach the work of God with the same passion, persistence, and perseverance as Jesus. And may I experience the same spiritual nourishment in so doing.

> **Jesus always did God's work, God's way, in order to receive God's supply.**

20/20 Vision

"Look, I tell you, lift up your eyes, and see that the fields are white for harvest." (John 4:35 ESV)

Sometimes that which is the most obvious can be the hardest to see. The disciples often were spiritually shortsighted and frequently confused about Jesus's teachings. They repeatedly made the mistake of reducing His teachings to something less than the spiritual message He intended to communicate. One such opportunity the disciples had trouble seeing was the evident divine harvest of souls coming their way, individuals who needed the hope and salvation that Jesus offered. As Jesus continued to speak, He helped the disciples recognize the spiritual opportunity before them.

We, too, can suffer from similar spiritual shortsightedness by focusing on physical events rather than being mindful of the larger and often overlooked spiritual reality before our eyes. The Word of God is always the prescription for poor spiritual eyesight. The more we allow Jesus to speak into our lives, the less spiritually shortsighted we will be and the easier we'll be able to understand and follow the instruction God seeks to provide.

Jesus, speak to me when I'm having trouble seeing the obvious spiritual lessons before my eyes. Help me to lift my eyes past my selfish shortsightedness and see the obvious opportunities that You place in front of me. May I never miss those times when You have placed a field white for harvest before my eyes.

Jesus always will help us look through the lens of God's Word to see His will clearly.

Sowing and Growing

"For here the saying holds true, 'One sows and another reaps.'
" (John 4:37 ESV)

We all have a part to play in God's plans and purposes. Some plant and some pick, some scatter seed and some gather the harvest, some pray in private and some speak from a pulpit. All are necessary in God's kingdom work. Although God doesn't need us to accomplish His plans, He has graciously granted us the allowance to participate in His holy endeavors. The greatest of those endeavors revolves around God's desire that all people would be saved and come to the knowledge of the truth (see 1 Timothy 2:4).

God is working through His people to plant spiritual seeds and reap a spiritual harvest. He calls all of us to participate in this work by exercising our gifts for the sake of the gospel. We should appreciate the diversity of gifts, recognize and support the callings of others, and be content with how God has called, gifted, and assigned us to do His work. The nature of spiritual work is less about how we have been gifted and more about our willingness to do the work and our faithfulness to continue the work.

Lord, help me to focus on being faithful to the work You have called me to do. Work on my willingness to serve whenever, wherever, and however You lead. Take away my covetous concern for how others are used, and help me to seek to be used as You choose. Begin today by showing me how I can encourage Your will to be done right where You have placed me.

If we take care of the sowing, Jesus will take care of the growing.

The Miracle Worker

"Unless you people see signs and wonders you will by no means believe." (John 4:48 ESV)

Jesus certainly created a buzz everywhere He went. There's no getting around the wow factor associated with the signs and wonders of Jesus. But this wow factor was intended to do more than astound and amaze spectators. Signs and wonders were supposed to lead people to faith. They were intended to confirm the gospel message, attest to the God-given authority of Jesus's ministry, and authenticate His divinity. Unfortunately for some, the miracles of Jesus had become more about witnessing the spectacular and less about accepting the Savior.

Nothing has changed with the passage of time. Signs and wonders are not to be the focus of a ministry. Miracles can happen. The supernatural exists. God can heal. Jesus can still do the impossible. But the message of Jesus is not one of miracles; salvation isn't found in signs. The message has been—and always will be—that salvation is found in no other name but the name of Jesus. Don't seek experience above truth, and don't allow entertainment to distract from authenticity. Stay focused on Jesus, let His Word and Spirit guide you, and He will repeatedly astound and amaze you.

Thank you, God, for the miraculous message of salvation through Jesus. Let me never look to wonders to remain faithful. And may I only seek the miraculous from a position of faithful humility and trust in Your sovereign determination. Make it my priority to pursue growth and obedience above experience. Your wondrous works always should create a deeper love for You.

> **The miracles of Jesus were intended to confirm His authority and develop faith.**

Thunderstruck

But Jesus rebuked him, saying, **"Be silent, and come out of him!"**
(Mark 1:25 ESV)

With a thunderous command, the lightning strike of Jesus's words hit the rebellious demonic inhabitants possessing the man with enough energy to bring them into thunderstruck submission. The authority of Jesus shined bright in this flash of divine supremacy against the powers of darkness. Intellectually, these spiritual beings inhabiting the man in Capernaum recognized who Jesus was and comprehended His authority. But they refused to live in complete submission to Him.

When we look at Jesus, it must be with more than intellectual acknowledgement of His influence. We must accept His authority and live yielded to His supremacy. We cannot label any area of our lives as off-limits to God. Submitting to Jesus must be complete and comprehensive; there's no such thing as partial submission. Any lack of submission is rooted in selfish disobedience, placing our own desires and determination above God's. But as we receive help from the Holy Spirit and practice authentic obedience, we can faithfully live in loving submission to His authority.

Lord Jesus, help me to submit my will and my ways to You today and every day. May my gratitude for all You have done for me cause me to humbly walk in continuous submission to Your will, Your ways, and Your Word. May this thunderous example flash in my mind any time I'm tempted to question or resist Your divine authority.

> **Jesus wants us to have more than good theology; He wants us to love and worship Him.**

Seeing with His Eyes

"Let us go on to the next towns, that I may preach there also, for that is why I came out." (Mark 1:38 ESV)

Jesus loved people, and He made a point to go where the people were to proclaim His God-given message. In spite of the busy, full days of teaching, healing, and praying, Jesus still made it a priority to be purposeful in taking that message out to those who needed to hear it. The message Jesus came to proclaim was so important that He always made time to share it with others, whether one-on-one, in a small group, or with a large crowd.

Jesus still loves people, and He wants us to make a point to go where the people are to proclaim the same God-given message. As we look at the life of Jesus and allow it to impact us, it should boost our love for others and motivate us to take God's message to those who need to hear it. In spite of our full days and all the needed church work and ministry, we must keep going out. We cannot expect unbelievers to come on their own in search of Jesus. We must take Jesus to them. Whether spontaneously inspired or corporately organized and purposefully intentioned, we have a message to share and people who need to hear it.

Lord, Jesus, just as You used someone to share Your life-changing message of hope and salvation with me, help me to be someone You can use to speak words of hope, help, and faith into someone else's life. Open my heart to love others as you did, and open my eyes to see people as You do.

Jesus loved people, and it is our job to love people like He did.

Father Knows Best

"Why do you question these things in your hearts?"
(Mark 2:8 ESV)

Does anyone truly know us? After all, we don't advertise every thought that comes into our minds. We don't declare every desire that fills our hearts. We don't express every emotion that we feel. If we were candid, we would admit that we don't even truly know ourselves, because our hearts our untrustworthy and unknowable (see Jeremiah 17:9). But there is someone who does know us completely and wholly. Just as Jesus saw the questioning hearts of the scribes, He knows us from the inside out.

Jesus knows our every thought, because He knows our very hearts. Because God knows us better than we know ourselves, we are free to take a deep breath, take God at His word, and know that He has a plan and a purpose for everything He says and does. God has our best interests at heart through everything He allows in our lives. The more we let God take control of our hearts and minds, the more we'll be able to see Jesus clearly, hear His voice distinctly, and respond confidently. When we stop questioning God and start looking to Him for answers, we are in the best position to hear from heaven.

Even in the midst of my questions and uncertainties, I trust You, Lord. I know that You are always working my life circumstances for a greater, more glorious good. Work in me to depend on You more and on my own heart less, trust Your wisdom fully, and allow Your Word to guide me through life's events, tests, and trials.

Jesus knows what's best for us, because He knows us better than anyone.

Proof Positive

"But that you may know that the Son of Man has authority on earth to forgive sins"—he said to the paralytic— "I say to you, rise, pick up your bed, and go home." (Mark 2:10 ESV)

Standing in the middle of a mixed group of onlookers, holy men, and beggars, Jesus boldly declared to a man suffering from physical paralysis, "Your sins are forgiven" (Mark 2:5 ESV). That daring and dangerous statement immediately ruffled religious feathers. How could Jesus say such a thing? The power to forgive sins is reserved for God and God alone. But that was the point, wasn't it? Jesus made many declarations during His life and ministry, but the most daring were those testifying to His *God-ness*, His divinity.

Jesus wants us to know that He is God, and therefore He provides proof. In that moment and with that audience, Jesus decided He would demonstrate His divine authority through His miraculous control over the physical world. Here it was healing a lame man, another time it was feeding five thousand, and on another occasion it was calming a storm. The miracles of Jesus are proof positive that Jesus was who He said He was. That means we can take Him at His word. When He says that our sins are forgiven, we can know that "as far as the east is from the west, so far has He removed our transgressions from us" (Psalm 103:12).

Jesus, I am so thankful that You not only said that You are God, but You also demonstrated that You are God. You prove Your authority again and again throughout the Scriptures, and that strengthens and encourages my faith. I know and trust the authority of Your Word, and I'm building my life on it.

Jesus provided all the evidence needed to believe.

A Sinner's Friend

"Those who are well have no need of a physician, but those who are sick. I did not come to call the righteous, but sinners, to repentance." (Mark 2:17)

Jesus sees what a person can be. We typically see only what a person is.

Jesus was frequently found in the company of sinners, and therefore He was accused of being a friend to sinners. Jesus wasn't afraid to spend time with real people who had real problems, because they were the people He came to help. Jesus didn't isolate Himself from the needy. He reasoned with the lawbreaker, He sat with the adulterer, He ate with the extortionist, He talked to the prostitute, He noticed the beggar, and He recognized the outcast. He spent time with sinners and made Himself available to meet their needs. To those who accepted Him, He brought needed spiritual healing.

Jesus didn't tell people to clean themselves up and then come to Him. Instead, He invited them to come to Him, as they were, and then He would clean them up. Jesus sees not only who we are, but more importantly, who we were created to be. If Jesus didn't want to save sinners, then He never would have left heaven. Whether we're rich or poor, religious or skeptical, admired or cast away, we are all sinners in need of a Savior.

Dear Lord Jesus, I know I am a sinner, and I am forever thankful that You died on the cross for my sins and rose from the dead, defeating sin and death. The life I now live, I live by faith. Guide me and direct me as I seek to follow You and honor You every day of my life.

> **Jesus gladly spent time with sinners, not because He approved of sin but because He came to save us from it.**

The Wineskins of Our Ways

*"No one puts new wine into old wineskins; or else the
new wine bursts the wineskins, the wine is spilled, and the
wineskins are ruined." (Mark 2:22)*

Are you set in your spiritual ways? Are you open to new ideas and new opportunities when it comes to your spiritual walk and service to the Lord, or do you prefer to keep operating the way you always have?

Now, the Word of God is timeless, the life-changing message of faith in Jesus Christ is unchanging, and the spiritual gifts God has given us are enduring. But the work God is doing *in* your life personally and the work that He wants to do *through* your life visibly may bring you into a new season of spiritual growth. This new season might include new expressions of your spiritual gifts and service to God.

It's important to know that Jesus wants to do great things in your life, and He wants you to flourish in your faith. That loving purpose comes with cultivation and maturing life lessons. As Jesus looks for ways to develop and mature you, allow Him the freedom to stretch you in new ways, give you a renewed mindset, or create new habits or ways of serving Him.

Lord God, my heart longs to be fully devoted to You. I desire to hear Your voice and to walk in obedience to Your Word. I know that You are preparing me and maturing me so that I may better know You and serve You. Keep me open and flexible to Your Holy Spirit's leading in my life.

**Jesus wants us to remain flexible to the new
works He may be doing in our lives.**

Change is Never Easy

Now a certain man was there who had an infirmity thirty-eight years. When Jesus saw him lying there, and knew that he already had been in that condition a long time, He said to him, **"Do you want to be made well?"** *(John 5:5–6)*

If you've ever felt trapped by your emotions, an addiction, your choices, or your sin, then this question from Jesus is for you: "Do you want to be made well?" Perhaps you have gone so far as to make drastic life changes, only to predictably return to your habitual ways.

For the man who had been stricken thirty-eight years with a sickness, his response to Jesus's question wasn't an immediate "yes, I want to be healed!" Instead, it was a deflective answer, complete with excuses. Nevertheless, Jesus cut through the redirecting rationalizations and provided healing. We all can get stuck in the spiritual mud and struggle with our emotions, an addiction, our choices, or our sin, and we may even be stuck for a long time. But the question remains: "Do you want to be made well?"

To be made well, we must *abandon* the idea that we are in control, because our own efforts always fail to make the needed spiritual change. To be made well, we must *admit* that we need to be healed and that the solution is outside of ourselves. To be made well, we must *answer* the Lord's question with a resounding, yes.

Father, I know my struggles and my weaknesses, but today I'm taking a fresh step forward and ending the excuses. I want to be made well. Strengthen me to release my fears of failure, and keep me focused and surrendered to your holy desires.

Jesus is ready to deal with our limitations—if we are ready and willing to change.

Sin and Sickness

Afterward Jesus found him in the temple, and said to him, **"See, you have been made well. Sin no more, lest a worse thing come upon you."** *(John 5:14)*

Sickness *is* the result of original sin, but not all sickness is the result of personal sin. There's a very destructive school of thought that declares all sickness is the result of personal sin and that a lack of faith prevents a person from being healed. This is dangerous and damaging. It's dangerous because it isn't supported in the Scriptures, and it's damaging because it diminishes faith rather than develops it.

The message of healing in John 5 isn't "sin less, or God will punish you with greater sickness." The significance is that *sin* is the sickness, and if someone continues in sin and rejects righteousness, the worst thing that will happen to them is not physical infirmity but eternal separation from God. In God's presence is fullness of joy and spiritual well-being. Separation from Him is despair and sorrow.

Jesus cares about our physical condition, but His highest concern is for our spiritual welfare. Yes, Jesus healed this man's physical condition, but his healing wasn't primarily for physical restoration. This man was healed for holiness and holy living.

Heavenly Father, by the power of Your Holy Spirit that is at work in me, empower me to resist sin and walk in holiness. Give me a hunger for holy living, and show me what it means to be holy and how to live out holiness in my everyday life.

By trusting in Jesus, we have been healed for a life of holy living.

Doing Good

Then Jesus said to them, "I will ask you one thing: Is it lawful on the Sabbath to do good or to do evil, to save life or to destroy?"
(Luke 6:9)

There are some who would rather find fault than rejoice in blessing. During Jesus's earthly ministry, there were those who found fault with His mercy instead of being happy for a healing. Clinging to the security blanket of human effort, some oppose grace by becoming fixated on following the rules. Instead of seeking to better understand the difference between the letter of the law and the spirit of the law, some stress obedience over faith. As a result, they fall into legalism.

Legalism, at its core, is rooted in pride. Legalism equates behavior to right standing before God, whereas grace understands that our right standing before God is based on the redemptive work of Jesus on the cross. Legalism draws attention to man's ability to follow the law rather than living in the completed work of God. Legalism seeks to please God with a sweat-of-the-brow attitude, whereas grace understands that although we're called to live according to God's commands, our acceptance by God isn't based on our performance. Our adherence to God's moral law is our response to God's grace. It is not required for receiving His grace.

When religion and rituals replace salvation by faith in God, we're in danger of substituting legalism for grace.

Father, help me to remember that I do not gain Your acceptance by what I do or how well I follow Your commandments. I am accepted because of what Jesus already has done for me. Help me to live in the freedom of Your grace.

Jesus challenges us to choose grace and to be givers of grace.

God at Work

"My Father has been working until now, and I have been working." (John 5:17)

God is always working. He isn't an obsessive workaholic, but His work is never finished. His sovereignty never takes ten, His authority never ends, and His omniscience has no blind spots. God is working both visibly and behind the scenes to accomplish His plans and purposes. Some are heavenly, big-picture plans based on His sovereign determinations, and some are individual spiritual growth plans for His people.

God's continuous working means that He's working when we're resting, He's working when we're waiting, He's working when we're tested, He's working when we're tempted, and He's working when we're rejoicing. He's working when we're doubting, He's working when we're uncertain, He's working when we're hurting, He's working when we're aggravated, and He's working when we're cheerful. God is always working.

I may not always know what God is working to accomplish in my life or in a specific situation, but I do know that God's work is always good (see Romans 8:28). And although I may not always understand the ways in which God works and might be unclear about the timing of His work, I can always trust the nature of His work.

Dear God, I know that Your will is best and that all your work is established in Your goodness and grace. I know that all Your plans for me are good plans. May I never lose heart or grow discouraged, because You are always with me and working to accomplish Your good and perfect plans.

> **Jesus is always working good, because as God, He is good (see 1 Chronicles 16:34).**

FEBRUARY

Like Father, Like Son

"Most assuredly, I say to you, the Son can do nothing of Himself, but what He sees the Father do; for whatever He does, the Son also does in like manner." (John 5:19)

The character of Jesus is the character of God. As God thinks, Jesus speaks. As God feels, Jesus expresses. As God plans, Jesus accomplishes. As God loves, Jesus illustrates. Whatever God does, Jesus does in like manner. Jesus is manifestly unique but seamlessly united with the Father, one in nature but distinctly different in personification. Jesus never refuted the claims of the religious leaders when they accused Him of making Himself equal with God, but in His equality, He always chose to remain surrendered to the will of the Father.

The character of Jesus needs to be the character of every Christian. As Jesus speaks, we should speak. As Jesus loves, we should love. We are manifestly unique yet extraordinarily united with Christ (see Colossians 1:27). We have divine help working within us to accomplish God's plans and purposes (see Philippians 2:13). As the Son can do nothing of Himself, apart from Christ we can do nothing (see John 15:5). As Jesus observed the Father and followed His example, we should observe Jesus and follow His example as well. His life is the standard.

To see Jesus is to see You, Father. And through the life of Jesus, I have an example to follow. Help my life to be an example of Jesus's character, grace, and love. As I see Him doing, I seek to do in like manner.

Jesus is a reflection of the Father, and we should be reflections of the Son.

Give Honor Where Honor Is Due

"For the Father judges no one, but has committed all judgment to the Son, that all should honor the Son just as they honor the Father. He who does not honor the Son does not honor the Father who sent Him." (John 5:22–23)

Jesus is the most important individual you have never seen. He is the central figure throughout the Bible and the full and faultless image and expression of God the Father. Jesus has been given all judgment so that all humanity will acknowledge and esteem Him.

Sometimes the Bible gives us direct commands, and other times the Bible gives us information that ushers us into a deeper knowledge about God. Knowledge determines action. Therefore, what we know and believe about Jesus is the single most important influence that shapes how we live out our faith. Jesus gives us life, and He is the one to judge our lives. Believing in the substitutionary, sanctifying work of Jesus on the cross is the only requirement to escape judgment. And by so believing, we honor the Son and the Father who sent Him.

Practically, we honor Jesus by living our lives for the glory of God and not for our own glory. Daily, we honor Jesus by keeping Him in the center of the decisions we make with how we use our time and our resources, as well as the actions we take. Giving Jesus the honor He is due is a daily decision to put Him first.

Jesus, I seek to further honor You by allowing You to shape my thoughts, my knowledge, and my understanding of You and by letting those thoughts, knowledge, and understanding determine how I will live out my daily life.

Jesus must receive the same honor as the Father, because they are one.

Eternal Life

*"Truly, truly, I say to you, whoever hears my word and
believes him who sent me has eternal life. He does not come
into judgment but has passed from death to life.*
(John 5:24 ESV)

Every soul will live forever, but not every soul will experience eternal
life. Eternal life is more than endless life. Eternal life speaks of both
the quality of life and the quantity of life. Belief is the link that joins
us to Jesus and ushers us into eternal life. We take ownership of eternal
life the moment we believe in Jesus. It is not just a future experience but a correspondingly present possession.

The purpose of eternal life is knowing God the Father and Jesus
the Son (see John 17:3). The enjoyment of our current possession of
eternal life is growing in our intimate and personal fellowship with
God. The blessing of eternal life is endless fellowship with God.

It is not only my future with God that is important regarding
eternal life; it is also understanding that I can begin to experience and
enjoy the blessings of eternal life today by walking in the knowledge
and grace of how I have passed from death to life by believing in Jesus.

*Lord God, use the Holy Spirit to help me walk in the present reality
of the eternal life you have given to me—a reality that should help
me face the future with gratitude, generosity, and graciousness and
live for the glory of God.*

**Jesus gives an eternal life that can be
experienced today and forevermore.**

The Will of God

"I do not seek My own will but the will of the Father who sent Me." (John 5:30)

Knowing God's will can seem Herculean at times. With every new opportunity, challenge, or decision comes a question: *What does God want me to do in this situation?* We can further complicate the process by going to God with our predetermined expectations of how we presume God should direct us according to our limited understanding.

Jesus lived in the center of God's will his entire life. He lived to fully follow after God's will. Even in His final hours He prayed, "Not My will, but Yours, be done" (Luke 22:42). Jesus made the daily decision to trust and obey the Father's will over His own will. Seeking God's will is a daily discipline that requires a conscious, daily determination to trust and obey God's will above our own. May we constantly commit ourselves to pursue God's will and purpose to do it, because in the center of His will is well-being, safekeeping, and joy.

Dear God, my desire is to follow the remarkable and flawless example of Jesus. His perfect pursuit and surrender to Your will motivates me to seek God's will above my own. Don't let my desires blind me to Your will. Give me clarity and understanding to know Your will and live it. May Your will guide me, motivate me, and sustain me, just as it did for Jesus.

Jesus passionately pursued and remained perfectly surrendered to God's will.

Follow the Evidence

"But I have a greater witness than John's; for the works which the Father has given Me to finish—the very works that I do—bear witness of Me, that the Father has sent Me."
(John 5:36)

People have a natural hunger to see evidence. To accept something as true, we want to see the proof. Jesus understood this aspect of human nature and willingly provided confirmation that He was who He said He was. Witnesses establish truth, and Jesus had many of them. There was the testimony of John the Baptist, the testimony of God the Father, and, of course, the entirety of Scripture to back up His claims. But His works perhaps were the most compelling witness of all. They were designed to testify to the truth of who He was and authenticate what He said was true.

Jesus performed countless miracles, evidentially displaying His splendor and authority. The greatest of His works were His resurrection and ascension, boldly declaring in glorious display the proof and verification of His nature, sovereignty, and identity. Knowing there is proof of who Jesus is gives us the confidence to build our lives on His Word. It gives us the courage to face the ups and downs of each day, and it gives us the sureness to share Jesus with a skeptical world.

How wonderful and marvelous are the works of Jesus. Thank you, Lord, for the proofs You provide that establish and encourage my faith. May I live to declare your wondrous works.

Jesus's works are enough evidence for a profession of faith.

All About Jesus

"You search the Scriptures, for in them you think you have eternal life; and these are they which testify of Me." (John 5:39)

If your study of the Bible isn't bringing you closer to Jesus, then you're missing the point. Just as the religious leaders (who had spent their lives studying the Scriptures) missed the fact that the Messiah was standing right in front of them, we do not want to get so deep in our Bible studies that we miss the fact that Jesus stands in the center of them all. It is true that the span of the Bible is sweeping, its arrangement is amazing, and the narrative is inspired, but the message is unified. And the message is one of Jesus Christ.

There is one mediator between God and man: Jesus. As such, the entire Bible is the written declaration of that fact, and we always should be on the lookout for the connection to Christ in everything we read in the Bible. My study of the Scriptures not only should expand my knowledge of Jesus, but it also should deepen my love for Him and advance my relationship with Him. As I spend time studying the Bible, I should look at every passage and ask, "How does this declare Jesus?" The Bible is for us, but it's all about Jesus.

Jesus, You are at the center of all Scripture. Help me to never lose sight of You when I read Your Word. Just as You are at the center of all Scripture, I want You to always be at the center of my life.

Jesus can be found on every page of the Bible.

Poverty's Riches

"Blessed are the poor in spirit, for theirs is the kingdom of heaven." (Matthew 5:3)

We are most blessed when we realize we need God most. The Beatitudes are the gateway to living a happy Christian life. They provide both guidance for good behavior and consolation in hardships. Jesus opened up the most famous public speech ever with a roadmap to happiness—happiness not based on superficial merriment but grounded in blessing, joy, fulfillment, and an eternal perspective.

Jesus began with *"blessed are the poor in spirit."* In other words, we are happiest when we realize our absolute need for God. There is no other place to start, because in order to experience the blessings of God, this unique relationship must begin by recognizing that we are destitute without God. Our poverty is not financial; it is spiritual. It is recognition that apart from God, we are helpless, hopeless, and spiritually bankrupt. But with God resides blessings beyond measure.

In God's spiritual economy, poverty begets prosperity, scarcity leads to plenty, and impoverishment leads to inheritance. Our genuine awareness of our own bankruptcy opens the door to the kingdom of heaven.

Jesus, apart from You, I am spiritually empty. Daily I need You, and daily I need You to fill me up. When I find my satisfaction in You, I receive the riches of fulfillment and joy.

> **Jesus displayed His own poverty of Spirit by being totally dependent on God the Father.**

God of Comfort

"Blessed are those who mourn, for they shall be comforted."
(Matthew 5:4)

Charles Swindoll said, "There can be little comfort where there has been no grief."[2] Death often is the setting where mourning's magnitude moves us the deepest. As much as the consolation of God comforts us during the painful time of loss, the comfort of God extends beyond bereavement. Spiritual mourning naturally follows being poor in spirit and should lead to a place of brokenness over sin. As Dr. Swindoll points out, Christian mourning can extend into such places as grief concerning evil in the world and godly sorrow over sins committed against God.[3] It also can include heartache regarding the suffering and persecution of fellow believers.

The Bible tells us that Jesus was "a Man of sorrows and acquainted with grief" (Isaiah 53:3). Although we never will experience a sliver of Jesus's sufferings, we can experience the overflowing comfort of God. The apostle Paul felt he was the worst of all sinners, but the mercy and grace of God moved him to describe himself as "sorrowful yet always rejoicing" (2 Corinthians 6:10). When we comprehend our spiritual deficiency, fall before God in brokenness over our own iniquity, and mourn over our lack of righteousness, we are perfectly positioned to be comforted and filled with the righteousness of Christ. Though we may mourn, we don't wallow in self-pity, because the comfort of God moves us on.

May Your comfort, God, always move me to rejoicing, regardless of the depths of sorrow I may experience.

Jesus was comforted when He was most grief-stricken, and God always will be there to comfort us in our times of greatest grief.

The Magnitude of Meekness

"Blessed are the meek, for they shall inherit the earth."
(Matthew 5:5)

Meekness, or gentleness, is *not* weakness. Meekness *is* strength under control. It is remaining calm, cool, and collected when tensions rise. Meekness is the ability to bring calmness and clarity to conflicts and confusion, and meekness doesn't lash out because of mistreatment. Jesus personified bridled strength. He is the Lion of Judah and the Lamb of God, able to call upon the full arsenal of heavenly hosts. Yet He stayed fully submitted to fulfilling God's salvation plan.

Meekness does not mean you are a doormat to be trampled on. Being temperate doesn't mean that you tolerate wrong. Being self-controlled doesn't mean that you are spineless toward the truth. Meekness maintains a balance between being "wise as serpents and harmless as doves" (Matthew 10:16). It is being lionhearted but lamb-lipped.

Practicing meekness has both rewards in the present and the future. For example, practicing meekness today by surrendering and submitting to God reduces worry and eases anxiety. As for the future, good will triumph and the meek will rule with Christ.

May I faithfully walk in a spirit of meekness, a meekness found in Your strength, Lord. Help me to surrender, submit, and agree with your will for my life. Assist me to wait patiently for You to accomplish Your will instead of rushing ahead in my strength.

> **Jesus lived a life completely clothed in meekness and humility, resting in the power of His Father's strength.**

My Hope Is Built on Nothing Less

"Blessed are those who hunger and thirst for righteousness, for they shall be satisfied." (Matthew 5:6 ESV)

We normally measure others in terms of their accomplishments, but Jesus places the emphasis on character over achievements. One character trait that God encourages and blesses is having a healthy appetite for righteousness. In other words, happy is the person who desires to live rightly.

Righteousness sounds spiritually elusive, but it is more realistic if properly understood. Righteousness involves both *right living* and *right standing.* Our right standing with God is imparted to us through faith. As we place our faith in Jesus for our salvation, Jesus places His righteousness upon us, graciously giving us the *right standing* with God that we never could achieve in our own strength or by our own good works (see Philippians 3:9). Once we have *right standing* with God, we can then pursue *right living* for God. *Right living* involves staying connected to God, knowing God through His Word, communicating with God through prayer, and choosing to do what is right as defined by God. To those who keep a healthy appetite for righteousness as a regular part of their lives, Jesus promises *they shall be satisfied.*

Lord God, continue to give me a passion for righteousness. Help me not to settle for mediocre living or a half-hearted pursuit of You. Instead, help me to pursue right living with a heavenly hunger.

Jesus's righteousness gives me life and enables me to live rightly.

Mercy Begets Mercy

"Blessed are the merciful, for they shall obtain mercy."
(Matthew 5:7)

We all want God's mercy for ourselves. However, we often demand that others walk the plank of justice. In other words, we eagerly devour God's extravagant mercy, but we can be reluctant to extend that mercy to others. Mercy doesn't deny or ignore wrongdoing. It doesn't ignore offenses or sin. It only chooses to forgive, even when justice is deserved.

God "is rich in mercy" (Ephesians 2:4). His mercy is personally enduring, following us all the days of our lives. It is everlasting and eternal. It is saving and cleansing. And it is like manna from heaven, replenished daily (see Psalm 23:6; 103:17; Titus 3:5; Lamentations 3:23).

Mercy flows from our hearts as we personally understand and receive mercy from God. We are merciful when we have compassion and show kindness. We are merciful when our hands help others. And we are merciful when we are being patient, helping those who are hurting, forgiving those who have hurt us, and giving others a second chance. Mercy builds bridges, repairs broken relationships, and cares more about pointing people to Jesus than protecting our own pride.

Dear Lord, You are generous and gracious with Your mercy toward me. As I have received Your mercy countless times in my life, may I show mercy equally to my family, my friends, and to all my connections, both intimate and casual.

The mercy of Jesus has given us a pattern to follow.

Pure and Simple

"Blessed are the pure in heart, for they shall see God."
(Matthew 5:8)

Jesus wants to do more than clean up your act; He wants to transform your heart. Jesus is more interested in the inner self, because the root of an individual is buried in the unseen recesses of the heart. The heart is the seed of our thoughts, will, and emotions, and what we cultivate there will sprout and blossom into our words, actions, and attitudes.

A pure heart exhibits a single-mindedness toward God, an undivided devotion, and spiritual integrity. The purest heart is the one that desires nothing more than more of God. There is no rival to God, and there is no greater pursuit than God. A pure-hearted person will not let the things of this world override his or her affection and attention toward God. Jesus lived in the world, but the world did not distract Him from loving and serving God with His whole heart.

Take care of your heart, and your heart will take care of your character. Purify your heart, and you will see God more clearly, enabling you to discern His will more easily and serve Him more effectively.

Father God, forgive me for those times when my heart was far from You, for those times when my heart was distracted. Purge that which contaminates my heart, and create in me a pure heart. May my heart's desire be to find fulfillment and purpose in You. Then my life will be blessed as I see You more plainly.

Jesus's purity of heart gave Him true spiritual vision.

The Peacemaker

"Blessed are the peacemakers, for they shall be called sons of God." (Matthew 5:9)

It is easier to hold a grudge than to seek reconciliation. But conflict that goes unsettled can lead to bitterness, and bitterness left to ulcerate can be harmful physically, emotionally, and spiritually. It isn't enough to want peace; peace is something we have to work to promote. So how can we be peacemakers?

The first step is being at peace with God. The apostle Paul writes that "since we have been justified through faith, *we have peace with God through our Lord Jesus Christ*" (Romans 5:1 NIV, emphasis added). Knowing and surrendering your life to Jesus equips you to extend Christ's peace to others by sharing the message of the gospel.

The next step is to choose to live as a peacemaker, which means seeking solutions, choosing soft words in heated situations, and saying "I'm sorry" when we have wounded another. It means being willing to serve others, and it means seeking and supporting the reconciliation of relationships. Being a peacemaker doesn't always mean that we will achieve peace, but it does mean doing all that we can to live at peace and promote peace (see Romans 12:18). How are you doing as a peacemaker in your relationships?

Lord, help me to keep my eyes on You during disagreements. Help me to bring peace in the course of conflicts. Help me to point to Your glory and grace in the thick of transgressions.

> **Jesus came as the Prince of Peace so we could live at peace with God and others.**

Our Great Reward

"Blessed are you when others . . . utter all kinds of evil against you falsely on my account. Rejoice and be glad, for your reward is great in heaven" (Matthew 5:11–12 ESV)

Following Jesus isn't always sunshine and puppy dog kisses. I don't want to burst your spiritual bubble, but there will be times in your Christian life when you will suffer mistreatment because of your relationship with Jesus. Did you notice what Jesus said? It is not *if* but *when* others disparage you because you are connected to Him. Also note that Jesus didn't say, "Blessed are those who suffer for being foolish, or sinful, or bizarre." Not all persecution is because of righteousness.

To communicate that we live for God, we don't need to stand on a box in a busy town center and shout, "Repent!" All that is required is to seek to live as the Bible teaches. The result of living for Jesus and following His example is that some people will be bothered sometimes by our reflection of Jesus. We cannot control how others will react, but we can control how we choose to live. Even if insult arises or persecution comes, our calling is to remain faithful to God and focus on our future promises to get us through any present persecution. As we look to our marvelous future with God, rejoicing becomes easier, no matter who may be trying to extinguish our light.

My God, Give me the courage to stand and speak for You, even when I face opposition. Grant me the strength to live boldly for Jesus today, even if I'm reviled.

Jesus reminds us to rejoice and be glad, because He lavishly rewards those who suffer for His sake.

A Pinch of Salt

"You are the salt of the earth; but if the salt loses its flavor, how shall it be seasoned? It is then good for nothing but to be thrown out and trampled underfoot by men." (Matthew 5:13)

A juicy steak with a pinch of salt and twist of pepper . . . chewy caramel with a smidgeon of sea salt . . . lightly salted movie popcorn. There is no single seasoning more versatile and fundamental to food than salt. When properly applied, it enhances flavor, accentuates subtleties, and even prevents rotting. But salt that isn't salty isn't suited for the soil or the manure pile.

As Christians, we are called the salt of the earth because our presence should enhance life, accentuate truth, and prevent societal decay. It could be as simple as sharing an encouraging word, praying for someone, or serving people in need. It doesn't have to be huge. A pinch goes a long way.

Have you lost your saltiness? Has your faith become stale? The evidence will be easy to see. Are the relationships around you becoming better or worse spiritually because of your influence? If you have lost your ability to enhance the lives around you, if your impact no longer accentuates Jesus, then it is time to ask the Lord to refresh your walk.

Father, I don't want to be a flavorless follower of Christ. I want to enhance lives and bring the taste of Jesus to all my relationships.

Jesus enhances every relationship, and so should we.

"This Little Light of Mine"

"Let your light so shine before men, that they may see your good works and glorify your Father in heaven." (Matthew 5:16)

What good does it do to tell people how great God is if they cannot see how greatly He has impacted your life? When we live our lives in such a way that people see the light of God in us, they are more likely to believe what we have to say about Him.

Light makes something visible, and it also stimulates sight. As the light of the world, Jesus made God the Father visible and kindled our spiritual sight so that we could see God (see John 8:12). Jesus also calls *us* the light of the world (see Matthew 5:14). The mistake some people make is thinking they need to have a picture-perfect life before they can let their light shine. Wherever you are in your relationship with God, you can start shining the light of your Christian life today for others to see.

Be generous with your life, share what God has given you, and open up to others, because it will help them open up to you and provide an opportunity for you to shine Jesus into their situation. Be someone who inspires others to be more loving, more forgiving, more patient, and more kind. Be someone who is willing to walk into the darkness of another person's life and shine the light and love of God so they might experience His glorious grace.

Jesus, I know I am the light of the world because your light dwells in me. Your light is not for me to keep to myself but to shine brightly so that others can see You and seek to follow You.

Jesus is glorified when His people live lives that shine brightly.

The Goal of God's Law

*"Do not think that I came to destroy the Law or the Prophets.
I did not come to destroy but to fulfill." (Matthew 5:17)*

God's Law isn't just a list of *thou shalt nots*. It is more than rules, regulations, and the results of disobedience. Sure, there are warnings and boundaries. There are dos and don'ts. But the broader picture illustrates the indispensable relationship with the Creator of the universe. God's law isn't intended to grind us down; it's to grow us up. It isn't intended to hurt us; it's to heal us.

Throughout Jesus's life, He lived in perfect harmony with God's law. He was the only one able to follow it flawlessly and fully. He obeyed every commandment, He met every requirement, and He lived up to every standard. That is important, because the Law also required a perfect sacrifice for sin: "without the shedding of blood there is no remission" (Hebrews 9:22 NIV). Jesus fulfilled the Law through His righteousness, and He fulfilled the law by dying on the cross as the only acceptable payment for sin.

The Law never was intended to save humanity; it was intended to show us our need for a Savior. When we read the laws of God, they should convict us of our sins and point us to Christ.

Lord, I try to be a good person, but I know my best still isn't good enough. I can never fully follow Your law, but my trust is in Your Son, Jesus, who died for me so that I could truly live.

**Jesus alone fulfilled the Law and freely gives
His righteousness to all who believe.**

The Enduring Word

*"For assuredly, I say to you, till heaven and earth pass away,
one jot or one tittle will by no means pass from the law till all
is fulfilled." (Matthew 5:18)*

What if God wrote a book? What would He say? What would He tell
us about Himself? What would He say to the world? What would He
say about life? Well, God did write a book, and we call it the Bible. It
is divinely inspired, absolutely trustworthy, and entirely relevant for
modern life and godly living.

The Bible is so important that Jesus declared the durability and
dependability of the Scriptures down to the tiniest detail. He essentially said that every dot of the *i* and cross of the *t* made on the precious parchments of Scripture were supernaturally engineered, cate-
gorically sealed by the authority of God, and destined to be completed
just as God has declared. What does this mean for us today? If God
says something, His Word can be trusted. If God makes a promise,
we know He will keep it. If God predicts something, we know it will
come to pass. If God says it, that settles it!

What should we do with this God book? We should read it, hear
it, believe it, embrace it, speak it, obey it, pray it, preach it, trust it,
and meditate on it.

*Heavenly Father, thank you for Your inspired and enduring Word.
Give me the faith to receive all that it says, give me the understanding
to know what it means, and give me the will to do what it says.*

> **Jesus knew the Word of God was trustworthy
> and timeless, making it all we need for a
> healthy spiritual life.**

Getting Right with Each Other

"If you enter your place of worship and, about to make an offering, you suddenly remember a grudge a friend has against you, abandon your offering, leave immediately, go to this friend and make things right." (Matthew 5:23–24 MSG)

Martin Luther King, Jr. said, "We must learn to live together as brothers, or we will perish together as fools."[4] If our faith does not transform our relationships, then our faith is wishy-washy at best or lifeless at worst. Jesus blows the doors off old religious ideologies by saying that reconciliation is more important than religion. Jesus isn't interested in empty or shallow religion. Rather, He's interested in a religion that promotes a relationship with God and impacts lives personally and practically.

One area in which God expects His transformative power to impact our relationships is conflict resolution. And He says that to work toward reconciliation, you may have to make the first move. Jesus doesn't tell you to wait and see if the other person makes a move; He tells *you* to *go* without delay. "But wait," you may be thinking, "that's a little inconvenient. Why the urgency?" The longer you wait, the harder it is to actually go. Also, the longer you wait, the more it damages the relationship, making it harder to forgive. Then there's the fact that the longer you wait, the longer you are being disobedient to what God is asking you to do. Therefore, when it comes to getting right with one another, don't put off until tomorrow what you should make right today.

Father, You know how often I have offended someone else. Rather than justify or excuse my actions, help me to humbly seek forgiveness and restoration so that my worship is acceptable.

> **Jesus says that reconciliation is so important, it needs to be a top priority.**

Thoughts That Kill

"Whoever looks at a woman to lust for her has already committed adultery with her in his heart." (Matthew 5:28)

What's the harm in a thought? Why does God prohibit certain thoughts? God wired us, so He knows that if we think about something long enough, eventually we will act on those thoughts. Your thoughts become words, your words become actions, your actions become habits, your habits become character, and your character becomes your destiny.[5] The Bible says that as a man "thinks in his heart, so is he" (Proverbs 23:7).

We need to control our thoughts, because our thoughts control us. Our thoughts have a tremendous ability to shape our lives both for good or for bad. Jesus drives the point home by making the connection that our thoughts are where sin begins, and an uncontrolled mind is a breeding ground for sin.

Rather than changing our circumstances, God wants to change our thinking. The process of breaking a sin cycle begins by stopping a bad thought from beginning. Paul wrote, "I'd say you'll do best by filling your minds and meditating on things true, noble, reputable, authentic, compelling, gracious—the best, not the worst; the beautiful, not the ugly; things to praise, not things to curse" (Philippians 4:8–9 MSG). As you change your thinking, you will change the direction of your life.

Lord God, help me to let go of destructive thoughts and embrace God-honoring thinking. Replace unhelpful thinking with thoughts that align with Your love and agree with your Word.

Jesus wants us to think rightly so that we live righteously.

Cut It Out

"And if your right hand causes you to sin, cut it off and cast it from you; for it is more profitable for you that one of your members perish, than for your whole body to be cast into hell."
(Matthew 5:30)

Does Jesus actually mean that we should pluck out our own eye or sever a hand if we are prone to sin? We tend to respond to such extremism this way: "Yes, sin is bad, but isn't this a little over the top, Jesus? Wouldn't such actions just leave us in a blind and broken world?" That is why it's so important to know what the Bible *means*, not just what it *says*.

We know that Jesus is speaking figuratively, because the actual removal of a body part doesn't get the root of the problem. Sin doesn't start in the eye. Bad behavior doesn't begin in the hand. What Jesus is emphasizing through verbal shock therapy is that sin is so insidious, its effects so devastating, that it is a soul killer and a hell supplier. When our reverence for God slips, our tolerance of sin soars.

The snares of sin are subtle. Its enticements blind us to the truth, making it easy for us to stray from the path of holiness. Jesus breaks through the apathy toward our personal sin and reminds us that we may need to cut off bad habits, sever toxic relationships, chop off a cancerous career, or amputate deadly addictions.

Jesus, I know I never will be sin free this side of heaven, but help me to be free from the bondage of sin. May I radically reject sin rather than rationalize it.

Jesus wants us to sever our relationship with sin, because sin disrupts our relationship with Him.

When "I Do" Becomes "I'm Done"

"I say to you that whoever divorces his wife for any reason except sexual immorality causes her to commit adultery."
(Matthew 5:32)

No one ever goes into a marriage wanting it to fail. No one ever says, "I do," hoping to one day say, "I'm done!" It is true that God hates divorce (see Malachi 2:16), but it is also true that He has made an allowance for divorce. In the case of sexual immorality, God essentially says, "You can break your covenant. You can get out of your contract." But just because God gives you an exit clause doesn't mean that He supports immediately driving to divorce court. Divorce should be the last resort, not the first choice. Don't throw in the towel just because you may have to work to keep your marriage intact. Don't give up quickly on the love you once had for your spouse when that love has grown cold or has been wounded.

Divorce is messy, complicated, and painful. There is no one-size-fits-all approach when it comes to making that dreaded decision to divorce. However, we must remember that love is more than a feeling; it is the choice to live lovingly (see 1 Corinthians 13). Human love can fade, but the divine love of God remains forever brilliant and can revitalize the nastiest of marriages. The more we allow God's love to change us and flow through us, the more we can offer others a love that lasts.

Dear God, I know that marriage is complicated and challenging, but I want to do what pleases You. Give me the wisdom for today and the determination to choose to live lovingly in my marriage, even if feelings fade.

Jesus wants marriages to succeed. Even immorality can be overcome with God's love.

Promises, Promises

"Let your 'Yes' be 'Yes,' and your 'No,' 'No.' " (Matthew 5:37)

Do others believe what you say, or do they take everything that comes out of your mouth with a grain of salt? When you say that you will pray for someone, do you? Do you pay back what you promise? Granted, no one is perfect, and we all make mistakes, but can people take you at your word?

God takes our words very seriously, and He wants us to do the same. One area in which Jesus speaks regarding how we use our words is making promises. We do not need to say, "I swear to God" for a promise to pack a punch. Some of Jesus's harshest rebukes were directed toward those whose words didn't match their lives. The way God sees it, if we say one thing and do another, we are guilty of hypocrisy and empty promises. The Bible says that people who promise things they never give are like "clouds and wind without rain" (Proverbs 25:14).

So, what should we do? Don't try to look more religious to others by making promises that you don't intend to keep. Here are a few rules to remember: (1) Don't say it if you don't mean it, (2) don't make a promise that you don't intend to keep, and (3) if you say "yes" to something, then do it no matter what. When you break a promise, you open the door for bitterness to creep into a relationship. And when your words are meaningless, you weaken your witness.

Father, let my actions and my words be one and the same. Help me not to be careless with my words or say things that I don't mean.

Jesus wants us to mean what we say and say what we mean.

A Slap in the Face

"Whoever slaps you on your right cheek, turn the other to him also." (Matthew 5:39)

We all have been mistreated in life. Most of us have been insulted, mocked, or taken advantage of. When wrong happens to us, God wants us to respond with grace. Jesus is not saying that Christians need to be namby-pamby pushovers or that we should never stand up, speak up, or defend ourselves. This is not about enduring physical violence; it has more to do with a disrespectful offense.

Refuse to retaliate. Instead, respond by representing Jesus. Pride wants to retaliate, but Jesus wants you to resist the urge to fight back. When you are ready to lay down your rights, you are ready to walk in the righteousness of Christ. When you refuse to give in to retaliation, you reflect Jesus and honor God. This isn't easy, and it certainly isn't natural. In fact, it's supernatural.

How can you do this? Start by taking a step back. Don't let your emotions get the better of you. Allow God time to work on your attitude. Next, let it go and give it to God. A bruised ego takes longer to heal than a slap on the face—unless you surrender it to God. Holding on to hurt will hurt you the most. Lastly, pray. Prayer keeps your connection with God open and allows God's nature to transform and heal your hurts.

Dear God, help me to be forgiving and not hold grudges. Let my behavior bring peace and healing to relationships.

Jesus demonstrated righteous restraint, and He works in us so that we can do the same.

Living in the Extra Mile

"And whoever compels you to go one mile, go with him two."
(Matthew 5:41)

In Jesus's day, a Roman soldier could require a subject of Rome to carry his marching pack one mile. Jesus dropped a bombshell by adding, "And whoever compels you to go one mile, go with him two." *What? Why would we do that? These people have conquered us, and you want us to go above and beyond for them?*

Yes. Certainly we need to tell people about the love of God, but Jesus also wants us to show people the love of God in real and practical ways. And one such way to do that is by going the extra mile. Imagine how the situation and conversation changed when, after one mile of compulsory service, the servant of God kept walking. The extra mile would have immediately transformed their relationship.

You see, it is in the extra mile where we are not only transformed, but our relationships are transformed as well. Living in the extra mile means going above and beyond, even when it is not convenient, and it means living that way across all our earthly relationships. Living in the extra mile will cause people to stop and take notice. This breaks down barriers and creates opportunities to build bridges for sharing that Jesus is the reason we go the extra mile. Where can you go the extra mile today?

Father, thank You for all You do and have done for me. Show me how I can not only go the extra mile for someone today but how I can live an extra-mile life.

Jesus's entire life was lived in the extra mile.

Selfless Generosity

"Give to him who asks you, and from him who wants to borrow from you do not turn away." (Matthew 5:42)

The people who have had the most impact in my life are not those who took the most from me but gave me the most. For example, the single greatest influence in my life is Jesus. There is no question that Jesus is a giver, and it is no surprise that He instructs us to be givers too. Givers are influencers, and as we seek to influence the world for Jesus, one way to accomplish this is by giving.

Giving includes giving of our time, talents, and treasures. However, there are obstacles to giving, and the biggest obstacle is selfishness. Selfishness is very powerful in our hearts, but we can counter its effects as we focus on thankfulness and contentment. The more we appreciate what we have been given and the more content we are with what we have, the more we will cultivate generosity.

There are certainly some exceptions to giving, because Jesus didn't say that we should give to everyone, every time, and everything they ask. Look at it this way: when in doubt, give. It's better to give to someone and look like Jesus than not to. How can we not consider giving to others when God has given us so much?

Father, I thank You for Your radical generosity toward me. I also thank You for those who have given to me and blessed my life. May I learn to be more radical with my generosity.

> **Jesus is the greatest giver of all time, and when we give selflessly, we are like Him.**

Praying for Our Persecutors

"Pray for those who spitefully use you and persecute you."
(Matthew 5:44)

Oh, I will pray for those who persecute me all right: "God, give it to them good!" Let's be honest. Isn't that our first thought when someone is cruel or unkind to us—or worse, persecutes us for our belief in God? As much as it might be our natural reaction, it is not the action God calls His children to apply.

God challenges us to rise above the normal response to hate our enemies and wish them harm. Of course, this isn't easy, but it is an opportunity for God to bring out the best in us, not the worst. When someone gives us a hard time, we are to respond with blessing. It is then that we are being who we were created to be: our God-centered selves.

So, how should we pray for our enemies? Any prayer for our enemy that fails to include their forgiveness and turning to Jesus falls short. A good prayer to present to God on behalf of our enemies is the very one He gave us to pray for ourselves: the Lord's Prayer (see Matthew 6:9–13). In this prayer we can ask God to lead our persecutors to hallow His name, accept and accomplish His will, trust Him and His provision, forgive and be forgiven, and to resist evil. What a model prayer both for ourselves and our enemies.

Father, fill my heart with love, especially for my enemies. May I love without limitations and give grace without reservation.

> **Jesus prayed for those nailing Him to the cross. How can we do anything less?**

Nobody's Perfect, Are They?

"Therefore, you shall be perfect, as your heavenly Father is perfect" (Matthew 5:48 NASB).

Have you ever read the Bible and thought, "Okay, now you have gone too far, God! How in the world am I supposed to be perfect? I mean, what You have said so far has been hard enough. Now it seems like You are asking for the impossible." God's standard always has been and always will be perfect holiness. But apart from Christ, we can never attain that lofty standard.

It is not so much an issue of reaching a state of moral perfection as it is receiving His perfection and letting it work in us and through our lives. In God's eyes, we have been perfected by virtue of being joined to Jesus by faith, which frees us from needing to earn His approval. But it also does not erase His holy standard.

God is perfect, and we must move on in the direction of His perfect standard. Pursuing the standard of perfection does not mean that we never will fail, but it does mean that when we fail, we turn to God with it. Jesus gives us positional perfection through justification, and He calls us to live out practical perfection through the sanctification process. He also promises future perfection through glorification. So focus fully and completely on being perfectly devoted to God, and you will be moving in the perfection direction.

Father, perfect my obedience. Bring my will into perfect alignment with Yours, and help me to perfectly follow the example of Jesus.

> **Jesus's perfection allows me to follow Him, even in my imperfection.**

Thankfulness

"Father, I thank You that You have heard Me." *(John 11:41)*

Why do we need to be reminded to be thankful? Perhaps it's because difficult situations make it more challenging for us to give thanks. But God wants us to be regular givers of thanks, because God has a specific purpose for gratitude in our lives.

Jesus made it a habit to give God thanks, and He expressed His thanks to God publicly for the benefit of others so that we, too, might learn to be grateful to God. Jesus gave thanks for food (see John 6:11; Mark 8:6), He gave thanks for God's approach to revelation (see Luke 10:21), He gave thanks for God's attentiveness (see John 11:41), and He even gave thanks for the opportunity to give His life as a sacrifice (see Matthew 26:27–28). Jesus lived in thankfulness to God, but His thanksgiving wasn't just a token of gratitude to God, although it was that. It also prepared the way for the miracles that would follow.

Now, gratitude may not change our circumstances, but it will help us become more aware of God's presence. Gratitude creates fellowship, and it also leads to a lifestyle of worship. Giving thanks helps us to seek God's purposes in our situation, giving thanks positions our hearts to see the goodness of God in any given situation, and giving thanks prepares us to accept however God will work out our situation.

Thank you, Jesus, for the good in my life, and thank you for life's challenges, because I know that everything is an opportunity to experience Your presence. Work in me to give you thanks in all things and for all things.

> **Jesus lived in thankfulness so that we would be radically thankful people.**

MARCH

Good Work

*"Watch out! Don't do your good deeds publicly, to be admired
by others, for you will lose the reward from your Father in
heaven. (Matthew 6:1 NLT)*

When you give to charity, do you seek the applause of others? Do you
only lend a hand when someone else can see it? In the Sermon on the
Mount, Jesus called His followers to let their light shine so that others
would see their good works and glorify God. But just one chapter
later, He is warning us to beware of practicing good works so that others notice them. So what is the difference? In a word, it's motivation.

Whatever we do, whether we're giving, helping, serving, or
worshiping, God is looking at our hearts. Motive is everything. We
shouldn't do what we do for a pat on the back. We shouldn't give to
get. It's been said that "God is more pleased by one work, however
small, done secretly, without desire that it be known, than a thousand
done with the desire that people know of them."[6] Our good works
should not be done to draw attention to our goodness but should
point to God. Our good deeds are evidence that our faith is genuine
(see James 2:18, 20). Good works are not bad; they are good. And
as Christians, we should want to do them because we love God. We
should not want to do good works because they makes us look good,
but because they glorify God. If a compliment comes our way because
of a good deed, then we should pass the praise on to God.

*Heavenly Father, You see my motives. Purify my heart so that my
works are always done because of your goodness and for your glory.*

**My good works should seek to point to Jesus
and not promote myself.**

Pray with Purpose

"And when you pray, do not use vain repetitions as the heathen do." (Matthew 6:7)

Prayer is not a magical wand that we wave while repeating some incantation to get God to do something for us. God is not impressed with verbose vocabularies or pseudo intellectual recitations. Prayer's purpose is less about getting God to do things for us and more about setting our eyes on God.

When we are praying, we are talking with God. It is meant to be a conversation from the heart, not a script we recite. The condemnation here is not about repeating a phrase, a Scripture verse, or a thought in our prayers; it is a criticism of meaningless prayers. When we establish prayer in superstition over significance and tradition over relationship, it becomes formulaic rather than conversational—and we miss the mark. If we have disengaged our minds, prayer has become nothing more than paying God lip service. Soliloquies devoid of sincerity are skeleton prayers. They have no meat and therefore no substance.

When prayer is a heartfelt extension of our devotion to God and cultivates our communion with Christ, a heartfelt "God help me" can mean more than a thousand empty words.

God, help me to pray with purpose. May my prayers always be heart-felt extensions of my faith that draw me closer to You and cultivate my communion with You.

> **Jesus cares about the condition of our hearts more than the construction of our prayers.**

Why Forgive?

"For if you forgive others their trespasses, your heavenly Father will also forgive you." (Matthew 6:14 ESV)

Why should I forgive that person? You don't know how much they hurt me! Deep hurts happen, and emotional pain is real. But God wants us to extend grace and be forgiving. Why should we forgive? Because unforgiveness can bring our walks with God to a screeching halt. Why should we forgive? Because unforgiveness is not an option with God. Why should we forgive? Because we cannot receive from God that which we will not give to others.

Forgiveness, like works, must be present in the believer's life. Just as faith without works is dead (see James 2:14–17), we cannot say that we have faith if we are unwilling to forgive. A Christian who refuses to forgive is in conflict with God, which is not a good place to be, by the way. Forgiveness doesn't mean that we always will forgive perfectly, but we must be willing to forgive positively. The ability to forgive comes from God, and the willingness to forgive comes from us. Forgiveness is not a condition of our salvation; it is fruit stemming from our salvation.

Are you blocking the fullness and freedom of God's forgiveness by refusing to extend the same grace of forgiveness that God has extended to you? Being a Christian is to forgive as you have been forgiven, which is graciously and completely.

Father, thank you for the forgiveness I have through the work of Jesus on the cross. And thank you that knowing this forgiveness frees me to forgive others.

> **Having been forgiven by Jesus, we must forgive others.**

Hungry for God

"But you, when you fast, anoint your head and wash your
face, so that you do not appear to men to be fasting."
(Mathew 6:17–18)

Fasting is like a turnip. It's good for you. But just as no one is going out of their way to eat more turnips, Christians are not going out of their way to fast more. Let's get real for a moment. Jesus assumed that fasting would be a regular part of the Christian's life, because He didn't say *if* you fast but *when* you fast. So why don't most Christians fast?

Perhaps the best place to start is by answering this question: Why should we fast? Fasting is a way of letting God know that He's a priority. Fasting is not about punishing our bodies by depriving them of food; it is about consecrating our lives by feeding our souls. We fast to remind ourselves of our dependence on God. We fast to express grief. We fast to humble ourselves. We fast to strengthen our prayer lives. We fast to seek repentance for sin. And we fast to hear from God. A unique aspect built into fasting that isn't found in any of the other spiritual disciplines is the physical prompt, via hunger pangs, that serves as a recurring reminder of why we are fasting. Biblical fasting can serve to reposition our hearts to receive God's truth, greater insight, or direction. God has called us to consecrate ourselves and come to Him, at times, in fasting.

Father, touch my heart and give me a greater desire to draw closer to You through prayer and fasting. May I be purposeful in my fasting, recognizing that denial devoid of devotion empties fasting of its spiritual value.

A hunger for more of Jesus should lead you into times of fasting.

Investing in Eternity

"Do not lay up for yourselves treasures on earth, where moth and rust destroy and where thieves break in and steal; but lay up for yourselves treasures in heaven." (Matthew 6:19–20)

No one sees a hearse towing a U-Haul, because everyone knows you can't take your stuff with you when you die. Even though we know that, it can be very easy to get caught up in the here and now and lose sight of the then and there of heaven. But when you give your time, riches, and resources to heavenly matters, you invest in that which will be enjoyed forever.

So, how are you using what God has given you to serve Him?

When we are strategically and sacrificially using our various gifts and resources to serve others and to advance God's kingdom, we are investing in eternity. People are important to God, and they have been created to last forever. Investing in the spiritual health and well-being of others not only profits them, but it also adds to our spiritual bank accounts. Storing up treasures in heaven begins by helping others get to heaven.

When we keep in plain sight the big picture of how people matter to God, it should motivate us to invest in the lives of others. We never will lose what we have invested in eternity.

Lord God, help me to remember that what I do for You is what will remain for eternity. Help me to encourage, exhort, evangelize, and devote effort to the spiritual needs of others.

According to Jesus, investing in God's work pays eternal rewards.

The Money Trap

"You cannot serve God and money." *(Matthew 6:24 ESV)*

Money isn't evil, but money is dangerous. It's dangerous because if you have it, then you are inclined to turn to it and trust in it. That will trap you. If you don't have it, then you are inclined to work for it and want more of it. That, too, will trap you. The money trap can be as subtle as thinking, "If I just had that car" or "If I just had that house" or "If I could just travel a little more." So you work a little harder to make a little more money and to buy a little more, only to find out that more is never enough.

Chasing after money conflicts with faith in God. Either we are looking to God to solve our problems and bring us fulfillment and joy, or we are looking to money to solve our problems and bring us fulfillment and happiness. Following after God rather than money doesn't mean that we have to take a vow of poverty to prove our devotion to God.

Either we have power over money, or money has power over us. Money itself is not evil, because it is possible to be wealthy and serve God. However, it's easy for us to think we are serving God when we are really serving the god of stuff. Serving God with our whole hearts and making Him first in our lives will bring wealth to our souls, peace to our pursuits, and joy to our lives. Money never will. The choice is yours.

God, help me to align my priorities with Yours. Keep my thoughts and heart centered on eternal things, making me generous, gracious, and content with what You give me.

Jesus wants us to trust Him with everything, including our checkbooks.

Fear Not

"Do not worry." (Matthew 6:31)

Does worry keep you up at night? Is worrying a way of life for you? We know that life has its difficulties. We must cope with concerns about our health, family, finances, and more. But how we cope with these difficulties is a choice, and according to God, choosing worry isn't an option. Just to be clear, concern is not the same as worry. Concern is thoughtful consideration about an issue that leads us to take appropriate action. Worry is fearful negativity that exaggerates a problem, overtakes our minds, and takes no action. When we worry, we focus more on our problems and less on God's promises.

It takes more than willpower to overcome worry. We need God's help. Start by handing your worry over to God and trust Him to take care of you, because He loves you (see 1 Peter 5:7). When worry increases, faith decreases. So the next time you're tempted to worry, stop and do the things that build faith: put your eyes on Jesus, pray (see Philippians 4:6–7), and spend time in God's Word. Avoiding this will only feed fear. Next, choose to take life one day at a time, because worry ruins today and provides no remedies for tomorrow (see Matthew 6:34). Lastly, cultivate thankfulness and contentment, because God promises to meet all our *needs*, not all our *wants* (see Philippians 4:19).

Dear God, grant me peace of mind and calm my troubled heart when I begin to worry. Help me remember that You are always working in my life, and I have no reason to fear.

Jesus will give you His peace when you hand your worry over to Him.

First Things First

"But seek first the kingdom of God and His righteousness, and all these things shall be added to you." (Matthew 6:33)

The key to living an abundant life filled with blessings and joy is to put God first and keep Him there. Consistently and continually putting God first every day is a discipline, but determining to seek God first always will put you in the perfect position for God to work in and through your life.

Seeking God is not to be a casual pursuit. It is not intended to be a half-hearted pastime. If Christianity is nothing more than a hobby to you, then you are shortchanging your faith. You will be disappointed and dissatisfied with life and left longing and looking for more. The problem is that all too often we want God's blessings, but we also want to live life on our terms. What we often fail to realize is that when we put our relationship with God first, what He gives us far exceeds any so-called sacrifices that we make. We're willing to put God first on Sundays, but what about the rest of the week?

Seeking God means that we set our minds and hearts on God. It is a conscious choice we must make to daily direct our thoughts toward Him. The comforting promise from the Bible is that if we seek God in this way, we will find Him (see Jeremiah 29:13), and He will take care of our needs. Are you seeking God first in everything you are doing?

Help me, Lord, to keep You first today, tomorrow, and every day after that. Remind me to always look to You first, because You are my supply.

> **Jesus first means, that God will meet your needs not your wants.**

Passing Judgment

"Judge not, that you be not judged." (Matthew 7:1)

I've fallen victim to judging someone else. I had my ideas about a certain person and ministry, and I had determined they were watering down the truth and compromising the Word of God. The problem was the more that I actually listened to what this person taught, the more I couldn't find anything that I disagreed with. This taught me that we're not in a position to judge others, because our judgments are ill-informed and misguided.

Being judgmental thinks the worst instead of looking for the best. Judgementalism is negativity personified. The Enemy likes to keep us busy pointing at others so we'll ignore the problems in our own lives and neglect to make the changes *we* need to make.

Judging doesn't mean that we ignore making an evaluation, discard our discernment, or walk away from using wisdom. But it does mean that we should exercise extreme caution when making judgments about others. It's wrong to judge before hearing the facts. It's wrong to judge based on outward appearance. And it's wrong to judge if restoration isn't involved. The bottom line is that we should be more concerned about our own conduct and conscience before we worry about someone else's. It's best to leave judgment in the hands of God.

Help me to change the way I view other people, and forgive me for the times I've had judgmental thoughts. I want to see others with Your eyes of love and compassion.

> **Jesus essentially gave us this warning: judge at your own risk.**

Take off the Mask

*"Hypocrite! First remove the plank from your own eye,
and then you will see clearly to remove the speck from your
brother's eye." (Matthew 7:5)*

If Christianity is true, why are there hypocrites in church? Or, if Christianity is really supposed to change people, then why do some profess to believe in Jesus yet set such bad examples? In other words, why do some believers not seem to practice what they preach?

Christians are often accused of being a "bunch of hypocrites," and it is true that we make the same mistakes that non-Christians make. But just because we speak about sin and yet still sin doesn't make us hypocrites; it just makes us human. As Christians, we don't claim to be perfect or sinless (see 1 John 1:8), but we should confess our sins and work to overcome them. Hypocrites will call attention to others' sins yet conceal their own. Hypocrites want others to see them as picture-perfect, even though they are flawed.

Pretending to be someone you aren't is exhausting. Hiding who you really are builds walls, not trust. If you are different on social media than you are in person, or if you are different at home than you are at church, stop wasting time and energy by wearing a mask and start working to become the person God made you to be.

Father God, thank You for loving me unconditionally and knowing me completely. Help me, Lord, to be honest, authentic, and real with those around me and to encourage others to be the same.

> **Jesus has freed you from pretending to be
> something you are not.**

Pigs and Pearls

"Do not give what is holy to the dogs; nor cast your pearls before swine, lest they trample them under their feet, and turn and tear you in pieces." (Matthew 7:6)

Is there ever a time when it is okay *not* to share the gospel with someone? After all, sometimes people just don't want to hear what you have to say. The Bible says that when Jesus was brought before King Herod, He didn't say a word. Why? Wasn't this a great opportunity to proclaim the Good News to a powerful leader? Jesus didn't speak even a word, because King Herod didn't want to hear the truth. He wanted to be entertained instead, and Jesus refused to perform (see Luke 23:6–11).

Let's face it. Some people are unaffected by spiritual truth. They are so closed that their continued rebelliousness is an indication to the discerning that it's time to turn your attention elsewhere. There comes a point when continuing to speak truth to someone who ridicules, scoffs, or rejects it is a waste of time and energy. We should never give up hope, but we should be wise enough to know when it is time to move on.

Prayerful persistence and enduring faithfulness to share the truth with someone is commendable. Jesus wasn't telling us to avoid people who are in spiritual need or to refuse to offer the gospel to difficult or challenging people. But Jesus was teaching there will be occasions when those resisting the gospel should be left alone (see Matthew 10:14).

God, You can penetrate the hardest of hearts, and the work of salvation is Yours alone. Help me to be wise and humble when it comes to sharing the truth of Your Word.

Jesus wants everyone to be saved, but sometimes the wise thing to do is take the gospel to someone who wants to hear it.

Keep on Keeping On

"Ask, and it will be given to you; seek, and you will find; knock, and it will be opened to you." (Matthew 7:7)

Prayer often has become a last option when, in fact, it is a great opportunity that we should choose before we do or decide anything. As Dr. A. J. Gordon pointed out, "You can do more than pray after you have prayed, but you cannot do more than pray until you have prayed."[7]

Do you need something? Ask! Do you want to know something important? Seek! Are you looking for a door to open? Knock! There is no need to bargain with God. There are no magic spells, and there is no secret password. There is nothing but the most difficult thing for busy souls to do: simply ask. The best translation of Matthew 7 is "keep on asking, keep on seeking, keep on knocking." Persistence should characterize our prayers.

There's a progression we should note in this verse as well: movement from passive praying to increased action. When we ask, we realize our need and ask God for help. When we seek, we are praying plus pursuing. There's effort involved. When we knock, we are praying plus pursuing plus persevering. God's answer might be yes, it might be no, or it might be not right now. We don't always know what the will of God is, but finding the answer is a process that begins with prayer, continues with pursuit, and usually requires perseverance.

Dear God, I know that as I persevere in my prayers, in Your time I will see the answer. I will find what I seek, and I will be able to walk through the open door.

Jesus is ready to give to those who ask, seek, and knock.

The Golden Rule

"Do to others whatever you would like them to do to you. This is the essence of all that is taught in the law and the prophets."
(Matthew 7:12 NLT)

Do you want to have a better relationship with your spouse? How about improving your relationship with your parents, in-laws, coworkers, church family, and neighbors? The Golden Rule is not some sappy, feel-good, fortune cookie mumbo-jumbo. It is the distilled essence of God's desire for how we live relationally with others.

To actually live out this pragmatic principle, we must keep God in the Golden Rule. We cannot truly love others until we are truly in love with God. We cannot properly live relationally with others until we are living properly in our relationship with God. We cannot truly live this out until we are living selflessly, which means that we do so regardless of whether we receive anything for it.

What's the best part of the Golden Rule? It's so simple. It's concise, comprehensive, complete, and complementary with the totality of Scripture. Living this way prevents the need for an endless list of rules and regulations. It doesn't remove or diminish the entirety of the law and the prophets; it merely fulfills it.

Father God, help me to live positively toward others today, extending to them the same love, grace, and respect that I seek to receive and that You demonstrate.

Jesus gives us a rule that works in every situation and sums up righteousness.

Warning: False Prophets Ahead!

*"Beware of false prophets, who come to you in sheep's clothing,
but inwardly they are ravenous wolves." (Matthew 7:15)*

Wouldn't it be great if there were a sign that flashed every time a false teacher stood up to speak for God? Whether it is the recent teachings of Universalists, the individual teachings of someone like Jim Jones or David Koresh, or even the early philosophies of the Docetists or Gnostics, people always have fallen under the spell of false teachers. And the sad reality is that every generation faces false teachers and false teaching. So in the absence of a flashing neon sign warning of false teachers ahead, how can we spot the wolves among us?

False teachers will diminish the importance of Jesus, dilute the truths of Scripture, display significant moral flaws, disseminate easy believism or a health-and-wealth gospel, and disguise their lies with pieces of truth. But a strategic offense is the best defense. Knowing God's Word is the best way to spot a fake. Just like holding up counterfeit currency to the light reveals the imperfections, holding up someone's teaching to the light of God's Word will reveal the imperfections. Finally, be sure to examine the fruit, making sure that a teacher's deeds and doctrine line up.

Jesus, keep me watchful when it comes to safeguarding my spiritual health, always comparing what I hear with what You have said and demonstrated in Your Word.

> **Stay close to Jesus, and you won't walk with wolves.**

Superficial Spirituality

"Not everyone who says to me, 'Lord, Lord,' will enter the kingdom of heaven, but the one who does the will of my Father who is in heaven." (Matthew 7:21)

Most people think they will go to heaven when they die, but the truth is that not everyone who says they are a Christian will wind up in heaven. A person can know all the right Christian words but still not go to heaven. A person can be born into a Christian home and still not go to heaven. A person can even go to a Christian church and still not go to heaven. Getting into heaven is more than looking and sounding like a Christian.

If you want to ensure that you have more than a superficial spirituality, then you need to have more than just a belief in God (see James 2:19). You need to live your life dedicated to doing what God says. A profession of faith is essential, but it must be followed by a practicing faith. Faith without the follow-through of obedience is not genuine faith, and partial obedience is still disobedience.

To be clear, we are saved by faith alone in God alone, but a genuine faith in God is never alone. Righteous words and religious works must be accompanied by right living. As we do God's will, we'll experience His best and enjoy the blessings of pleasing Him.

Jesus, help me to live a life of obedience. Be with me today as I seek to fully live out the will of the Father.

> **Jesus lived to do God's will, and all who follow Jesus will do the same.**

Solid Rock or Sinking Sand?

*"Therefore whoever hears these sayings of mine and does them,
I will liken him to a wise man who built his house on the rock:
and the rain descended, . . . and the winds blew . . . ; and it
did not fall, for it was founded on the rock."*
(Matthew 7:24–25)

Living in California, I see many homes built on hillsides and sea-shores. Every time I drive past one of those particular constructions, I think, "I sure hope they have the right foundation." But even more important than building our homes on the right foundation is to make sure our lives have the right foundation.

Church attendance, ministry work, and community service are good, but they are no substitute for a solid foundation of faith built on Jesus Christ. Building a life on possessions, passions, popularity, or even the pursuit of happiness are all sandy foundations. Jesus clearly declared that our foundation must be built on obedience and trust in His words. When we trust and obey Him, our lives find the solid rock of God's power, provision, and peace.

Jesus doesn't promise us that we never will face wind and rain, but He does say that when the strong winds blow and the torrential rains fall, our faith will not be washed away. We will not drown in spiritual disaster when our faith is built on the Rock. On what foundation are you building your life? Don't build on the sinking sand of the world's ways. Listen to Jesus, learn from His words, and build your life on the solid rock of Jesus Christ and His Word.

Jesus, You are my rock and my foundation, and in You I am safe and secure.

Stand on the solid rock of Jesus, and you always will stand secure.

Marvelous Faith

"Assuredly, I say to you, I have not found such great faith, not even in Israel!" (Matthew 8:10)

Did you know there was a person in the Bible who amazed Jesus? It wasn't a priest or prominent religious leader who made Him marvel. Instead, it was a Roman soldier. A centurion in the Roman army had such a great faith that Jesus actually stopped, took notice, admired his faith, and performed a miracle for him. What made this centurion's faith worth admiring? And how can we have a faith that Jesus notices?

I believe the answer is found in the soldier's statement to Jesus: "Lord, I am not worthy that you should come under my roof. But only speak a word, and my servant will be healed" (Matthew 8:8). The greatness of this man's faith is seen first in his humility. Although he is a high-ranking military officer and a great supporter of the Jews, he sees himself as utterly unworthy. We should all come to Jesus from a position of complete humility, not demandingly or with perceived entitlement. Next, the centurion believed in the power and authority of Jesus to accomplish this great miracle. The Bible tells us that when you ask, "You must *believe* and not *doubt"* (James 1:6 NIV, italics added). Lastly, this man believed in the mere word of Jesus. He had some understanding that Jesus's word had the omnipotent power to do what it was commanded to do.

Father, work in me to come to You in humility of spirit, believing and never doubting, fully trusting in the power of Your Word.

Jesus notices when faith is loving, humble, and trusting.

Overcoming Disappointment

"And blessed is he who is not offended because of Me."
(Luke 7:23)

Has God ever disappointed you? Did you expect God to come through for you in some way, but then He didn't? God's ways are not our ways, and God's thoughts are so much higher than our thoughts (see Isaiah 55:8–9). We never will fully understand the hows and whys of God's ways. And being offended at God is, in one way or another, not trusting in His will or His way. When life's outcomes don't match what we believe they should be, we can be left with doubts and feeling offended at how God is working.

In the context of today's verse, John the Baptist's ministry had come to a screeching halt when he was imprisoned. John had given up everything to prepare the way for Jesus, and his supporters were wondering why Jesus let this happen. When our expectations don't match God's plans, disappointment can be close at hand, and our thoughts can jump to questioning God's love. God must have the final word when it comes to His will. We cannot let unanswered prayers, unchanged circumstances, or unexplained situations drive us to doubt God's perfect will and complete sovereignty. If you feel yourself drifting toward disappointment in God, let those uncertainties prompt you to find comfort in His grace, peace in His presence, hope in His love, and strength from His Word.

Jesus, I know there will be times in my life that I do not understand Your will or Your ways. Protect me from feelings of hurt and disappointment, and help me to walk by faith and not by sight when I cannot see what You are doing.

A faith in Jesus that doesn't falter always will be blessed.

The Great Privilege

"For I say to you, among those born of women there is not a greater prophet than John the Baptist; but he who is least in the kingdom of God is greater than he." (Luke 7:28)

What we think of ourselves or what others think of us is not as important as what God thinks. John the Baptist was not half-hearted, nor did he sit on the spiritual fence, no matter what people said or did to him. He did not waver, weaken, or kowtow to pressure. But that isn't what made him the greatest of the Old Testament prophets. John was considered the greatest prophet because he had the great privilege of seeing and preparing the way for Jesus Christ.

So how is it, as today's verse points out, that the least in the kingdom of God is greater than John? Are they greater in works, character, or ministry? Certainly not! Are they greater in position, privileges, and knowledge? Beyond a doubt. All who have come to faith in Christ after the Cross are greater in the sense that we live in the light of the knowledge of the redemptive work of Christ. We have received a fuller revelation of truth than any person from the Old Testament, because we see all things through the lens of the life, ministry, death, and resurrection of Jesus, and we have the presence of the Holy Spirit within us.

Just think, if God used John the Baptist in such a powerful way and called him the greatest prophet to ever live, then how much more should God be able to use us because we have a fuller knowledge of Jesus? Let's follow this great prophet's example.

Dear God, as John prepared the way and pointed people to Jesus, help me to prepare the way for people to know Jesus, and let my life point people to You.

Greatness is always tied to a greater understanding of Jesus.

Wisdom's Offspring

"Wisdom is justified by all her children." (Luke 7:35)

Living in the information age, we have quick and easy access to an abundance of knowledge. If you want to know something, all you have to do is grab your phone and, in a few seconds, *voilà!* You have the answer you're looking for. But one thing I've noticed is that people can be gluttons of information while there's a scarcity of wisdom.

Wisdom is the proper application of knowledge. More definitively, biblical wisdom is the proper application of biblical knowledge. This wisdom helps you to know what to do, when to do it, and how to do it in a way that pleases God. When "wisdom is justified by all her children," it means that wisdom is demonstrated over time. The Bible is full of God's wisdom, and those who live according to God's Word prove its wisdom by the fruit and faithfulness borne out in their lives.

The wisest people in the world always will be those who know God and live according to His Word. The wisdom of God transforms people, freeing them from sin and empowering them to live productive and pleasing lives. The fruit of godly wisdom makes a person more discerning, compassionate, understanding, wholesome, gentle, peace loving, merciful, sincere, and humble.

May I walk closer to You, Jesus, and be a living example of Your wisdom and grace. May Your wisdom bear its fruit in my life.

Live surrendered to Jesus, and you will cultivate godly wisdom.

Loving God

"Therefore, I tell you, her many sins have been forgiven—as her great love has shown. But whoever has been forgiven little loves little." (Luke 7:47 NIV)

It is easy to judge what we don't understand. For the woman in Luke 7, a former prostitute, the grace and forgiveness of God that Jesus showed her made her see the ugliness of her sin and the magnitude of God's love for her.

Are we able to do the same? Think of how many sins we have already committed in our lifetime. The number is probably staggering. We must never lose sight of the atrociousness of sin. We can be quick to abhor it when we see it in others, but our sin is just as appalling to God. The degree to which we understand the depth of God's forgiveness and the ugliness of our own sins is the degree to which we will love God. For this woman, her love was extreme, extravagant, and exuberant as she washed, wiped, kissed, and anointed Jesus's feet. If your love for God has grown cold, perhaps it is because you have forgotten the depth of the sin from which you've been delivered. A forgiven heart always should be a fountain of godly love, first toward the One who forgave and, second, toward those who need forgiving.

Can others see our love for God? Would someone look at us and say that we love God with an extreme, extravagant, and exuberant love?

Lord, You have blessed me beyond measure through the forgiveness of my sins. Even though I am undeserving I want to be one who loves much.

> **The secret to loving Jesus much is to realize how wonderful it is to hear the words "your sins are forgiven."**

Showing Compassion

"But if you had known what this means, 'I desire mercy and not sacrifice,' you would not have condemned the guiltless."
(Matthew 12:7)

God prefers relationship to ritual. The role of sacrifice should not surpass the need for compassion. Sacrifice has its place, but God rather would see His people demonstrate kindness through acts of compassion than merely go through the religious motions. One of the problems Jesus saw in the Pharisees was they were very good at being religious, but they were terrible at showing mercy or compassion. The natural human tendency is to try and please God through external religious works. And it's true that we should give our time, talent, and treasures to God, because external actions often reveal an internal change. However, God wants us to move past merely doing that which is perceived as religious good works and take our relationship deeper.

Jesus wants to use us as conduits of His compassion. The mercy and compassion we have received from Jesus are also what we need to extend to others. Many of the "works" Jesus did were acts of compassion in which He healed the sick, raised the dead, comforted the afflicted, and afflicted the comfortable. Compassion takes action; it cannot sit idly by. It moves toward those who are hurting. Are you ready and willing to let your life be lived with a Jesus kind of compassion?

Jesus, I know that You are more concerned with my heart than my religious habits. Break my heart of stone, and make it a heart that beats with compassion for others.

Jesus followers should be known for their compassion.

Rest and Relaxation

"For the Son of Man is Lord even of the Sabbath."
(Matthew 12:8)

Our days revolve around our calendars. Our phones have scheduled to-do lists that beep, appointments that pop up, and weekly occurrences that send out reminders. It has become difficult to unplug, unwind, and take it easy, because we often overwork, overcommit, and overlook our need to take a Sabbath rest. Perhaps you are like me and can see God chipping away in those areas of your life in which you're displaying a lack of trust. How you observe the Sabbath might be one of those strongholds in your life. Do you trust God to help you get your work done in just six days?

Taking a day of rest made it on God's Top Ten List (see Exodus 34:21), and Jesus reminds us that the Sabbath was a gift for us so that we would be regularly refreshed and renewed, both physically and spiritually (see Mark 2:27). God created a need for Sabbath rest deep within us, not just for our bodies, but for our spiritual health, which is why it's so important. It doesn't matter what day of the week your Sabbath is. It just matters that you have one. The Lord wants us to take a rest not only from all the fixations of work, but also from all the fixations of working to earn His favor.

Lord, show me the areas of my life in which I haven't fully submitted to You, and help me learn how to accept Your gift of rest and practice honoring You with my rest.

Jesus needs to be the Lord of every day, including our day of rest.

The Great Divide

"And if a house is divided against itself, that house will not be able to stand." (Matthew 12:25 ESV)

There's a lot of conflict in our world. Our planet is filled with wars, disputes, discrimination, racism, terrorism, and partisanship. As a result, we have broken relationships and division. It is something we see in every area of life. Whether it's a business, sports team, government, church, or marriage, there must be unity for success, survival, and fruitfulness. Without unity, organizations and relationships are vulnerable to attack and inevitably will collapse, wither, and die. It's only a matter of time.

The apostle Paul warned the churches there should be no divisions among them and to avoid people who cause division (see 1 Corinthians 1:10; Romans 16:17). Division obstructs growth and hinders progress. This should first be a warning to us. Is there unity in our relationships? Would others consider us as people who bring unity or division to a situation, relationship, or the church?

Unity comes as we live submitted to the Holy Spirit, allowing God to control our thoughts, attitudes, and emotions. Fostering unity in our relationships requires us to be loving toward others, demonstrate patience, show gentleness, and cultivate humility (see Ephesians 4:2–3). This way, we can stand united instead of falling divided.

God, give me the discernment to recognize strife and division in relationships, and grant me the wisdom to be an ambassador of unity.

> **Unity across all relationships is easiest when Jesus is at the center.**

Choosing Sides

"He who is not with Me is against Me." (Matthew 12:30)

Every day we decide what we're going to do for the next twenty-four hours. We choose what to wear, what to have for breakfast, and what we need to be accomplish. Every day we also decide whom we are serving. Are we serving ourselves and our own desires? Or, are we serving God and what He desires?

The way we choose to live each day is the true standard by which our priorities are determined. Everyone has a choice to make, and for the Christian, the most important choice we must make, day in and day out, is whether or not we're going to live for Jesus. If we are not making choices *for* God, the reality is that we are making choices *against* God. "Oh now wait," you may be thinking, "I never would refuse to choose God." But the reality is that if we are making self-first decisions, then we are making choices against God.

Choosing to serve the Lord isn't always an easy decision to make, but the battle of choosing God or choosing ourselves begins the moment we wake up in the morning. It is a choice that we must renew daily. It is a choice that says, "I will draw near to God today, and I will let God shape my thoughts, words, and actions throughout the day." It is a choice that's made easier when we decide to start our days by spending time with God. It isn't always easy making those God-first decisions, but if you begin each day by choosing God first, it will make all the difference in choosing Him again and again.

Father, help me to make God-centered decisions today. May I make choices that put You first and not me first.

> **Choosing Jesus isn't a one-time decision; it is one that we must make every day.**

BLASPHEMY!

"Therefore I say to you, every sin and blasphemy will be forgiven men, but the blasphemy against the Spirit will not be forgiven men." (Matthew 12:31)

Is there such a thing as a sin that God won't forgive? The thought that there could be a sin so bad that God would not forgive it makes many people eager to know if they have ever committed the unpardonable sin. There are Christians who have been divorced, had abortions, or committed adultery and thought that God could never forgive them. Others think that suicide is the one thing that God won't forgive.

When Jesus cast out demons, His critics accused Him of being in cahoots with Satan. Essentially, they said that He was an agent of the Devil. Blasphemy of the Spirit, however, is not the occasional wrong thought or bad behavior. Sin is sin, and we never want to diminish the severity of it. But those sins are not the persistent, deliberate resistance and rejection of Jesus or the willful ascription of Jesus's actions to Satan. That is the core of blasphemy of the Holy Spirit. It is not that God is unwilling to forgive someone. Rather, it's that someone who is guilty of such a sin has fully and finally turned their back on God and hardened their heart against God's grace.

Christian, you can rest easy, knowing that you did not, cannot, and could not commit such a sin. The Spirit of God within you would prevent you from ever crossing that line.

Jesus, I know I cannot commit the unpardonable sin, but I also know that all sin is hurtful and harmful. Work in me by the power of your Holy Spirit to resist sin.

Jesus forgives all sin except the willful opposition and rejection of God.

Apples and Oranges

"A tree is known by its fruit." (Matthew 12:33)

In my backyard here in California, I have a couple of fruit trees that supply my wife and I with tasty homegrown oranges and lemons. Some years the trees bear more fruit than others, but every year we can count on them to bear their respective fruit. Those trees always remind me of Jesus's words: "A tree is known by its fruit" (Matthew 12:33).

Spiritual fruit is important, and all believers should be bearing fruit in their lives. The fruit we bear is a reflection of our spiritual health and what we cultivate in our spiritual lives. Jesus condemned the religious leaders for producing bad fruit, because they rejected Jesus and spoke evil of His works. The spiritual fruit that God wants us to produce is listed in Galatians 5:22–23: "But the fruit of the Spirit is love, joy, peace, longsuffering, kindness, goodness, faithfulness, gentleness, self-control." We will bear good fruit when we deepen our relationship with Christ and allow the Holy Spirit to nourish and grow us, producing Christlikeness. Our words and actions are the result of our choices, and those choices determine the fruit we produce. The quality and the quantity of the fruit we grow in our lives will be a reflection of how much we water our lives with the Word of God.

Jesus, help me to follow Your words and walk in the Spirit so that I can produce good spiritual fruit.

Jesus will help you produce a life of good fruit.

The Last Word

"I tell you, on the day of judgment people will give account for every careless word they speak." (Matthew 12:36 ESV)

"I appreciate you." "I believe in you." Sometimes words feel like a hug, warm and comforting. At other times, words can be like a wood-chipper, destructive and devastating. *"You will never amount to any-thing." "You are so stupid."* We all know the weight that words possess, because we all have experienced their force.

The Bible admonishes us to make the best use of our words, because words express what is in our hearts (see Matthew 12:34). There is no better gauge of our hearts than the words that come from our mouths. Just like a good tree produces good fruit and bad trees produces bad fruit, so the mouth reveals our spiritual condition. What do your words say about you? Even the words you speak about yourself are important. Your words speak volumes, and one day the words we have spoken either will speak good of us or bad of us as we stand before God.

God takes our words very seriously, and so should we. We should be using our words to build up and to bless, not to break down or belittle.

May these words of my mouth and this meditation of my heart be pleasing in your sight, LORD. (Psalm 19:14 NIV).

> **Speak like Jesus, and you always will speak loving truth.**

Something Smells Fishy

"For as Jonah was three days and three nights in the belly of the great fish, so will the Son of Man be three days and three nights in the heart of the earth." (Matthew 12:40)

What does it take for someone to believe in Jesus? Some say that seeing is believing. They want solid, convincing proof, or they won't believe. There must be some sort of clear evidence that God is real and that Jesus is who He said He was. The critics of Jesus fell into this category of disbelief, wanting to see some mind-blowing sign as proof of Jesus's divinity. Jesus refused to indulge them. Instead, He said the sign they were to accept was the sign of Jonah. But how is this fish story proof?

Jesus's death and resurrection are to be the definitive proof of His divinity and the foundation of our faith. Sure, I could say the proof of Jesus's resurrection is the empty tomb, the five hundred-plus post-Resurrection witnesses, the changed and emboldened lives of the disciples, or the spread and presence of Christianity today. Yet despite the evidence, some simply do not want to believe. There always will be those who look at the story of Jonah, say that something smells fishy, and doubt the authenticity of biblical evidence. It has been, is, and always will be a matter of faith, and "faith comes from hearing, and hearing through the word of Christ" (Romans 10:17 ESV).

Jesus, Your resurrection is all the proof anyone needs, and it gives my life meaning, purpose, and the power to walk in victory over all of life's circumstances.

Christianity stands on the basis of the resurrection of Jesus.

Running from God

"The men of Nineveh will rise up in the judgment with this generation and condemn it, because they repented at the preaching of Jonah." (Matthew 12:41)

Have you ever found yourself refusing to follow God's direction? Your aspirations pull you one way, and God's convictions pull you another. Jonah knew what God was calling him to do, yet he resisted anyway. Jonah knew what was right, yet he struggled all the same. It took some drastic intervention by God for Jonah to realize his rebellion. You see, before Jonah could be used by God, he had to learn a lesson in mercy and forgiveness. During his time in the belly of the great fish, Jonah was impressively persuaded that God is the one who decides how His mercy and forgiveness will be demonstrated.

Following God is a process, and we don't always get things right the first time. But God is gracious, and He doesn't give up on us. Is God trying to get your attention? Is He asking you to do something that you are struggling with? Don't run away from what God is showing you. Running from God's commands doesn't release you from them; it just means that it will take you longer to learn them. Every step away from God is a step in the wrong direction.

Lord God, when I am tempted to run from Your will or Your ways, train me to do the opposite and run to You instead.

When Jesus gives you something to do, don't waste time running from it.

Family Resemblance

"Who is my mother, and who are my brothers? . . . For whoever does the will of my Father in heaven is my brother and sister and mother." (Matthew 12:48, 50 ESV)

I know the power of adoption, because I was adopted. I know nothing about my biological parents, except that they were drug addicts. And I don't know whether I have any biological doppelgängers walking around in the world. What I do know is that one day, a loving couple, Chuck and Ann, brought me home and made me part of their family. When we believe in Jesus Christ, we immediately become adopted into God's family, God becomes our Father, and we become His children (see John 1:12–13; Matthew 6:9; Galatians 3:26).

As grateful as I am to have been adopted into a wonderful and loving family, being part of God's family transcends all physical ties. When Jesus spoke this way about family, He was not diminishing the importance of our physical family ties; He was redefining the family. As adopted children of God, we are led by the Spirit of God, have received the Spirit of adoption, and have been made fellow heirs with Christ. God's loving and gracious decision to adopt us into His family should show itself in our lives. In other words, there should be a family resemblance that shows itself in how we love others and live for God, our Heavenly Father.

Father, thank You for making me part of Your family. I look forward to the day when I am at home with You in heaven.

Obedience to Jesus displays our adoption into the family of God.

APRIL

The Sower and the Seed

*"A sower went out to sow. . . . Some seeds fell along the path,
and the birds came and devoured them. Other seeds fell on
rocky ground, . . . and immediately they sprang up. . . . And
since they had no root, they withered away. Other seeds fell
among thorns, and the thorns grew up and choked them.
Other seeds fell on good soil and produced grain."*
(Matthew 13:3–8 ESV)

So much of horticulture is outside of human control. We cannot control the wind, rain, or blight. Sowing the Word of God is similar. There is much we cannot control. Some people will outright reject the message of the gospel. Others, as soon as tough times hit, will walk away from God. Still others will walk with God, but over time they become increasingly distracted by the worries of the world and the deceitfulness of wealth. However, there is a fourth group: those who will hear the Word of God, receive it, and go on to be fruitful and faithful followers (see Matthew 13:19–23).

Despite the fact that much lies outside of our control, the farmer still sows, and the Christian still proclaims. As sowers of the Word of God, we must spread the gospel seed so that others can hear it and respond to it in faith (see Romans 10:14–17). However, we must trust God for the results, because it is God who gives the increase (see 1 Corinthians 3:6).

Some people may not respond to the gospel, but by the Spirit's work of tilling the soil of a person's heart, others will respond. Just as the sower goes out to sow, we need to go out and tell others about Jesus. Some will respond in faith and become faithful and fruitful followers of Jesus, and some will not. But there's no greater privilege than being involved in the process.

*Father, May I share Your Word with hope, joy, and faithfulness. Give
me opportunities to sow into people's lives with great power.*

**Share Jesus with a hopeful heart, and leave
the results to God.**

Getting Your Hands Dirty

"Still other seed fell on good soil, where it produced a crop—a hundred, sixty or thirty times what was sown. Whoever has ears, let them hear." (Matthew 13:8–9 NIV)

Have you ever seen a gardener's hands? They are rough and soiled. That's because the process of cultivating requires getting your hands dirty. Ground requires cultivation to ensure the soil is prepared for fruitfulness. And in the same way that soil needs *tilling* and *fertilizing* for fruitfulness, the soil of our hearts needs cultivation for fruitfulness.

There are two great impediments to the soil of our hearts: busyness and self-confidence. Just as *tilling* loosens soil and removes weeds, a properly tilled spirit will loosen the constraints of busyness and remove the weeds of self-confidence, producing humility. God's Word loves to grow in the soil of humble hearts. *Fertilizing* provides essential nourishment required for optimal growth, and the proper balance of water and nutrients leads to the greatest growth. It's the same with the soil of our hearts, which needs the constant watering of God's Word and the nutritive work of prayer.

You are the one who determines what kind of soil your heart will have. If the soil of your heart has become hard and dry or too overcrowded to welcome God's Word, then it's time to get your hands dirty as you loosen up the ground, remove some weeds, and begin to fertilize the soil so that God's Word can grow.

Jesus, help me to do the dirty work of tilling and fertilizing the soil of my heart. I always want to have a receptive heart for Your Word so that I can be productive for You.

Cultivating the soil of your heart will allow Jesus to produce an abundant harvest in your life.

The Purpose of Parables

"This is why I speak to them in parables, because seeing
they do not see, and hearing they do not hear, nor do they
understand." (Matthew 13:11–13 ESV)

"We are, as a species, addicted to story," says Jonathan Gottschall. "Even when the body goes to sleep, the mind stays up all night, telling itself stories."[8] Good stories do more than transfer information; they cultivate passion, inspire action, and build connections. Jesus was a master storyteller, and people came from all around to hear Him preach and teach. One of His most effective communication techniques was telling a spiritual story using easily recognizable imagery. We call them parables. Jesus spoke over thirty unique parables in which He sought to reveal truth to those seeking God and hide truth from those who wrongly flocked to Him.

Jesus used parables because they were easy to understand and easy to remember. And let's be honest. You won't use what you can't remember. Jesus used parables to cultivate a passion for God, to inspire godly living, and to build personal connections with God.

There's power in a good story. And as believers, we can use our stories to cultivate godliness, inspire holiness, and encourage godly relationships.

God, I know You seek to work in people's lives, so help me to be ready
to share Your truth with others in a way that creates passion, inspires
action, and builds connections.

The parables of Jesus capture our attention
and create a connection with God.

S-H-I-N-E

"When someone lights a lamp, does he put a box over it to shut out the light? Of course not! . . . A lamp is placed on a stand to shine and be useful. (Mark 4:21 TLB)

Living for God means putting yourself out there. Whether you like it or not, as a Christian your life is on display for others to see. *But I don't like being the center of attention. I am uncomfortable in the spotlight.* As true as that may be, God still wants you to S-H-IN-E for Him.

Whether you realize it or not, people are watching you to see how you will react in life's many diverse situations. They watch how you dress, how you take care of your home, how you work, how you treat other people, and how you handle difficulties. Some people may not read the Bible, but they are reading your lives. For many, you are the living embodiment of the pages of Scripture, read by those in your life.

So how can you shine brightly for God? Consider Moses. After he came down from spending time in God's presence, his face shone brightly (see Exodus 34:29). This serves as a reminder that we don't need to overcomplicate the process. The more time we spend in the presence of God, the brighter our lives will shine for Him. A light bulb shines because it is connected to power. Stay connected to God's power, and you will S-H-I-N-E in brilliant ways.

Lord, thank You for being the light within me so that I can shine brightly to the world around me. May I be a light that helps others see you more clearly.

SHINE for Jesus—Show Him IN Everything.

Wheat and Tares

"Let both grow together until the harvest, and at the time of harvest I will say to the reapers, 'First gather together the tares and bind them in bundles to burn them, but gather the wheat into my barn.' " (Matthew 13:24–30)

Satan is a deceiver. He's also a fraud and a copycat, and what you may not know is that he has infiltrated the church. We certainly know that outside the church there will be those who appear to be Christians but are not. But what is more disturbing is that Satan plants such people within the church.

The tares that Jesus described in the parable of the wheat and the tares look almost like wheat in the beginning stages of growth. But after they grow a little more, it becomes clear they are weeds that can undermine the growth of the wheat. We always will have tares that infiltrate our ranks, satanic plants like Judas Iscariot, Diotrephes, Demas, and Ananias and Sapphira who can undermine the work of God (see John 13; 3 John 1:9–10; Acts 5). But it is not our job to clear those people out. It's God's responsibility to take care of the tares. The day is coming when the Lord will separate the good from the bad, because He alone knows what is in a person's heart, and He alone is able to know whether someone's faith is real.

Just as the wheat's job is to grow and be productive, our job is to make sure that *we* have an authentic, personal, and productive relationship with God and, through the process of sanctification, grow closer to Jesus.

Lord God, keep me rooted and grounded in Your Word so that I will grow and glorify You.

> **Jesus will separate the wheat from the tares.
> Until then, be productive in your corner of
> God's field.**

Tiny but Mighty

"To what shall we liken the kingdom of God? . . . It is like a mustard seed which . . . is smaller than all the seeds on earth; but when it is sown, it grows up and becomes greater than all herbs, and shoots out large branches." (Mark 4:30–32)

Bigger is better, or so it seems. Our society values bigger numbers, bigger churches, bigger bank accounts, and bigger houses. But God's kingdom is different. Small things can produce big results. A mustard seed may look insignificant at only one millimeter in diameter, yet the smallest seed in the garden can produce the largest plant.

God loves small beginnings, because He gets the glory. The church is a perfect example, because from eleven unlikely men, Jesus grew His church. When the kingdom of God began to spread, it wasn't because of a great social media campaign or millions of dollars spent on global advertising. It was the Spirit of God drawing, convicting, and working.

The greater the platform, the greater chance of success. This is the world's way of thinking. But God's way is to take mustard seeds, those small, ordinary starts with inconspicuous, unknown people, and supply them with the power of the Holy Spirit. No step of faith is too small for God to do something big. The smallest step, done God's way, in God's time, and with God's power, is never unimportant or unproductive.

God, may I never despise the days of "small beginnings" (Zechariah 4:10 NLT). I know that You waste nothing, and any act of obedience is never a small thing with You.

With Jesus, small beginnings can have big endings.

Immeasurable Treasure

"The kingdom of heaven is like treasure hidden in a field, which a man found and hid; and for joy over it he goes and sells all that he has and buys that field." (Matthew 13:44)

Your values form the foundation of your life. They control the choices you make, and they determine the direction your life goes. They influence your relationships, your career, and how you spend your time and money. The problem is that too many Christians don't take the time to reflect on what is important to them and then recalibrate, making the necessary adjustments to their lives. As John Calvin pointed out, "We are so captivated by the allurements of the world, that eternal life fades from our view; and in consequence of our carnality, the spiritual graces of God are far from being held by us in the estimation which they deserve."[9]

Jesus makes it abundantly clear that nothing is more valuable than the kingdom of heaven. The kingdom of heaven is of such immeasurable value that when we truly understand its worth, we will do whatever it takes to possess it. We will pursue it with urgency, and our ownership of it will bring us the greatest joy.

The proper valuation of God's kingdom will properly position our priorities, appropriately adjust our attitudes. and aptly alter our actions. What value have you placed on your pursuit of God?

God, help me never to diminish the value of being part of Your kingdom. May this be a reminder for me to pause today and reflect on the values and priorities I hold dear.

There should be no person, place, or thing worth more than your relationship with Jesus.

The Reality of Hell

"The angels will come forth, separate the wicked from among the just, and cast them into the furnace of fire. There will be wailing and gnashing of teeth." (Matthew 13:49–50)

Hell—now there's a subject for polite dinner conversation, right? Not exactly. But as uncomfortable as the subject may be, we should not ignore its importance. Jesus talked more about hell than anyone else in the Bible, so it is clearly significant. Why did Jesus speak about hell as much as He did? Because He doesn't want anyone to go there.

What should we know about hell? First of all, hell is a real place. It is a place of torment, and it is place that lasts forever. The exact conditions of hell may be a bit mysterious, but one thing is certain: part of what makes it hell is the absence of God. The good news is that God doesn't want anyone to go to hell (see 2 Peter 3:9). God loves us so much that He sent Jesus to die for us so that no one has to go there (see John 3:16–17).

Hell isn't God's choice for anyone. Hell is an individual's choice. As much as God doesn't want you to go to hell, the choice is yours to make. Choosing to live apart from God on Earth also will follow you into eternity. Hell is the default destination for those who reject Jesus.

God, I know I cannot find goodness, blessing, and joy apart from You. Even though the reality of hell is hard to grasp, living for heaven means that I understand I'm saved from hell.

Salvation from hell can be found by placing your faith in Jesus.

Priorities

"Follow Me, and let the dead bury their own dead."
(Matthew 8:22)

Not everyone is quick to follow Jesus. But we can be quick to provide a reason for why we aren't ready to make God first in our lives: *I'm too busy. I will do it later. I have to get my life together first.* One day Jesus met a young disciple who seemed eager to join Him, but when Jesus asked this disciple to follow Him, he made an excuse as to why he wasn't quite ready to give up everything to do as Jesus asked.

There is speculation as to whether this man's father was already dead or whether he wanted to wait around until after his father died so that he could receive his portion of the inheritance. That's not the important issue. Jesus was challenging the man's priorities. He was preoccupied with the cares and concerns of this life, and Jesus was telling him that following Him supersedes all other obligations, relationships, and responsibilities. We should not prioritize our personal interests over our personal relationship with Jesus.

Don't let any *thing* hold you back from following Jesus. Equally, don't let any *person* hold you back from following Jesus. He isn't looking for admirers or fans; He is looking for faithful followers.

> *Dear Lord, I admit to You there have been times when I have not made following You my first priority. Forgive me for those moments, and grant me the strength keep you first today and every day. In Jesus' name, amen.*

When Jesus says, "Follow me," it means that we should drop everything and follow Him.

A Cure for Weak Faith

*"Why are you afraid, O you of little faith?" Then he rose and
rebuked the winds and the sea, and there was a great calm. And the
men marveled. (Matthew 8:26–27 ESV)*

How do you know whether your faith is weak or strong? God often
tests our faith to show us where our faith has faults, because a faith
that falters in the face of adversity is a little faith. And a faith that is
not tested cannot be trusted.

Our faith often falters because we have the wrong mindset.
The most common faith issues that reveal a weak or little faith are
worry, fear, forgetfulness, and lack of focus. We worry about our circumstances and God's provision, we fear because we can't see God's
answer, and we forget God's faithfulness and His past provision. All of
these faith issues stem from a lack of focus. We focus on our circumstances more than on Christ, we see our shortages rather than God's
abundant supply, and we keep our eyes set on our current problems
while failing to remember God's past provisions.

If we want a strong faith that not only remains steady in the face
of adversity but also is a faith that changes things and accomplishes
much, then we must do the following: set our minds on the truth of
Scripture, remember the faithfulness of God (past and present), and
look for His hand in our present situation.

*God, I know that just as I would study to take a test, I must study
Your Word so that my faith is ready for testings that will come. As my
mind is strongly set on You, my faith will be stronger.*

**Sometimes it takes a storm to remind us of
what Jesus can do.**

Overcoming Obstacles

"Somebody touched Me, for I perceived power
going out from Me." (Luke 8:46)

Let's face it. We all have issues, and we all have obstacles to overcome. But if you want something bad enough, then you will go after it, because pursuit is the proof of passion. The Bible tells us about a woman whose passionate pursuit of Jesus brought her healing.

This woman had issues and obstacles to overcome. She had a menstrual blood flow issue for twelve years, a condition that made her ceremonial unclean. The repercussions were a life of isolation as a social outcast. In addition, she had financial problems. In search of healing, she had spent all her money on doctors who provided no relief and no cure (see Luke 8:43). She was broke. The world left her feeling helpless, hopeless, penniless, and friendless. But she wasn't faithless. Despite obvious obstacles, her faith sent her in pursuit of Jesus, a pursuit so passionate that she wouldn't let her social standing or the large crowd surrounding Jesus keep her from Him. As she approached Jesus, she reached out, knowing that making a connection with Him would change her life. And it did.

Jesus, I know when I face an obstacle or heartache, it is my connection with You that brings me complete confidence knowing that no matter how You choose to handle my problem, Your solution is always in my best interest.

> **The way to overcome obstacles, pain, and heartache is by reaching out to Jesus and allowing Him to change your situation.**

Only Believe

"Your daughter is dead. Do not trouble the Teacher." But when Jesus heard it, He answered him, saying, **"Do not be afraid; only believe, and she will be made well."** *(Luke 8:49–50)*

Sooner or later, we all face fearful situations, situations in which hindrances and setbacks can shake our confidence in God, and we don't know what to do, situations in which the bottom suddenly drops out from under us, and we find ourselves in the midst of a tragedy, desperate situation, or at the end of our emotional, physical, or spiritual rope. When our world comes crashing down around us, believing in Jesus isn't easy. Those around us may even laugh and say, "What a fool to trust in Jesus!" But we must look past these situations and look directly at Jesus.

Jairus went to Jesus for the healing of his sick daughter. Then the situation went from bad to terribly worse, and she died. Those around Jairus told him to leave Jesus alone, because the situation was irreversible. But Jesus told Jairus to face his fear and *only believe*.

It isn't easy to drive out fear. The only one way to do it is by believing—believing in the presence, promises, and power of God in Jesus Christ. Jesus can bring new life to a situation that seems dead. Jesus can make a way when we come to a dead end. Jesus is the One who makes all things new if we only believe.

Jesus, just as you challenged Jairus to believe, help me to look to You and believe that You can bring new life to my relationships, finances, health, or spiritual walk.

> **Jesus can bring new life to our fearful situations if we *only believe*.**

Free of Charge

"Freely you have received, freely give." (Matthew 10:8)

God doesn't like cheapskates when it comes giving away that which He has freely given to us. If we hold on to what God has given us with a closed fist, then we are ignoring the fact that every good thing that we have has come to us from God (see James 1:17).

When Jesus sent His disciples to preach the gospel, He gave them gifts to accomplish their mission. Jesus gave them power and authority to drive out evil spirits and heal every disease and sickness. He even provided them with the power to raise the dead (see Matthew 10:8). He added that since they freely received their empowerment from God, they were to freely give out what God had given them.

We can easily and incorrectly claim a sense of ownership to all we posses. We can be stingy in dispensing forgiveness when we have been freely forgiven. We can be greedy with God's grace when God has been abundantly gracious to us. We can be uncharitable with compassion when God's compassion never fails us.

Jesus reminds us to be prepared to give as freely as we have received from God and to give joyfully (see 2 Corinthians 9:7). We have been chosen to be conduits of God to bless others, not impediments that cause people to stumble.

Father, as I meditate on all that You have given me, may I always express my gratitude by freely, fully, and joyfully giving.

> **Lasting joy comes when we freely give that which God has given to us.**

Sheep, Wolves, Snakes and Doves

"Behold, I send you out as sheep in the midst of wolves.
Therefore be wise as serpents and harmless as doves."
(Matthew 10:16)

The world is a hostile place, and it should come as no surprise that many people are antagonistic and even aggressively opposed to the gospel message. Jesus was profoundly aware of the dangers that would face those who were willing to share the Good News, so He gave us a vivid forewarning. As we go out to share Jesus with others, we go out like sheep among wolves.

It's no secret that sheep are staggeringly simpleminded and significantly vulnerable. Therefore, Jesus gave the disciples a piece of advice: They were to be as wise as serpents and as harmless as doves. Jesus's instruction means that we are to have a balance of snakelike intelligence and dovelike innocence.

A Christian who goes into the world as wise as a serpent will use good sense and wisdom. Wisdom is the proper application of spiritually right-minded thinking and biblically sound judgment. Wisdom naturally protects and advances God's purposes. Being dovelike means relating to unbelievers with purity of intent, a gentle approach, and peaceable behavior. The enemy wants to keep people from realizing God's wonderful plan for their lives, so we must share the gospel with the proper balance of wisdom and vulnerability in order to properly promote Jesus.

God, help me to maneuver wisely and gently so that I can be mindful of the warfare around me. Grant me boldness to share, and the love to do so, with truthful humility.

Jesus wants us to be resourceful and respectful as we live in a hostile world.

Being a Servant

"It is enough for a disciple that he be like his teacher, and a servant like his master." (Matthew 10:25)

Do you remember being asked as a child, "What do you want to be when you grow up?" I doubt anyone answered that question by saying, "I want to be a servant." But servants are exactly what God wants us to grow up to be. Therefore, God is building into His people the same servant qualities that characterized Jesus.

Being a servant like Jesus means that we have to change our attitudes. We spend most of our time focused on serving ourselves, but following Jesus's example means that we should spend more time focused on serving others. Being a servant like Jesus means realizing that our lives belong to God. Everything we are and have is from Him and for Him. We are merely managers. Being a servant like Jesus also means becoming more interested in glorifying God than gaining personal greatness. Our lives aren't measured by the success we receive; they are measured by how successfully we allow God to work in and through them.

Our identity is to be found in Christ, and our Christlikeness is most evident when we love and serve others.

Jesus, help me to let go of my selfishness and humbly seek to serve others to the glory of God.

> **We will find our greatest fulfillment serving as Jesus served.**

Truth Triumphs

"Therefore do not fear them. For there is nothing covered that will not be revealed and hidden that will not be known."
(Matthew 10:26)

It is important to remember that good wins in the end. Truth triumphs, and lies will be exposed. That being said, every believer at some point is likely to face evil opposition in the form of false accusations. That's because the Enemy is a liar and a deceiver (see Genesis 3:1; Revelation 12:9). Some people will rise up maliciously to tarnish the reputation of another. Others may manipulate or exaggerate facts about your integrity, hoping to defame or malign your character. Joseph dealt with the false accusation of sexual assault (see Genesis 39:11–14), Jeremiah was falsely imprisoned for being a deserter (see Jeremiah 37:11–16), and false witnesses lied about Jesus during His trial (see Mark 14:55–59), but God saw to it that the truth came out.

False accusations can sting and can even be devastating. But we have nothing to fear, because God will one day reveal the secrets of people's hearts, expose them, and judge them (see Romans 2:16). At the final judgment, those who have persecuted Christians will be exposed, and those who have been faithful to God will be exonerated. Present trials should not frighten us, because we are living in the light of God's truth, and truth ultimately will triumph.

Let God be your strength, let God be the judge, and trust in Him to deal with deception.

Father, thank you that I can rest in the knowledge that one day, truth will triumph, wrongs will be made right, and falsehoods will lie in ruins.

Jesus knows the truth, and one day He will silence all the lies and right all the wrongs.

A Healthy Fear

"Don't be afraid of those who can kill only your bodies—but can't touch your souls! Fear only God who can destroy both soul and body in hell." (Matthew 10:28 TLB)

Normally the Bible talks about being fearless, because fear and faith cannot coexist. When we let fear get a foothold, we are dowsing the embers of our faith. However, there is one type of fear that is healthy and faith filled, and it is the fear of God.

What does it mean to have a healthy fear of God? The Bible tells us that "the fear of the LORD is the beginning of knowledge" (Proverbs 1:7). God is the ultimate source of truth, knowledge, and wisdom, and fearing God has more to do with knowledge and love than trembling in terror. Fearing God has more to do with understanding and respecting the majesty and immensity of God and less to do with cowering in a corner or disingenuously kowtowing to God to avoid punishment. The fear of God accentuates our insufficiency in the presence of God and immediately drops us to our knees in righteous abasement. It is a fear from which Isaiah's vision of God made him cry, "Woe is me!" and confess, "I am undone! Because I am a man of unclean lips" (Isaiah 6:5).

Godly fear is a paradox, because when you fear God, you fear nothing else. If there is anything you fear more than God, then you are allowing that fear to be bigger than God.

Jesus, I know that as I fear God, I will trust You more, know You better, live more cleanly, and fear others less.

Jesus knows that a healthy fear of God is helpful for our spiritual walk.

God Cares!

*"Are not two sparrows sold for a copper coin? And not one
of them falls to the ground apart from your Father's will.
But the very hairs of your head are all numbered. Do not
fear therefore; you are of more value than many sparrows."*
(Matthew 10:29–31)

It is easy to feel insignificant in a world of nearly eight billion people. Feelings of inadequacy, insecurity, and even questioning the importance of our lives can regularly apprehend our thoughts. The result is that we can question whether God really cares about what's going on in our lives.

Even though God can feel a million miles away, He isn't! One thing we must always remember is that God is omnipresent, omniscient, and omnibenevolent. In other words, God is everywhere at all times. He knows everything at all times, and He is infinitely loving at all times. That means that God knows every detail of your life. He knows the pain in your body. He is aware of the financial worries you have. He sees how your boss is treating you. He understands the hurts you have in your heart. He is entirely and accurately aware of everything at all times, both visible and invisible, and He sees it all through His loving eyes.

Does God care, then? The answer is a resounding yes. God cares. In fact, He cares more than you care. He wants to help you more than you want His help. He knows what you need more than you know what you need. Yes, He cares.

*God, when I am tempted to wonder if You care, remind me that I
am the object of Your attention every moment of every day of my life!*

**You are not invisible to Jesus, you are
not overlooked by Jesus, and you are not
insignificant to Jesus.**

Working with Purpose

"Do not labor for the food which perishes, but for the food which endures to everlasting life, which the Son of Man will give you, because God the Father has set His seal on Him."
(John 6:27)

How bad you want something will determine how hard you work for it, which begs the question: What are you working for? Most people spend the majority of their lives working a joyless job, devoid of any purpose other than earning a paycheck to pay the bills and buy the desired creature comforts with what's left. We often have to work harder and longer because we overspend and over leverage ourselves just so we can have the nicest and newest. But shouldn't work be more than that?

Work is important, and there is no doubt that God expects us to work for food (see Genesis 3:19; 2 Thessalonians 3:10), but Jesus did not mean that satisfying our physical appetites is to be all-important and all-consuming. Instead, the purpose and priority of our work is to produce food that endures forever.

No matter what your job is, your work is meaningful, because God has placed you there to reflect His nature and character in the workplace.

Dear God, help me not to see work as a grind, but as something You have given to me with the purpose of serving others and introducing them to Jesus.

Your greatest purpose at work is to represent and reflect Jesus to your coworkers.

Soul Food

"I am the bread of life." (John 6:35)

Nothing is more important than Jesus. You can do without many things, but you cannot do without Jesus. The problem is that not everyone understands that. So how can a limitless God communicate to limited humanity our undeniable and unconditional need for Jesus? Well, perhaps there is something to the old adage, "The quickest way to a man's heart is through his stomach."

Bread, specifically in the Bible, is a significant food. It came in the form of manna in the desert for the Israelites. It was broken time and again at Passover meals, and earlier in John, chapter six, Jesus fed five thousand-plus people with two fish and five loaves of bread. Jesus piggybacks on that miracle to make the point that bread may satisfy the stomach, but He satisfies the soul.

Ultimately, life just doesn't work unless you believe that Jesus is the main thing you need to survive. The Bread of Life is the most important thing in your home, in your marriage, in your job, and in your relationships. Nothing should surpass Jesus, and nothing is a substitute for Jesus.

So how hungry are you for the Bread of Life? Is Jesus really at the center of everything you do?

God, I know You are calling me out of humdrum dreariness and into a deeper, more satisfying walk with You—a walk where You sustain me, support me, and strengthen me.

> **Until we make Jesus the most important thing in our lives, we will be settling for bread crumbs instead of feasting on the Bread of Life.**

The Mystery of Grace

"All that the Father gives Me will come to Me, and the one who comes to Me I will by no means cast out." (John 6:37)

God is sovereign. His sovereignty is not partial; it is total, and it is not subject to any conditions or forces outside of God Himself. That is a straightforward truth and somewhat easy to understand. What is not so easy to understand is reconciling our responsibility and God's sovereignty when it comes to salvation.

Coming to Jesus is not a decision made apart from God or His sovereignty. The Bible teaches that we are responsible, and God is sovereign. In other words, God is absolutely in control of everything, but at the same time, we also are responsible to choose to believe in God. Throughout the Bible, people are responsible to believe and respond in faith (see Romans 10:9; John 3:16). But Jesus also makes it perfectly clear that no one comes to the Son unless the Father draws them (see John 6:44). Trying to bring these two seemingly opposite truths together is enough to make your head hurt. But the reality is that our choice and God's choice are not mutually exclusive concepts. Rather, they're opposite sides of the same coin. The choice is yours to make, but it is a choice made possible by the Holy Spirit. Our responsibility and God's sovereignty are a mystery held together by God's grace.

Father, I am so grateful for Your eternal purposes, which allow me to rest in deep gratitude for Your grace, mercy and complete sovereignty.

Jesus welcomes all who come to Him.

Is Tradition a Bad Word?

"And why do you break the commandment of God for the sake of your tradition?" (Matthew 15:3 ESV)

Some of us just don't like change. We sit in the same seat at church, and heaven help the person who dares to sit there before we arrive. *Don't they know that's our spot?* Then, God forbid, someone goes against the that's-the-way-we've-always-done-it church engine. However, there are good traditions too. For example, holding on to the authority of Scripture, committing ourselves to gathering in worship, and taking communion all can offer important benefits that grow our understanding of truth and enhance our worship of the dynamic splendor of God. The apostle Paul even encourages us to "stand firm and hold to the traditions that you were taught" (2 Thessalonians 2:15 ESV). Traditions can be good if they honor God, promote unity, and remain workable with—and not resistant to—the will of God and the work of the Holy Spirit.

On the other hand, holding fast to a custom or tradition blindly and being suspicious of anything new or different can inhibit the freedom and freshness of the Spirit of God. Tradition is bad if it hinders growth, is resistant to change, disregards clear biblical teaching, and causes division. If a religious tradition becomes more focused on an experience, expression, or execution of faith rather than rightly glorifying God and His Word, it needs to go. Appreciate tradition when it's helpful, but never let tradition undermine truth.

Father God, may I never let rituals come before my relationship with You. May they always and only enhance my spiritual life and never hinder it.

> **Jesus doesn't condemn all traditions—only traditions that resist His Word, His work, or His will.**

Lip Service

"These people honor me with their lips, but their hearts are far from me." (Matthew 15:8 NIV)

Have you ever been distracted in church? One minute you are worshiping in song, and the next minute you are thinking about what you want to have for lunch. Or have you ever sat down to have a daily devotion, only to realize that your mind wandered the entire time you were trying to pray? We have all been there. We have all had those moments when we spent more time wondering what we were going to do that day than what God was trying to show us in that moment. The problem isn't with an occasional lack of focus. The problem is when all we ever do is pay God lip service. When Jesus saw some religious people going through the spiritual motions, He said they had a big problem.

God has great things in store for our lives. But if we want our lives to be as fruitful and blessed as God wants them to be, there must be a willingness to do what God says. We must do more than speak of our love and devotion to God; we must live it. Loving God is not something we just say. It is something we must do. God didn't just *say* that He loved us. Rather, God demonstrated "His own love toward us, in that while we were still sinners, Christ died for us" (Romans 5:8) If our hearts are drifting from God or our worship of God wanders into lesser things, it takes discipline to reposition our thoughts on God so that our hearts will follow and our lives will reflect it.

Dear Lord, help me to cultivate my love for You so that I am not just speaking of my love for You but am living for You. Help me to honor You, Lord, with both my lips and my life.

> **If Jesus has your heart, then your lips and your life will show it.**

Dealing with Defilement

"Hear and understand: it is not what goes into the mouth that defiles a person, but what comes out of the mouth; this defiles a person." (Matthew 15:10–11 ESV)

What comes out of our mouth shows what is inside our hearts. That means our words are an indicator of where we are spiritually. Our words either glorify God, because our hearts seek to glorify God, or we struggle with wholesome words, because our hearts struggle to stay pure. It is true that God seeks purity for His people, but purity comes from a heart surrendered to God.

The heart represents the center of the mind, will, and emotions. The problem is that no ritual can cleanse your mind, no outward ceremony can purify your will, and no amount of church attendance can free you from your emotional struggles with sin and selfishness. Only the blood of Christ purifies our conscience, and only the blood of Christ gives us the freedom to draw near to God with clean hearts (see Hebrews 9:14; 10:19–22). So if defilement comes from sinfulness rooted in the heart, then holy living comes from a sanctified heart.

So how can you deal with the defilement in your heart? First, choose to change. Either you are moving closer to God, or you are drifting further away. There is no middle ground. Next, confess and turn away from past failures. Don't wallow in your wickedness. Surrender everything to God and leave it with Him. Don't keep carrying it around with you. Finally, commit to improving your communion with God through prayer and Bible reading.

Father God, I seek to keep my heart pure so that the words of my mouth are a reflection of Jesus in my life.

> **We will have a heart like Jesus if we purpose to pursue Jesus daily.**

The Not Enoughs

"How many loaves do you have?" (Mark 8:5)

It does not matter how little we have. What matters is what we do with what we have. Many of us struggle with a case of the "not enoughs." We can feel as though we are not smart enough, eloquent enough, or talented enough for God. We often feel insecure, inadequate, or intimidated, and therefore, we can hesitate to step out and serve God when opportunities come our way. But being focused on what we don't have to offer or looking at what we have as being insufficient obstructs all that we can accomplish, and be, in Jesus.

Do you remember the story of Jesus feeding four thousand people with only seven loaves of bread? Well, when the disciples (who, by the way, already had seen Jesus perform the miracle of feeding the five thousand) saw their current situation, they basically said to Jesus, "What we have to offer is *not enough* to get the job done." It's hard to imagine anyone actually saying to Jesus's face that they don't have enough to get the job done. But we do the same thing when we entertain those not-enough thoughts. After all, God is more than standing among us; He dwells *within* us (see 1 Corinthians 3:16).

It is easy to focus on what we don't have or what we need in the moment rather than realizing that with God, we always have enough to get His work done. Let God start with where you are and with what you have, and let Him show you that He is enough in every situation.

God, sometimes I need You to remind me that I am enough, because You are enough. You always will supply all that I need to live for You.

Jesus always will give you what you need to do whatever He asks you to do.

Good Man or God-Man?

"Who do you say that I am?" (Matthew 16:15 ESV)

The time had come. The question had been asked. Now the disciples had a decision to make: either accept Jesus for who He said He was or deny Him and walk away.

Today there are many ideas floating around as to who Jesus was. Some say He was a good teacher, others say He was a wonder-worker, and others say He was a Jewish rabbi. But the reality is there are only two options: either Jesus was who He said He was, or He wasn't. C. S. Lewis, once an agnostic, said it this way: "You can shut Him up for a fool, you can spit at Him and kill Him as a demon; or you can fall at His feet and call Him Lord and God. But let us not come with any patronizing nonsense about His being a great human Teacher. He has not left that open to us. He did not intend to."[10] Either Jesus is God, or He is a deluded liar.

So how can you know for sure that Jesus was God, as He claimed? Let's face it. Other people have claimed to be God, and they were not. So what makes Jesus different? Simply put, it's the evidence—evidence that includes fulfilled prophecy, historical confirmation, and the recorded miracles of Jesus. But Jesus said many times that the ultimate proof of His divine nature would be His resurrection from the dead. And that is precisely what happened.

The proof is there. The only reason someone doesn't choose faith in Jesus is because they don't want to be responsible for such a decision. It isn't because of a lack of evidence. \

Jesus, trusting in You as God means that I must live a life centered around a commitment to honor You with my life and obey Your Word. Help me to live out what I know is true.

Who do you say Jesus was?

Blessed

"Blessed are you, Simon son of Jonah, for this was not revealed
to you by flesh and blood, but by my Father in heaven."
(Matthew 16:17 NIV)

We all have our own ideas of what we think "blessed" means. Some see it as health, wealth, or happiness. Certainly a good job, good grades, or good relationships are blessings. But there has to be more to being blessed than that, right?

Actually, if Jesus is speaking about being blessed, then I want to know how to experience more of His blessing in my life. Don't you? Peter had plenty of foot-in-mouth moments, but on this occasion, he nailed it. He answered Jesus's probing question of "Who do you say I am?" with, "You are the Messiah, the Son of the living God" and passed the test with flying colors (Matthew 16:15–16 NIV). And the result? Blessing. In other words, "Blessed are you, Simon Peter, because you received insight through divine revelation, not through human inspiration, and you responded to it." In that moment, Peter made the decision to allow godly revelation to override any and all human thinking.

What is blessing, then? Blessing is anything God gives us that makes us fully satisfied in Him. Anything that draws us closer to Jesus is a blessing. Anything that makes us more like Jesus is a blessing, as well as anything that increases my love for, knowledge of, and response to Jesus. Simply put, more Jesus equals more blessing.

Jesus, I long to know You more and to be more like You. I want more of You, Jesus, for in You are found the deepest and richest blessings in this life and in the life to come.

God's greatest blessings come through God's greatest gift, Jesus Himself.

Upon the Rock

"On this rock I will build my church..."
(Matthew 16:18 ESV)

All too often the church is seen as a democracy instead of a theocracy. Jesus, in a divine declaration, affirmed that He would establish, build, and protect the eternal, global society of His people called the church. As the founder, sustainer, and defender of the church, Jesus is the principal authority over it and the ultimate head of the church (see Ephesians 5:23).

When Peter gave the sure and inspired response that Jesus was "the Christ, the Son of the living God" (Matthew 16:16 ESV), Jesus made it clear that He was to be the foundation and the cornerstone of this newly established heavenly people. The solid rock of Jesus, as the Son of God, was to be the rock and foundation of the church—not Peter. Jesus did not, nor would He ever, build His kingdom of people on anything less than the supreme perfection of Himself. Peter deserves kudos for his proclamation, but he does not deserve veneration.

Christ's headship over the church implies that every denomination and every individual congregation is to follow the plan and purpose Jesus has for the church. Any church that does otherwise is rejecting the authority of Jesus by attempting to operate autonomously. Because the church is built on Jesus, and because Jesus is the head of the church, His plans, purposes, and will must always guide and direct His people, the church.

Thank you, Lord, for the great and glorious assurance of knowing that nothing, not even hell itself, can overwhelm or overpower Your precious and protected people.

Jesus alone is the only foundation and head of the church.

Why Go to Church?

"On this rock I will build my church, and the gates of hell shall not prevail against it." (Matthew 16:18 ESV)

Is church really necessary? Despite the cynical critics that might say church is old-fashioned or out-of-date in such a modern, technologically advanced society, I can assure you that it is not out-of-date, irrelevant, or discretionary.

Why is church important, then? The church is a community established by Jesus to draw people to Himself, to conform people into His image, and to encourage and edify people in the love of Jesus. The Christian life is not designed to be lived alone. God has created you and me to be part of a community—His community, the church. Being a part of the church community is important, because it helps people live lives that honor God and fulfill His purposes. The church community is where significant spiritual growth occurs through the teaching of God's Word. The church community is stronger together and can accomplish more together than apart. In this community that God has created, we are worshiping with others, praying for others, hurting with others, serving with others, and connecting our lives with others. Don't let excuses keep you from going to church as the Bible instructs us (see Hebrews 10:25) and from being a part of this beautiful community that God has created and keeps protected.

Oh God, capture my heart in a fresh way, and stir in my spirit a renewed commitment to meet with Your people to praise You, love others, and shine the hope of Christ to those who desperately need You.

We must go to church if we are going to be the church Jesus expects us to be.

Getting in God's Way

"Get behind me, Satan! You are a hindrance to me. For you are not setting your mind on the things of God, but on the things of man." (Matthew 16:23 ESV)

God's way is always best. His plans are always better than my plans. I may not always understand what God is doing, but I certainly want to do my best not to get in His way. There are plenty of obstacles when it comes to living for God, but I should not be one of them.

"Get behind me, Satan" had to hurt Peter's ego. After all, it was only moments ago that Jesus commended Peter for proclaiming the divinity of Jesus Christ. Now, Peter was rebuking Jesus for the His plan to go to the Cross. He was telling Jesus, "No way! This can't happen. I won't let it!" What Peter didn't realize was that by trying to stop Jesus from accomplishing God's redemptive plan, he actually was being influenced by Satan.

It should come as no surprise that Satan wants God's plans and people to fail, consequently we must be careful not to allow worldly thinking to get in the way of God's will and work. We don't know what God knows, and we can't see what God sees. Therefore, we can't fully understand the mind of God. We can get into trouble when we think we know what's best. Even our good intentions are no good if they get in the way of God's plans.

Jesus, help me to let go of self-centered attitudes and actions that may cloud my ability to see Your will and Your ways. Help me to spend more time with You so that I can better follow You.

Sometimes we need to be reminded to step aside and let Jesus do what He needs to do.

MAY

The Way of the Cross

"The Son of Man must suffer many things and be rejected by the elders and chief priests and scribes, and be killed, and be raised the third day." (Luke 9:22)

If there is no cross, there is no Christianity. We cheapen grace if we soften the cross. At the cross, eternal life and everlasting darkness intersected, time divided, and good and evil collided. The cross was used by man as an instrument of shame and suffering, but God used it as an instrument of redemption and glory.

God had predetermined that His Son would suffer, be rejected, and ultimately be killed in order to provide the redemptive road back to relationship with God for a people who had become separated from Him because of sin (see Romans 3:23). God's punishment for sin was death, and if Jesus was going to bring life back where death had entered, He would have to die to do it (see Romans 6:23). That's because only by the blood of Christ can we be reconciled to God (see Romans 5:8). Jesus understood His mission, and He predicted His suffering to His followers so they would know that God meant for it to happen. Jesus showed them He was not running from it but willingly moving toward its fulfillment. And after the suffering, shame, and death, He would rise again in exactly three days. His death was prearranged, His resurrection was predetermined, and everything happened according to God's sacred schedule. Nothing was accidental.

Never lose sight of what it cost God to make our salvation possible. It has been, and always will be, God's glorious plan to provide a way back to relationship with His creation.

Father, life can get busy, and it's easy to forget Your amazing grace. Because of the Cross, I have received forgiveness incomprehensible, love inexhaustible, and a life unimaginable.

Jesus willingly went to the Cross because of His great love for us.

Carrying My Cross

"If anyone desires to come after Me, let him deny himself, and take up his cross daily, and follow Me." (Luke 9:23)

Challenges come to everyone. Hardships hit us all. Trials touch each of us. But having a difficult boss, a prickly spouse, or a just an average teenager is not what is meant by "carrying our cross." We cannot classify any personal hassle or daily difficulty as a cross to bear. A cross is an extra hardship that comes to us as a result of our obedience to Christ.

Following Christ is a costly but rewarding choice. It calls for an across-the-board examination into our self-centered lifestyles. Yes, that's easier said than done, but it is necessary nonetheless. When we consider Jesus's denial statement in Luke 9:23, a couple of things jump out. First, those who desire to follow Him must come to terms with self-denial. Self-denial is inseparable from discipleship and is admittedly arduous in its daily obligation. Self-denial, at its core, is seeing and surrendering to the higher and holier will of God. Second, this cross bearing is not forced upon us; it is voluntarily taken up, fully accepting whatever hardships come from carrying our cross. Through our cross bearing, we are uniquely connected to Jesus as we live in obedience to His commands. This isn't wishy-washy believism; it is a radical commitment to faithfully live for God, come what may.

God, I know that carrying my cross will affect every aspect of my life, but the result will be life as it was meant to be lived. Help me to daily deny my selfishness and live selflessly as I take up my cross in agreement with Your will.

Jesus says that salvation is free, but following Him will cost you a cross to bear.

Losing Your Life to Save It

"For whoever desires to save his life will lose it, but whoever loses his life for My sake will save it." (Luke 9:24)

God has created you to be happiest and most satisfied when you give Him your life. If your attitude is to save your life now by hoarding it, holding it, esteeming it, trusting in it, and looking at every situation with the attitude of what's in it for you, then you're living to save your life. The irony is that you will lose out in the end. As you make personal pursuits your primary goal, you will suffer spiritual loss. You will lose intimacy with God and will lose out on the blessings of usefulness in God's intended work for you now and on blessings in the hereafter.

Jesus did not come to call us to depressing darkness and death. He called us to abundant life and joyful fulfillment, which come from serving and giving our lives away as Jesus did. What's involved in giving our lives away? Jesus modeled this by serving others, sacrificing for others, and ultimately dying for others. God has wired us in such a way that the more we give of ourselves, the happier and more fulfilled we will be. In giving we gain, but in saving we squander.

Father, it is the selfless life that truly satisfies. May I make daily choices to give myself away, even when it is hard and humbling.

> **We are to follow Jesus with the commitment, courage, and willingness to risk all for Him.**

Profit and Loss

*"For what profit is it to a man if he gains the whole world,
and is himself destroyed or lost?" (Luke 9:25)*

Is Christianity worth it? Everything in life costs us something. Saying yes to one thing means saying no to something else. Some people will spend their lives chasing after affluence, accomplishments, prominence, or influence. Nothing is intrinsically wrong with obtaining any of these. Where we can go wrong, however, is when we make these pursuits greater than our pursuit of God. Jesus tells us that a life given to the pursuit of worldly profit will, in fact, cost us heaven in the end.

Some people do not realize they are losing their souls as they chase worldly advantage. Jesus makes it plain: You can't put a price tag on your soul. Eternity is infinitely more valuable than the sum of all earthly gain. The apostle Paul came to this realization, writing, "I once thought these things were valuable, but now I consider them worthless because of what Christ has done. Yes, everything else is worthless when compared with the infinite value of knowing Christ Jesus my Lord. For his sake I have discarded everything else, counting it all as garbage, so that I could gain Christ" (Philippians 3:7–8 NLT). When Jesus becomes your greatest source of joy, you will understand the profit of knowing Him and the resulting loss of pursuing anything but Him. Your soul is priceless. Don't waste it for perishable profit.

God, I know You want to bless my life, but help me to never make my pursuit of blessing greater than my pursuit of You. My relationship with You is priceless and is my greatest blessing.

Nothing is of greater worth than knowing Jesus.

I Will Not Be Ashamed

"For whoever is ashamed of Me and My words, of him the Son of Man will be ashamed when He comes in His own glory, and in His Father's, and of the holy angels." (Luke 9:26)

You should never be embarrassed for believing in Jesus. You should never be ashamed for trusting the Bible. Words can be hurtful, but they won't kill you. What other people think of you isn't as important as what God thinks of you. There always will be people who dislike you or look disapprovingly at your life choices. Freedom comes when you value God's opinion more than the opinion of others.

Being ashamed of Jesus does not mean that if we falter one time by being ashamed of Him, we are no longer heaven bound. Peter, after all, was so embarrassed of Jesus that he denied Him three times. But Jesus forgave Peter and even used him greatly after his failure. There is always forgiveness in Jesus for the repentant. But someone's persistent and reoccurring denial of their relationship with Jesus is a sign there may be no relationship at all.

God is honored when we show courage for Him. God is honored when we live a life that openly glorifies Him. It isn't always easy standing up for Jesus, and yes, living a life that unashamedly esteems Jesus can be challenging. It may even cause us to be ridiculed when our choices go against the social current. But what little we may suffer for our faith is nothing compared to what Jesus endured so that we could part of His family.

Father, I never will be ashamed of my faith. My relationship with You, Jesus, is my hope and strength. May I never hesitate or be slow to stand for You.

> **Jesus is not ashamed to call us His own. We should not be ashamed to call Him our Lord.**

Genuine Greatness

*"Whoever receives this little child in My name receives Me;
and whoever receives Me receives Him who sent Me. For he
who is least among you all will be great." (Luke 9:48)*

Greatness is often ascribed to the person with power, popularity, or position. But there is a great contrast between what the world places value on and what God recognizes as true greatness.

One day Jesus's disciples got into an argument about which of them would be the greatest. Jesus stepped in to immediately redirect their prideful dispute by taking a little child in His arms and explaining that loving others was the path to genuine greatness.

As believers, we cannot allow the priorities if a society to determine the purposes of Gods people. God's purposes must take priority for Gods people. Carelessness here will result in God becoming smaller in our lives and worldly standards becoming larger. The outcome is that God will move from the center of our world and be conveniently relocated to the perimeter, allowing self-importance and self-confidence to grow stronger while dependence on God weakens. Prideful behavior will increase, and genuine humility will decrease.

Our care and concern for others is the true gauge of our greatness. Ask yourself, then, how much concern you have for others. In God's eyes, your love for others (especially the helpless, the needy, the poor, and those who can't return your care and concern) will give you a good idea of your true greatness.

Jesus, whenever I am tempted to think of myself more highly than I ought to, remind me that genuine greatness is shown by caring for and serving others.

> **Our greatness comes from our connection to
> Jesus and concern for others.**

We're on the Same Side

"Do not forbid him, for he who is not against us is on our side." (Luke 9:50)

Divisions and diversity of opinions undeniably exist, even among Christians. Splits and separations continually arise within churches concerning church government, styles of worship, preaching methods, and more. Should we split over these issues? Should we denounce those who do things differently than we do? The answer is absolutely not.

The disciples found someone who wasn't part of their group and had been casting out demons in Jesus's name. They didn't like it and told him to stop. Surely Jesus would agree with them and be glad they stopped someone who wasn't doing ministry their way. But unexpectedly, Jesus said to the disciples, "He who is not against us is on our side" (Luke 9:50).

We make a mistake when we exclude anyone who is not part of our particular church group or who does ministry differently than we do. God's kingdom is bigger than a single church or a particular denomination. We can praise the work of other Christians without compromising the essentials of the faith. We can have unity without uniformity. We can care for each other without seeing eye to eye on every nonessential issue. None of us should think that we have the perfect view of truth or a monopoly on ministry methods. If Jesus is being preached, the Bible is being faithfully and fully taught, and sin is being opposed, then most likely we're on the same side.

Father, help us to be uncompromising with Your truth but also to be discerning, understanding, and welcoming of other believers. The true church is not confined to a single congregation, denomination, or organization.

Everyone who has faith in Jesus Christ is part of God's family.

Distracted or Devoted?

"No one, having put his hand to the plow, and looking back, is fit for the kingdom of God." (Luke 9:62)

Life is filled with distractions, and one of life's biggest challenges is accomplishing what we set out to do, especially when it comes to following God. We all have lost focus on a project or started something, only to leave it for another day. Small distractions can stop us from accomplishing big things. Distractions destroy progress. And when it comes to following God, distractions can be a disqualifier.

Jesus made it clear that if we want to follow Him, we need to stay focused on living for Him and making Him our priority. Is something distracting you from following Jesus today? Just as no one can plow a straight line if they're looking backward, no one can follow Jesus if they continue to allow distractions to own their attention. Maybe materialism has your gaze, perhaps a relationship has divided your attention, or an unhelpful activity holds your focus. The most dangerous distractions are the ones you don't want to give up.

If you are going to follow God and live to serve Him, then your relationship with Jesus needs to come first. Total dedication, not half-hearted commitment, is what it takes to follow Jesus. If there is something in your life that isn't helping you live for God, don't focus on it.

Lord, help me to stay focused and pursue those things You call me to do. Deliver me from distractions that take my focus off Your plans and purposes for my life.

> **Don't allow yourself to be distracted by something that hinders your devotion to Jesus.**

Prone to Wander

"What do you think? If a man has a hundred sheep, and one of them goes astray, does he not leave the ninety-nine and go to the mountains to seek the one that is straying?"
(Matthew 18:12)

As much as we would like our lives to be marked by perfect obedience and nonstop faithfulness, the simple truth is that we can go astray now and again. Even though we cannot lose our salvation (see John 10:28), Jesus tells a story about how we can drift in our faithfulness to God.

When we give our lives to Jesus, we are given a new nature. But unfortunately, our old nature doesn't go away. Like sheep that wander off in pursuit of greener grass, we can take our eyes off the Shepherd and begin looking for the greener grass of newer opportunities or better situations, and before we know it, there is distance between God and us. In our wandering, we neglect God's Word, prayer, worship, and fellowship.

One of the most wonderful things about God is that people matter to Him. Just as a shepherd will pursue a sheep that has gone astray, God makes people His priority, and He will pursue a wayward individual. God's pursuit of the careless believer is real, and He won't rest until we are done drifting. If you have drifted away from Jesus and have wandered off, thinking you would be happier going it alone, you need to know that you never will. The grass isn't greener without God. So turn around and come back to the fold.

God, You know my heart is prone to wander. Thank you for pursuing me whenever I drift. Teach me to trust You more and to wander less. In Jesus's name, amen.

> **Jesus will relentlessly pursue us if we wander from His loving care.**

That Hurt!

"Moreover if your brother sins against you, go and tell him his fault between you and him alone. If he hears you, you have gained your brother." (Matthew 18:15)

Relationships come with their fair share of hurts. That means there are times when confrontation is an important step in the healing and reconciliation process. But confrontation also comes with a cost, because it is never easy, and there's no guarantee that the other person will respond agreeably. But sometimes we need to take the step anyway, because it is good for our own healing, and the Bible urges us to take restorative action.

Confrontation is not an attack. If you are going looking for a fight, then you probably will get one. Don't live by the bumper-sticker philosophy that says, "Don't get mad, get even." If there is animosity in your heart, then you need to wait until you can go to the person with an attitude of humility, gentleness, and long-suffering. If you aren't ready to forgive, then you aren't ready for a face-to-face conversation. Stop and pray, and ask God to work on your heart. When you are ready to go, keep in mind that you're going as a peacemaker seeking to represent Jesus throughout the process.

If someone has sinned against you, begin the process of reconciliation, and pray about taking the time to go and talk with them.

God, when conflicts arise and hurts have happened, help me to resolve those issues with love and the goal of restoration.

> **Jesus wants us to make an effort to quickly and quietly resolve our conflicts with other Christians when hurts have happened.**

Conflict Resolution

"But if he will not hear, take with you one or two more, that 'by the mouth of two or three witnesses every word may be established.' " (Matthew 18:16)

Sometimes life doesn't go as planned. There may be those times in life when you make an attempt at bringing resolution to a personal conflict, only to have it blow up in your face. Don't give up. It's time to get some help. But how do you know whether the issue is serious enough to get others involved? If the issue is dishonoring Christ, if it is damaging your relationship with the other person, or if it is hurting others, then it's time to get help.

This should not be seen as an opportunity to gang up on the other person but to bring in some objective observers who have wisdom, discernment, and can speak impartial truth and promote comprehensive healing. Conflict is two-sided, and even if you are the one who has been wronged, there still may be something you need to admit or accept. This is where godly mentors can evaluate and advise both parties on how to reach reconciliation.

No matter who you are in this scenario (the offended, offender, or adviser), you are to approach the situation in love and also speak lovingly (Ephesians 5:2; 4:15). Love is our responsibility and priority (see 1 Corinthians 13). We can't force someone to reconcile. But as Romans 12:18 urges us, "If it is possible, as far as it depends on you, live at peace with everyone" (NIV)

Jesus, show me any relationships in my life that may need attention. Help me to settle any outstanding disagreements so the focus of my mind and energy will be on serving You.

Jesus doesn't want us to avoid confrontation when hurts are involved. It's an opportunity to show grace and seek healing.

God with Me

"For where two or three are gathered together in My name, I am there in the midst of them." (Matthew 18:20)

Context is everything when it comes to proper biblical interpretation. If we are not careful, taking a Bible verse out of context can lead to misinterpretation, misrepresentation, and misapplication. A verse should not be severed from its surrounding context. The surrounding context is connected to the passage as a whole, the passage as a whole is connected to chapters, the chapters create the book, and the books make up the Bible in its entirety.

One verse that is often taken out of context is Matthew 18:20. We like this verse because it sounds nice in prayer meetings and in small group settings. But the context of it deals with settling conflicts and disputes. Here Jesus is talking about God's presence in church discipline. Context is important, because otherwise a person may be left asking, "Is God only present when two or three people are gathered together?"

Jesus is present with all believers at all times, but there is an aspect of His support that is present when two or three have gathered biblically to resolve conflict. In other words, when His people make holiness a priority in conflict resolution, He will be there in the midst.

God, I know You never will leave me nor forsake me, and that You are with me until the end of the age. Thank you for Your added support during biblical conflict resolution.

Jesus gives us His approval and authority when we follow His approach to resolving conflict.

Limitless

"Lord, how many times shall I forgive my brother or sister who sins against me? Up to seven times?" Jesus answered, 'I tell you, not seven times, but seventy times seven.'
(Matthew 18:21–22)

Forgiveness is one of the hardest things we do in life. We live in a world where we hurt others and others hurt us. Sometimes those hurts happen intentionally, and at other times they are accidental. Forgiveness doesn't change the past, but it does set us free to live a brighter future.

Back in the time of Jesus, forgiveness had its limits. According to Jewish law, you were to forgive a person three times, and after that, you didn't have to forgive them anymore. So Peter was probably thinking, "Jesus will be impressed with this question: Shall we forgive up to seven times?" But Jesus came back with an unexpected response, basically telling him, "Wrong! You're not even close, Peter! Try seventy times seven." The point Jesus was making is that we shouldn't keep count; we should just keep on forgiving. Whether a person deserves it or not, forgive! Whether a person asks for it or not, forgive! Whether a person offends over and over again, forgive! But why? Why should we forgive someone again and again and again? The answer is because God's forgiveness has no limit. We don't deserve it, yet He forgives! We offend God again and again and again, yet He forgives us. It isn't easy, but with God's help, we can forgive like He forgives.

Father, thank you for Your forgiveness. Even when I repeat the same mistakes, You still forgive me when I confess my faults and failures to You. Help me to show that same forgiveness to others.

Jesus forgives with limitless measure.

Loved by God, Hated by Man

"The world cannot hate you, but it hates Me because I testify of it that its works are evil." *(John 7:7)*

Who in their right mind would refuse to accept a life preserver if they were drowning? So why is it that people reject the glorious gift of God's grace? People reject God's grace because they love their sin more then they love Jesus.

Jesus explains that the world hates Him because He made the world aware of its depravity and disobedience. Now the world has no excuse. No one can claim they're ignorant of God's moral law. That means we have no one to blame but ourselves for our sin. Since the beginning, people have sought to blame others for their sinful behavior. Immediately after the first sin, when God asked Adam if he ate from the forbidden tree, he blamed Eve (see Genesis 3:12). So when Jesus shines the light of God's truth and exposes people's evil behavior, they don't like it. In fact, they hate it. They also hate Jesus for shinning a light on it. Basically, people don't want God interfering in their business. They want to be left alone to live as they please and do what they want.

If the world is your friend, then you need to question whether Jesus is your Lord. If your life reflects your belief in Jesus, then you will experience adversity. A life lived for Jesus inevitably will make some people uncomfortable, because it exposes their sin and disobedience.

Jesus, give me love and grace for those who exhibit hatred toward me just because I live for You. Open their eyes so they may turn from their sin and be saved.

Jesus's followers will be hated by the world for their commitment to righteousness.

The God Experience

"Anyone who wants to do the will of God will know whether my teaching is from God or is merely my own. (*John 7:17 NLT*)

You just have to experience some things in life for yourself. Seeing a picture of a sunset is different than watching one. Looking at a picture of a chocolate cake is different than tasting one. And reading about God is different than experiencing God. Spiritual understanding is a combination of knowing truth and personally experiencing truth through obedience, and obedience always brings blessing.

Jesus's words are divine truth, originating from God, and every person who faithfully puts them into practice continually discerns the soundness of God's Word and the sanctity of God's Word. God's Word, therefore, is self-authenticating. Simply put, try it, and you will see that it is true and that it works. A person doesn't have to go to seminary or take a course in Christian apologetics to find assurance that the Bible is inspired. Spiritual understanding comes by the exercising of faith through obedience.

So become a student of God's Word, because the more you know God's Word, the better you will understand God's will. Also, be determined to be obedient. Determining to do God's will and living according to God's Word brings greater revelation of God's will for your life. Obedience unlocks revelation.

God, give me a humble heart to yield to Your instructions at all times, and help me to obey Your Word and follow when you lead.

> **Jesus affirms that steps of faith produce lives of surety.**

The Glory Issue

"He who speaks from himself seeks his own glory."
(John 7:18)

Success is like a drug, and we can become addicted to the need to succeed. Who doesn't appreciate a pat on the back or hearing "job well done"? And there is absolutely nothing wrong with wanting to do a good job or even being the best at what you do. After all, shouldn't Christians endeavor to be the best at everything they do? But *why* you do what you do is what really matters. Do you want to be the best because of your need to be applauded? Are you addicted to gaining greatness? Or, are you motivated to bring glory to God?

God makes it clear that "to seek one's own glory is not glory" (Proverbs 25:27) and that we should not be motivated by selfish ambition (see Philippians 2:3). Rather, whatever we do, we should do it all for the glory of God (see 1 Corinthians 10:31). The reality for most of us, however, is that although we may truly desire to bring glory to God, there's a powerful pull of receiving praise from people. For Christians, success should be measured by our faithfulness to fulfill the work God has given us, not the accolades we may receive along the way.

If you find that you are struggling with the pursuit of greatness or popularity, then you may need to experience more of God's glory in order to bring Him more glory. God's glory is revealed in His creation, His love, and His Word. Spending time in God's presence will help you regain a sense of God's glory and realign your priorities.

Jesus, deliver my heart from the empty pursuit of my own greatness!
May I make daily choices that exalt Jesus and bring Him glory.

> **Promote Jesus more than you promote yourself.**

Looking Beyond Appearances

"Do not judge according to appearance, but judge with righteous judgment." (John 7:24)

Despite our best efforts, we all judge others. How someone looks, how they dress, and how they carry themselves all factor into judgments we make. Sure, appearances matter. But Christians, of all people, should be able to look past outward appearances, past people's flaws, mistakes, bad days, or whatever else may be influencing their behavior and go deeper than superficialities. If judging a book by its cover can leave you missing out on a great story, then judging someone by their appearance may leave you missing out on a great relationship.

Jesus felt the judgmentalism of the religious leaders many times. In John 7, we see them judging Jesus because, as far as they were concerned, He broke the law prohibiting work on the Sabbath. They judged based on appearances instead of looking to the truth below the surface. Jesus followed up by saying that we are to have a right-minded, Spirit-led approach when we make judgments.

We need to recognize that we are all works in progress, and that means approaching people with grace. Do we need to make judgments as Christians? Yes. But judging does not mean that we should be judgmental. When we need to make a judgment, we must evaluate situations through the filter of God's Word. His Word is the standard, and His Holy Spirit provides the wisdom and discernment to apply His truth correctly to every situation.

Father, help me avoid making quick judgments based on appearances, because they can be deceiving, and they fail to show love.

> **Jesus expects us to look beyond appearances and make godly judgments.**

A River Runs through Me

"If anyone thirsts, let him come to Me and drink. He who believes in Me, as the Scripture has said, out of his heart will flow rivers of living water." (John 7:37–38)

Water is life. Just look around the world. If water is present, life can be found. In the same way, Jesus is spiritual life. Just look around the world. If Jesus is present, spiritual life can be found.

It was the last and greatest day of the Feast of Tabernacles. Every day during this Jewish feast, priests marched from the pool of Siloam to the temple and poured out water at the base of the altar. It was during this ritual that Jesus made his declaration, "If anyone thirsts, let him come to Me" (John 7:37 NKJV). Inside all of us there is a thirst that nothing in this world can quench. Jesus invites the thirsty to come to Him, because He is the only the soul-quenching source of life.

Are you currently dissatisfied? Are you thirsty for more out of life? Jesus satisfies the deepest longing of our souls. Nothing else will. So go to Jesus and drink, and you will find complete satisfaction in Him. Then you will be able to experience a consistent fullness of joy in Jesus that flows from you to others. There is a difference between having the Holy Spirit and having the Holy Spirit overflowing in your life. Overflowing joy and abundant fruitfulness comes to those who drink deeply from Jesus and allow the Holy Spirit to direct their lives. Rivers of living water are to flow in us so they can flow through us and bless others.

Jesus, keep me forever thirsty for the things of God. Keep me seeking daily to be quenched with the living water of Your presence so that I may also show others where to drink.

> **Water is the lifeblood of our bodies, and Jesus is the lifeblood of our spirits.**

Glass Houses

"He who is without sin among you, let him throw a stone at her first." (John 8:7)

How does Jesus respond when we mess up? Simply stated, mercifully. We all mess up, and sometimes we mess up royally. But there is no sin so great that God can't forgive.

A woman who was caught in the act of adultery was brought before Jesus by the Pharisees. Not only were these religious leaders trying to corner Jesus between Roman Law and Mosaic Law, but they were guilty of hypocrisy, and Jesus knew it. Knowing that the Law of Moses demanded she be stoned to death, Jesus turned the tables and said if there was anyone there who had never sinned, let them throw the first stone. Jesus alone could have cast that first stone, because Jesus alone was without sin. But He chose to exercise mercy instead, telling the woman to "go and sin no more" (John 8:11). Jesus protected the dignity of the woman, but He also didn't ignore her misconduct. Jesus didn't condemn her, but He didn't condone her actions, either. Instead, He extended mercy to her. God's mercy forgives and frees us from past mistakes.

If people in glass houses shouldn't throw stones, then people saved by grace should be slow to throw stones of condemnation. This does not mean there isn't a place to confront someone who is sinning. But let us put down the stones of self-righteous condemnation and leave judgment at the feet of Jesus where it belongs.

Jesus, You chose to love me when I was still a sinner. In thankfulness to You, I desire to imitate Your grace and mercy to others, especially those who may be trapped in sin.

> **Jesus shows us how to extend mercy instead of throwing stones of condemnation.**

Sin No More

"Neither do I condemn you; go and sin no more."
(John 8:11)

God wants the best for our lives. It is true that God loves us and forgives us, but it is also true that He wants to change us. All too often the reason we do not experience some of the blessings God has is because we're not living the way He wants. Sin gets in the way of blessing. Sin damages our relationship with God, and it damages our relationships with one another. Sin harms our lives and causes emotional, physical, spiritual, and psychological injury. The reason God wants us to stop sinning is because God wants what is best for us, and sin does not result in God's best.

Jesus did not come to condemn; He came to forgive. But His forgiveness comes with a challenge, like it did for this woman: Do not keep living a sinful lifestyle. A life of gratitude for all we have been forgiven of means refusing to keep living a lifestyle that tolerates and practices sin. Yes, we are not going to be living in sinless perfection in this life, but we should be living a life that is marked by sinning less.

How does someone live out Jesus's command to sin no more? Well, it isn't by trying harder to avoid sin. Human effort cannot overcome spiritual influences. The only way to overcome sin is to walk with Jesus and invite Him to shine His light in the dark places of your life.

Jesus, forgive me of my sins and give me the strength to face the sins that are before me. Show me those sins I am unaware of so that I may sin no more.

We are not sinless, but our relationship with Jesus should cause us to sin less.

Light of the World

"I am the light of the world. He who follows Me shall not walk in darkness but have the light of life." (John 8:12)

Each day the sun rises to warm, illuminate, and provide growth on the earth. The moon and stars light the night, serving as a Global Positioning System long before smartphones. We reach for a light switch when we enter a dark room, and we rely on our knowledge to shed light on our lives. Light permeates every crack and crevice of our lives, whether visible, intellectual, or spiritual. Many people live with a *whatever-works-for-you* spirituality where they believe multiple lights can bring spiritual illumination. But Jesus makes it undeniably clear and unavoidably conclusive that only one way and one light leads to God.

Verse 12 of John 8 is the second of seven great "I am" statements made by Jesus. They are *all* bold, they are *all* gospel-centric, and they *all* light the way to God. But this one may be the most powerful and personal of them all. It is perhaps the clearest depiction of God's glory shining through to humanity in the brightest possible of ways: the physical manifestation of God, Jesus Christ.

If we believe that Jesus is the light, then we will walk in the light of His holiness and truth. We walk one step at a time as God illuminates our path, and we determine not to be distracted by the darkness around us.

God, may I walk not in the light of my own understanding but in the light of Your Word.

> **Whenever we see light, we are to remember that Jesus is the only spiritual light in this world.**

Pleasing God

"The Father has not left Me alone, for I always do those things that please Him." (John 8:28–29)

If I asked you whether you want to live a life that is pleasing to God, I suspect that your answer would be yes. However, if I asked you whether you believe that your life is currently pleasing to God, would you still be able to give the same answer? I think most of us feel forgiven and loved by God, but we may not feel like we are pleasing God with our daily lives.

It is so easy to be concerned with human opinions and long for human approval, but God didn't make us to be what others want us to be. The apostle Paul wrote, "Our purpose is to please God, not people" (1 Thessalonians 2:4 NLT). Faith is what pleases God more than anything else, because it is impossible to please God without faith (see Hebrews 11:1). A faith that pleases God is first a faith that believes God. Pleasing God is all about relationship. Spirituality is not a substitute for pleasing God, and religion is not a substitute for pleasing God. Genuine relationship is essential if we are to do anything pleasing to God, and that relationship starts with faith in God. Also, a faith that pleases God is a *doing* faith (see James 1:21–22). Our faith is confirmed by our actions. As we trust and obey, our faith is proven and pleasing to God. If we live and walk by faith, we will be doing those things that please our heavenly Father.

God, I come to You in faith, seeking to renew my commitment to live my life for Your pleasure and according to Your plan for me. May my relationship with You grow deeper and my life be an expression of my faith.

Jesus's top priority was to please God. May our lives share this priority.

Abiding and Thriving

"If you abide in My word, you are My disciples indeed."
(John 8:31 ESV)

Too many people come to the Bible and flounder around, flipping back and forth through the pages but never really thriving. If your daily Bible reading has become a humdrum routine devoid of substantive value, then a look at the meaning of "abide in My word" should provide some encouragement and unlock more of the life-changing power of Scripture in your life.

Reading the Bible to check it off your to-do list will not give you what you need to thrive spiritually. Abiding in God's Word must involve purposeful contemplation, or meditation (see Psalm 1:2; Joshua 1:8). Reading the Bible with the purpose of grabbing hold of every word that God has for you and then deliberately reflecting on what you've read (not just in the moment but throughout the day) is mediating on God's Word. That type of thoughtful consideration will be caffeine for your soul. Every meaningful relationship has lasting fellowship, and that's why abiding involves continuance. We abide in lasting fellowship by continuing to believe, by continuing to trust, and by continuing to obey.

If we are not looking to hear from God when we open the Bible, then we won't. If we are not expecting to be transformed by the Bible, then we won't. Let's get rid of the casual approach to God's Word and come to the Bible expectantly, excitedly, purposefully, and regularly.

Jesus, help me to live in an abiding lifestyle with Your Word and to be immersive and reflective with Your Word so that I might thrive.

Jesus's disciples are devoted to His Word.

A Slave to Sin

"Everyone who practices sin is a slave to sin." (John 8:34 ESV)

I think we all can agree that Christians are anything but perfect. But God is more interested in who we are becoming than the mistakes we make along the way (and there will be plenty of mistakes). That is not an excuse to sin, but it is a recognition that sin happens in our lives, even after we become believers. The sin and disobedience of humanity is seen throughout the entirety of the Bible—there is no escaping it, and there is no excusing it, either. You might think that you're not where you want to be when it comes to dealing with sin in your life, but there is a world of difference between struggling with your sin and deciding to live in sin as an acceptable lifestyle. Deliberately living in sin is impossible for believers.

If sin irritated us the same way sand in the eye does, then we might deal with sin more quickly. God wants us to be free from every type of bondage that prevents us from becoming the person He created us to be. Freedom like this does not come by trying harder; it comes by trusting greatly. It is not accomplished only by saying no to what is wrong; it is accomplished by saying yes to Jesus. By a determined submission to that which is spiritually nourishing to our souls, we can gain freedom from sin.

Father, thank you that I am no longer a slave to sin. I am alive in Christ. Your Spirit empowers me to say no to sin and say yes to that which is spiritually beneficial to my soul.

Living for Jesus will free you from being a slave to sin.

Living Free

"So, if the Son sets you free, you will be free indeed."
(John 8:36 NIV)

Freedom for many people might be described as being able to do what you want when you want. We think, "If only I . . . had more money . . . had a better job . . . had more success . . . could lose twenty-five pounds . . . could get away from all the stress . . . could get a new car. Then I would be free to do what I want." But when you realize how much God loves you, you will begin to understand that true freedom is not freedom from external constraints but from internal constraints.

When we read about how Jesus delivered people from illness or demonic oppression, the emphasis again and again is on what He saved them from. His purpose was to restore their lives and give them the ability to no longer live in spiritual defeat. He broke the chains that kept them under the control of sin. We never read of Jesus saying, "Okay, now you can go and do what you want when you want." Rather, He instructed people to leave their lives of sin.

Jesus doesn't want you to live a defeated Christian life. He wants you to live a full and free life. We no longer need to be controlled by sin but instead can be set free to live an abundant and victorious life by His power. Do you want this kind of freedom? Then genuine freedom comes by living a life fully surrendered to Jesus and completely committed to God's Word.

Jesus, thank you for setting me free from the power and penalty of sin. I no longer need to live controlled by sin but have been given the power to live free indeed.

> **Surrendering to Jesus and submitting to His Word will bring true freedom in life.**

Father God

"If God were your Father, you would love Me, for I proceeded forth and came from God; nor have I come of Myself, but He sent Me." (John 8:42)

Of all the names of God, Father is my favorite. God loves to be called Father, and Father was the name that Jesus most often used when referring to God. Jesus shocked many of His contemporaries by referring to God as His Father and by inviting His followers to address God as Father as well (see Luke 11:2).

Jesus came to explain the Father to us, and He depicted God primarily as a compassionate Father who lovingly and lavishly looks for ways to extend grace to His children. For example, our heavenly Father willingly paid the highest price in order to save us (see Romans 8:32). Every good gift comes to us from our heavenly Father (see James 1:17). Our heavenly Father wants to pour out His blessings in our lives when we come to Him (see Matthew 7:7–11). Our heavenly Father's love is not conditionally based upon our love for Him. Rather, He loves us before we love Him (see 1 John 4:19). Our Heavenly Father listens when we come to talk with Him (see 1 John 5:14).

Jesus demonstrated the importance of having fellowship with the Father through His deep, personal relationship with Him. Jesus has both the knowledge and the authority to teach us about God the Father, because He is God the Son and the only one who has seen and fully knows God the Father.

Our Father, hallowed be Your name! Let Your kingdom come and Your will be done here on Earth and in my life.

> **Looking at Jesus will give us the clearest picture of God the Father.**

Liar, Liar

"You are of your father the devil. . . . He was a murderer from the beginning, and does not stand in the truth, because there is no truth in him. When he speaks a lie, he speaks from his own resources, for he is a liar and the father of it." (John 8:44)

Satan. The Devil. The Serpent of Old. Some call him Beelzebub, Belial, the Beast, the Tempter, the Evil One, the Accuser, the ruler of this world, or the prince of the power of the air. Whatever you call him, he is the enemy, and he is a real and present danger. He is not the cute and harmless character portrayed in the cartoons. He is invisible but not imaginary. He is opposed to God but not equal to God. He is a powerful fallen angel called Lucifer, who wanted God's position of authority and reverence. He rebelled against God and disobeys Him completely, and he wants us to do the same.

This terrorist has one objective: "to steal, and to kill, and to destroy" (John 10:10). He has never, ever spoken truth, and he never will. He hates the truth, and is he is is angry, very angry, because he knows his time is short (see Revelation 12:12). And not only does he lose in the end, but he will suffer great and eternal torment (see Revelation 20:10).

We do not have to fall for his lies or become casualties of his war with God. The only way to fight a lie is with the truth. By learning the truth of God, pursuing truth, walking in truth, and speaking truth we will resist the devil, and he will run (see James 4:7).

I know I cannot battle the Devil on my own, but greater is God in me than the god of this world. Help me, Lord, to stand in Your truth so I don't fall for the lies of the enemy.

> **Jesus shows us that using the truth of God is the best way to resist the lies of the Devil.**

Eternal Life

"Most assuredly, I say to you, if anyone keeps My word he shall never see death." (John 8:51)

Christians die. Tombstones around the world testify to this truth. So how are we to understand Jesus's daring statement in John 8:51 that if we keep His Word, we never will see death?

There is an all-purpose principle that is especially helpful with biblical interpretation, and it goes like this: When you don't know something, start with what you do know. We know our bodies perish, and we know "it is appointed for men to die once" (Hebrews 9:27). But we also know that God has promised eternal life to all who believe (see John 3:16), death is not the end of our story, and it does not have victory over the believer (see 1 Corinthians 15:55). Knowing this, I believe that Jesus's emphasis is not on physical death but on the fear of death. Perhaps the key to understanding His statement is found in the word "see." The word here implies preoccupation. For the one found faithful to God's Word, there is no need to be gripped with fear or preoccupied with the thought of death, because there is no true death for the believer. Jesus destroyed death and the power of death by rising triumphantly over sin and death.

For Christians the moment we were born again, we were instantly united with Christ. From that moment on, we never will be separated from God, not even when our physical bodies die. Death merely ushers us into a new and everlasting aspect of living. It's life where the hardships of earthly living are no more, because there will be no more suffering, pain, tears, or death.

Thank you, God, for the powerful reminder that You are greater than death and that the grave has no power over us, because You are the giver of everlasting life.

Nothing, not even death, can ever separate believers from their unity with Jesus.

The Great I AM

"Most assuredly, I say to you, before Abraham was, I AM."
(John 8:58)

How would you finish this statement: "I am . . ."? Would you say, "I am a Christian," or I am single (or married)," or "I am an athlete," or "I am short (or tall)"? Jesus was continually making religious people mad, and what made them the angriest was His claim to be God.

"I AM WHO I AM" was a name God used to identify Himself in the Old Testament (Exodus 3:14). When Jesus described Himself in John 8:58, He didn't describe His job, His appearance, or some singular aspect of Himself. Rather, He described the entirety of His being. I AM speaks of God's eternal nature and His self-sufficiency. God does not need anything, because He has everything within Himself. By saying "before Abraham was, I AM," Jesus not only claimed divinity, but He claimed eternality. Jesus asserted that He existed before the creation of the world, He exists in the present, and He exists tomorrow. Jesus's existence did not begin in a manger in Bethlehem. He always has been, because He always has been God.

Throughout the gospel of John, Jesus uses more "I am" statements to describe different aspects of His self-sufficiency and the various blessings believers receive through their relationship with Jesus. But through this "I am" statement, we see His self-sufficiency and how He is all-sufficient for whatever we need, whenever we need it, wherever we need it.

Thank you, God, that you are not the I WAS or I WILL BE. You are always and forever the great I AM, all-powerful and ever present for every need we have.

Jesus is the great I AM, not the great I WAS.

Having a Compassionate Heart

"But a Samaritan, as he journeyed, came to where he was,
and when he saw him, he had compassion." (Luke 10:33 ESV)

The more I learn about God's love, the more I realize how unloving I can be at times. But I suspect that I am not the only one, because in comparison to the perfect love of God, we all could use a little compassion calibration.

In this familiar story, "A man was going down from Jerusalem to Jericho, and fell among robbers, who stripped him and beat him and departed, leaving him half dead" (Luke 10:30 ESV). On the same day, two other men also were going down this road. The first one was a priest, and the second was a Levite. Both men served in the temple, so both were religious men, both saw the man lying in the road, and both did nothing to help. The next person to come down the road was a Samaritan. Now, the Jews and Samaritans despised each other, but when the Samaritan saw the injured Jewish man, "he had compassion" (verse 33 ESV). The prequel to any act of kindness is having a heart of compassion (see Colossians 3:12).

We learn compassion by practicing acts of loving-kindness. Compassion is not an emotion we feel, it is a commitment we make. Compassion is choosing to show love to someone, even when we might not feel like it. Compassion means that we are willing to give of ourselves for the benefit of another. The genuineness of our love for God will be demonstrated by our love for others.

God, help me to cultivate a heart of compassion. Let Your love flow
through me and overflow into the lives of others.

> **Jesus reminds us of our need to be living**
> **examples of compassion to the world**
> **around us.**

Living As Good Samaritans

"He gave him first aid, disinfecting and bandaging his wounds. Then he lifted him onto his donkey, led him to an inn, and made him comfortable." . . . *Jesus said, "Go and do the same." (Luke 10:34, 37 MSG)*

"I don't have time." "It's not my problem." "Someone else will help." These are all excuses we can use to ignore the needs of another and refuse to lend a helping hand. If we were to place ourselves in the famous story of the Good Samaritan (see Luke 10:25–37), as much as we wouldn't want to admit it, it's possible that many of us would have passed by this down-and-out character, using one of our comfortable go-to excuses as to why we just couldn't be bothered to lend a helping hand at the time. The Samaritan could have said, "This man is my enemy" or "I am on my way somewhere, therefore, I just can't help today." We expect the religious men to have done something, but disappointingly they were too holy to lend a hand. But the Samaritan is the unlikely hero of the story, going above and beyond to help the injured man at his own expense.

So what can we do? To start, we'll have to change our mindset and stop thinking, "I'll help when I have time," "I'll help when I have the energy," "I'll help when it's convenient," or "I'll help when it's someone I know and love." Interruptions happen, and loving others is often inconvenient. The simple truth is that loving others costs us time and energy. So the next time you encounter an opportunity to help, will you pass by, or will you stop and lend a hand?

God, make me willing to help others in need. I can't help everyone, but let me help those I know I can.

When you encounter hurting people, Jesus is giving you an opportunity to love others.

JUNE

Used by God

"The harvest truly is great, but the laborers are few; therefore pray the Lord of the harvest to send out laborers into His harvest." (Luke 10:2)

You are here for a purpose. God wants to use you. Yes, God can do all things. That is part of what makes Him God. Yes, God has created the universe and everything in it, yet He invites us to partner with Him. God alone saves, He alone changes hearts, and He alone convicts of sin. But one of the most amazing aspects of how God works is that He chooses to work through His people.

Jesus points out that although there is a great harvest, there is also a great need for workers. In the world there is a harvest of lost and needy souls, ready to receive salvation and healing. All that is needed is for someone to share with them the good news of Jesus Christ (Romans 10:14–15). God does not *need* our help, but He does *want* us to help.

It is natural to feel inadequate and underqualified to do the work of God. But that's because we spend too much time focusing on our limitations and not enough time remembering that God is limitless. Even with my limitations, God is able to do "exceedingly abundantly above all that we ask or think, according to the [His] power that works in us (Ephesians 3:20). God needs your availability more than He needs your ability.

Lord, I confess to You the selfishness of my heart when I have chosen comfort over compassion and closed fists over helping hands. Give me a deeper love for others so that I would be more willing to go work the harvest fields.

> **Jesus sees the great harvest. Are you willing to step out and be used by God?**

Falling from Grace

"I saw Satan fall like lightning from heaven." (Luke 10:18)

Why would a God of love create something as horrible as the Devil? The first problem with this reasoning is that it assumes we know more than God, and we don't. Second, God did not create Satan as we know of him currently. Originally, Lucifer was created as good. In fact, the Bible tells us that he was the "seal of perfection, full of wisdom and perfect in beauty . . . anointed as a guardian cherub, . . . blameless" from the day he was created (Ezekiel 28:12, 15 NIV).

But Lucifer allowed his perfection to be the cause of his pride. He was not satisfied with worshiping God. Instead, *he* wanted to be worshiped, and *he* wanted the praise and glory that is reserved only for God Almighty. Lucifer, the "morning star" (Isaiah 14:12), became Satan, the accuser, when He fell from grace. As punishment for his prideful disobedience and rebellion, God cast Lucifer out of heaven to Earth to be seen by all (see Ezekiel 28:17).

Pride tops the list of sins that God hates (see Proverbs 6:16–17). The pride that the Bible condemns refers to being obsessed with yourself, so much so that your mind never turns to God, and your heart never seeks Him (see Psalm 10:4). As Christians, we should not underestimate Satan or think we are immune to his attacks, but we do not need to live in fear, either. If you have said yes to Jesus, then you have God within you, and "the one who is in you is greater than the one who is in the world" (1 John 4:4).

God, help me remember that even though Satan can appear as an angel of light, I have the power, in the name of Jesus, to resist him and to overcome him.

> **Jesus conquered Satan at the Cross, and He is our strength against the enemy.**

The Joy of Jesus

At that time Jesus, full of joy through the Holy Spirit, said, "I
praise you, Father, Lord of heaven and earth, because you
have hidden these things from the wise and learned, and
revealed them to little children. Yes, Father, for this is what
you were pleased to do." (Luke 10:21)

What gives Jesus joy? This is the only time the Gospels describe Jesus
as filled with joy. But it isn't just Jesus who was rejoicing. Notice that
all three members of the Trinity were involved here. So, what was it
that brought such joy to the Trinity?

The seventy disciples had just returned from being sent out to
preach, and they were overjoyed and reported their successes to Jesus.
First, this profound joy of Jesus was directly due to the Holy Spirit.
The Holy Spirit had worked through the disciples and gave them vic-
tories over Satan as they cast out demons. Jesus also was rejoicing that
God chose belief, not brilliance, as the means to salvation. Salvation is
not found in the power or intellect of humanity; God's grace is what
saves lost souls. Second, Jesus was rejoicing because the redemptive
plan of God was at work (see Luke 10:20). Finally, Jesus's ultimate,
joy-producing element was the sovereignty of God. Knowing that
God the Father was pleased also pleased Jesus.

Do you want to make Jesus rejoice? Then find your joy where He
found His: in partnership with the Holy Spirit, in preaching the grace
of God, and in doing what pleases God the Father.

*God, regardless of my current circumstances, I always have reason to
rejoice in the Spirit. As You are at work in the world accomplishing
your plans and purposes, be at work in me to also accomplish Your
plans and purposes where you have me.*

**The ultimate joy for Jesus was found in
pleasing God the Father.**

Are You Too Busy for God?

"Martha, Martha, you are worried and troubled about many things. (Luke 10:41)

Busy! It's a word that describes most of our lives. We've got places to go and people to see, children to raise and appointments to keep, friends to connect with and families to take care of. Add to that the various church activities, ministries, and service projects that we are involved in, and we just might find ourselves having a Martha moment. Finding calm in chaos can be challenging, but there may be times when the chaos is self-inflicted.

Jesus had only a few cherished friendships outside of his band of brothers, the twelve disciples. One such friendship was found with the family of Mary, Martha, and their brother, Lazarus. It must have been immensely enjoyable for Jesus to have a place where He could kick off His sandals, recline, and really relax. But on one such visit, Martha allowed herself to get so busy that she had a mini-meltdown.

Martha's busyness, although well intended, was self-inflicted. She had allowed herself to get all bent out of shape because she was trying to do too much. And in so doing, she was missing out on spending time with Jesus. Jesus's response to Martha in that moment reminds us that it is better being with Jesus than being too busy for Him.

God, grant me the wisdom to be a good steward with my time. Help me to be still before You and not let busyness take me away from being in Your presence. When I get too busy, calm my heart and remind me of my greatest need, which is more of You.

Don't allow yourself to get so busy that you miss time with Jesus.

Finding Balance

*Mary has chosen that good part, which will not be taken away
from her." (Luke 10:41–42)*

Has hustle been substituted for holiness? As Christians, we need to be careful that we do not put serving Jesus before intimacy with Jesus. Serving is an important principle in Christianity, but a problem arises when serving distracts us from the purpose of our service. If serving becomes a never-ending to-do list, then you might be missing the point.

Balance is essential in every aspect of our lives if we want to be happy and healthy. This is true for our physical and emotional health, and it is especially true for our spiritual health. Whether you naturally have a Martha personality and are a go-getting, energetic, high-achieving, type A person, or you naturally have a Mary personality and are an introspective, deep-thinking, easygoing, steady, reflective person, balance is essential. Martha was busy serving, and Mary was busy worshiping. Both are good, both are needed, and both are necessary. The solution is not the extreme of either-or but a mixture of both.

Jesus was not chastising Martha's service but just her choice in that moment, which was to be preoccupied with it. Snacks would have done the job. There was no need to spend the day in the kitchen and miss fellowship with the Savior. And maybe Martha thought, "Well, if I don't do it, it won't get done." That may have been true, but Jesus was teaching that our highest priority needs to be our relationship with Him.

Jesus, spending quality time with You always will help me live a well-balanced life and keep me from being more focused on doing for You rather than being with You.

**Living a balanced life involves both sitting at
Jesus's feet and serving Him.**

Talking with God

"When you pray, . . ." (Luke 11:2)

Do you find prayer a struggle? Do you find it difficult to maintain a consistent prayer life? Does prayer even matter? If we are being authentic, we all would agree that we struggle with prayer. Whether it is making time for prayer, knowing what to pray, staying focused in prayer, or feeling stuck in a humdrum prayer rut, we all can benefit from a little prayer push. Christianity is not just what we believe about God; it is also about connecting with God. And one of the best ways to connect with God is in prayer.

After Jesus finished a private conversation with His Father, one of His disciples said to Him, "Lord, teach us to pray" (Luke 11:1). Hearing Jesus pray must have been captivating and attractive and created a deep desire in the disciples to pray more like Him. Prayer, in its simplest form, is nothing more than talking to God. It is a conversation with our Creator, and conversations make connections. Conversations tear down walls, build bridges, and build relationships. The Lord's Prayer isn't intended to be a rote repetition of empty words. It emphasizes relationship, it is designed to make a connection between our hearts and the heart of God, and it inspires us to talk transparently with Him. The more we spend time getting to know God, the more we will be able to engage in real, heartfelt conversations with Him.

Dear Lord, sometimes my prayer life may take purposeful effort. Help me to use Your prayer to establish connectivity with You, build genuine conversation with You, and deepen my relationship with You.

> **Jesus prayed because He could do nothing without God, and neither can we.**

Praying to Our Father

"Our Father in heaven, . . ." (Luke 11:2)

God not only expects us to pray, but He also shows us how to do it. The Lord's Prayer, as we call it, can be divided into two parts: the glory of God and the provision of our needs.

All prayer, all praise, and all worship begins by being able to come to God as His children. Beginning our prayers with "our Father" lets us know that we are not alone; we are part of a heavenly household. There is an aspect of God's holiness that makes Him unapproachable in the heavenlies, but Jesus tells us that as *our* Father, God extends an invitation for us to have intimacy with Him. He inhabits heaven, but He is not distant. His love for us as His children is transcendent, unique, unmatched, and extravagant (see 1 John 3:1). He is the all-powerful Creator of the universe, but He cares immeasurably for you personally. He is a good father. He is never too busy for you. When you talk to Him, He listens. He always knows what is best, and He delights in blessing His children.

When you pray, then, remember the kindheartedness that comes through a personal relationship with God as Father. When you pray, it's about trusting in who God is as our Father and understanding that He loves His children perfectly, will lead His children completely, and will protect and provide for His children entirely.

Father, I thank You that I can come to You personally and comfortably as your child yet humbly to You as my God. Thank you for caring for me and listening to me as a loving Father. Continue to teach me how You are both my God and my Father in Heaven.

Jesus's prayer encourages us to connect with God as Our Father.

The Act of Hallowing

"Hallowed be Your name." *(Luke 11:2)*

God is BIG. God is awe-inspiring. God is marvelous. God is mighty. God is to be praised. Although *hallowed* is not a word we use today, the significance behind it is far-reaching in how we are to worship and praise God. When we understand and acknowledge God for who He is, we cannot help but worship Him.

Hallowing God's name means that we are captivated by God's holiness, which in turn produces an awe-filled adoration within in us. When we pray, we come to God respecting His holiness, but we also come to Him asking that His name will become more holy, sacred, revered, and respected by us and by all. God's name being respected is the general starting point and overall spirit underpinning every prayer we pray. We may ask for God's direction or provision, and we may ask for God's healing or protection, but all our prayers should seek to uphold and encourage the glory and sanctity of God (see 1 Corinthians 10:31).

Hallowing God's name begins by believing in God and submitting to God. You cannot come to God unless you first believe that He exists (see Hebrews 11:6). Believing He exists is to believe that He is the Lord God who revealed Himself in and through the person of Jesus Christ. Then you must live in submission to God, because at the heart of hallowing is obeying. The result is the more we make of God in our lives, the more we will hallow Him in our prayers.

Father, I thank You that I can come to you in prayer, but keep me from rushing into Your presence without first falling to my knees with a hallowing respect and reverence.

> **Jesus teaches us that our prayers always should include uplifting the great name of God.**

Praying for God's Kingdom

"Your kingdom come." (Luke 11:2)

Humans have a longing for truth, justice, and righteousness to prevail. We long for something this world can never provide, which is a perfect king who will rule perfectly. We long for the kingdom of God, but do we really understand what God's kingdom is?

The kingdom of God, in its simplest form, is the rule of God and the realm of His rule. A central theme throughout the Bible is the establishment and expansion of the kingdom of God, but the kingdom of God both *has* come, and *is* coming. The kingdom of God is both spiritual and physical. The kingdom of God *has* come through Jesus Christ during His first coming, and all who have faith in Jesus and follow Him are spiritually part of God's kingdom. The kingdom of God is also *coming* in the future and will be completed when Jesus sets up His earthly rule.

It is easy to pray about our needs, our trials, and even our shortcomings, but when we pray "Your kingdom come," we are asking for the continued extension of God's reign on Earth. We are praying for God to convert hearts and bring people to salvation in Jesus, and we are praying for the coming of the day when all evil, all sin, and all rebellion against God is over. So let's keep praying for God's kingdom to come.

God, may Your kingdom come. May Your rule and reign expand over my life, and may Your kingdom spread across the Earth and bring many more people into relationship with You. Use me to faithfully be a part of Your kingdom work.

Jesus explains that fruitful prayers will be those calling for the kingdom of God to grow.

Praying for God's Will

"Your will be done." (Luke 11:2)

Seeking God's direction for each day not only should be a priority in our prayers, but it also should be the purpose of our daily living. The worship of God includes pursuing and practicing His will. Much of God's will is not mysterious or unknown; it is spelled out clearly in the Bible. If you are waiting for an audible voice to direct you or something to be written in the sky to point the way, then you will miss out on what He already has proclaimed in His Word.

God is always ready for His will to be done. The question is whether we're willing to do it. Part of connecting with God is seeking His will and purposing to do His will. This portion of the Lord's Prayer not only is for God's will to be done generally, but it's also for us to personally surrender to accomplishing His will in our lives. When we come to God in prayer, it is not with the attitude of "my will be done" but "Your will be done." Every day we have a choice: either we'll purpose to live in obedience to God's revealed will found in the Bible, or we'll choose to go our own way.

When Jesus prays for God's will to be done on Earth as it is in heaven, He is asking for us to follow God's will from God's Word by God's Spirit. Praying for God's will to be done is to ask that we not only submit to His will, but also that people everywhere would love God and live according to His Word.

God grant me the courage to live one day at a time, enjoying each moment, surrendering to Your will, and walking according to Your ways.

Jesus declares that balanced prayer includes being committed to God's will.

Heaven and Earth

"On earth as it is in heaven." (Luke 11:2)

Heaven is a real place. It is not, however, a place where we listen to harp music, float along on clouds, and walk around wearing white robes and halos. Sorry to disappoint you, but that isn't what heaven is all about.

Heaven is a perfect, pain-free place where the glory of God resides and where God rules and reigns. In heaven God's will is done without opposition and without question. What God decides is accomplished. What God determines is established. God's will in heaven is done happily, humbly, continually, and perfectly. In heaven believers will enjoy God forever, praise Him continually, worship Him wholly, and serve Him flawlessly. On Earth, however, that is not the current state of affairs. People disobey God, Satan is in rebellion against God, and the world as a whole is too busy for God. That is why Jesus encourages us to pray for God's will to be done on Earth as it is in heaven.

To pray this way is to declare our great need for God's presence, provision, love, and redemption. It is not a petition for heaven to come down as much as it is a reminder that we should live in light of heaven. Praying this way means that heavenly minded people should live heavenly minded lives. As God's will in heaven is done happily, humbly, continually, and perfectly, so should it be done in our lives here on Earth.

Father God, Your will being done on earth begins with me. Inspire me to first commit to seeking and doing Your will so that I can then help others live for You.

Jesus desires His kingdom to fill the earth, and He seeks to do it through His people.

Daily Dependence

"Give us day by day our daily bread." (Luke 11:3)

The Christian life is so day by day. Daily dependence is at the very heart of our relationship with God. As a result, total dependence on God is central to the prayer that Jesus models for us. God not only is concerned about our spiritual needs, but He also is concerned with our physical needs. Therefore, Jesus approvingly encourages us to pray daily for both.

God wants us to trust Him and depend on Him day by day for our needs. However, Jesus did not say, "Give me this day a Lamborghini." Jesus teaches us to pray about that which is essential, not that which is excessive. Trusting God does not release us from planning or imply that we can be careless about our future. Rather, trusting God daily keeps our relationship with Him in proper alignment and keeps our prayers in proper perspective. This portion of the Lord's Prayer calls us to a recognition and realization that God is our provider. We are not to worry about tomorrow's provision today (see Matthew 6:34), and we should receive all that God supplies with thanksgiving.

God gave the children of Israel enough manna for each day (see Exodus 16:4, 21), and so too, God gives us what we need for today, not for tomorrow. What He gives is enough for that day and that day alone. God looks after all our needs, not all our wants. Praying this way helps to keep us submitted, surrendered, and dependent on God to keep, guide, and provide for us day by day.

God, help me to come to You in a spirit of humble dependence, never asking for riches but making my needs known to You. Help me to trust You to provide what I need, when I need it.

Jesus stresses daily dependence on the sovereign provision of God.

Daily Forgiveness

"And forgive us our sins." (Luke 11:4)

Forgiveness is freeing. Guilt, however, weighs us down and makes it hard to move forward. Emotional clutter can hinder our spiritual growth and our service for God, but God has made a way for us to release our guilt, walk in freedom, and cleanse our hearts from sin. The answer comes to us through prayer.

Jesus teaches us to ask God for forgiveness every time we pray. Asking for forgiveness is hard, because we have to admit that we were wrong, and it forces us to come face to face with our failures. Asking God for forgiveness requires us to humble ourselves before Him and let go of our pride. Jesus knew that we would daily fall short of God's standard. We may not be breaking one of the Ten Commandments, but we all have sinful thoughts, say things that are unkind and unloving, and don't always do the good that we should do. Therefore, a day does not go by that we do not need to ask God to forgive us of our sins.

But when we pray, "Forgive us our sins," we are asking God to deliver what He promises: "If we confess our sins, he is faithful and just and will forgive us our sins and purify us from all unrighteousness" (1 John 1:9 NIV). This, in turn, cleanses our conscience, provides a sense of peace with God, and frees us to move forward spiritually.

God, thank you for Your forgiveness. As I confess my sins, faults, and failures to You, Your forgiveness frees me today to walk in your grace. I am truly thankful for Your compassionate mercy.

Jesus reminds us that we should be in the habit of asking God for forgiveness.

Forgiving Others

"For we also forgive everyone who sins against us."
(Luke 11:4 NIV)

God is forgiving, and if we are going to be His disciples, then we must follow His example. If God is willing to forgive even those who fight against Him (see Acts 9:1–19), then how could we do anything less than be forgiving as well? According to Jesus, our forgiveness of others should be the natural result of personally receiving the forgiveness of God.

Believers need to accept and apply the truth that forgiveness is the only response when someone transgresses our trust. Mercy, grace, and forgiveness not only is for us to receive, but it is also for us to give out. Forgiving others is an essential aspect of becoming more like Jesus, not to mention that unforgiveness holds us hostage, grieves God, and hinders us spiritually. Holding on to hate or bringing bitterness everywhere we go will gnaw at our souls and harm our health. Jesus did not qualify our forgiveness, make it conditional, optional, or exclude certain offenses as undeserving of forgiveness. We are to forgive as God forgives: unconditionally and fully.

When we find it difficult to forgive, we need to remember that we've been forgiven of our ugliest thoughts, dirtiest deeds, and nastiest words, freely and fully. And because of God's forgiveness, we have been spared from hell. This should enable us to forgive more freely and more fully.

Father, You forgive me quickly and completely. Although my forgiveness of others may not be perfect, I want forgiveness to be a part of my life.

Jesus expects forgiven people to be forgiving people.

The Truth about Temptation

"And do not lead us into temptation but deliver us from the evil one." (Luke 11:4)

Sooner or later temptation will knock on your door, and when it does, it will do you no good if you lock the door but leave the window open. Temptation is good at making its way past half-hearted barricades. Temptation itself is not sin. However, it should not be taken lightly, because it can quickly lead to sin.

First, let's be perfectly clear: God does not temp us to sin. He never has, and He never will (see James 1:13). Temptation comes to us from one of the following enemies: the world, the flesh, and the Devil. The world offers counterfeit and temporary fulfillment and external enticements that can never satisfy the soul. The flesh is the desire within us that is inclined and vulnerable to do the wrong thing. Then there is the Devil, with his self-serving, God-snubbing invitations to dishonor God and disobey His truth.

Temptation is a decoy that seeks to divert our attention away from God's best for our lives. Temptation is often the strongest when we are at our weakest, but we never will face a temptation so strong that God can't deliver us from it. That is why Jesus encourages us to make the prayerful appeal in Luke 11:4 regularly and repeatedly, asking God for help and deliverance when temptation comes knocking.

Father God, I recognize my inability to stand against temptation on my own. Help me to take my eyes off enticement when it comes. Allow me to see the way out that You provide, and give me the spiritual presence of mind to take it.

> **According to Jesus, my dependence on God is a key to resisting temptation.**

The Goodness of God

"If you then, being evil, know how to give good gifts to your children, how much more will your heavenly Father give the Holy Spirit to those who ask Him!" (Luke 11:13)

Do you trust God to hear your prayers and respond lovingly? God is not temperamental or fickle, and He doesn't listen to us halfheartedly. When you pray to God, you don't have to worry about whether or not you're going to catch Him having a bad day. He is rock solid, unswervingly consistent, and can be trusted to always have your best interest in mind.

In this passage Jesus was specifically talking about God the Father sending the Holy Spirit to believers. But it has a broader application as well. God is the giver of "every spiritual blessing in Christ" (Ephesians 1:3 ESV). Also, Romans 8:32 poses this question: "He who did not spare his own Son, but gave him up for us all—how will he not also, along with him, graciously give us all things?" (NIV).

God has given us His Son, His Holy Spirit, and His Word, and in these we have everything we need to meet any circumstance with confidence. Knowing that God will give us what we need to meet every situation should give us comfort and confidence. We can trust God's goodness and His graciousness to give us good gifts. We can trust that when we come to Him in prayer, He will respond lovingly, generously and perfectly. This doesn't mean we always will get what we ask for, but we always will get God's best for us.

Father God, I can altogether trust and wholly build my life on the fact that there is no variation in Your love or in the consistency of Your goodness and provision for me.

Every good gift comes to us from God in Jesus Christ.

Harmony at Home

"A house divided against itself will fall." (Luke 11:17 NIV)

It's been said that family is like fudge: mostly sweet with a few nuts. Your heavenly Father knows all the idiosyncrasies of your family. He knows their weaknesses, trials, and difficulties. But He also longs to inspire and empower families so they can experience the wonders of God.

Jesus was being accused of driving out demons by the power of demons, to which He responded that such an accusation was baseless and senseless. Why would Satan work against himself and undermine his own authority? Jesus declared that His work is done by the power of God, and He made it clear that where there is division and disunity, kingdoms fall and households are injured. Division and disunity destroy growth, hinder progress, and devastate relationships.

The Lord created us to be in community with one another, and there is no closer community than family. Is there strife in your family? Maybe get-togethers are awkward or always end in an argument. Some issues are tough and may take a lot of prayer to work through. And yes, there is no perfect family, but God has placed you in your family, and He wants to work intentionally and purposefully through you and your family. We need to guard our households and our marriages against division, because if division takes root, damage is sure to follow.

God, I know that unity starts in the home. Keep me surrendered to You and Your will so that in my house, we are working together for Your good and Your glory rather than seeking our own selfish interests.

When a family lives surrendered to Jesus, there is harmony in the home.

The Pharisee Trap

Then the LORD *said to him, "Now then, you Pharisees clean the outside of the cup and dish, but inside you are full of greed and wickedness." (Luke 11:39 NIV)*

It is easy to agree with Jesus when He points the finger and condemns the hypocritical religious elite. But have we stopped to consider how we might be just like them?

Jesus's harshest condemnations often were leveled against the Pharisees, but who were these religious hypocrites? On one hand, they were holy men who kept the law, pursued purity with a passion, and wanted nothing more than to live lives that pleased God. On the other hand, they were the largest religious faction in Jesus's day and wielded considerable control over Jewish society and in the synagogues, which made many of them prideful. They were sincere but sincerely misguided. And in many ways, Jesus considered the Pharisees to be the worst of the worst because they were cold, uncaring, and legalistic. They cared more for the letter of the law than lovingly living the essence of the law. They were outwardly immaculate but inwardly defiled. Simply put, they did not practice what they preached.

We must be cautious of having outward religiosity without an inward transformation. A callous religion that doesn't care about people misses the heart of God. A Christian is not a Christian who is one only outwardly. There must be inward purification—not perfection but a renewing of the mind, sanctifying of the spirit, and a grace washing of the heart.

God, may I be less focused on appearances and more concerned with personal obedience. May the external be a reflection of my commitment to internal godliness at work.

> **Jesus wants both our internal and external selves to practice godliness.**

Bearing Burdens

*"And you experts in the law, woe to you, because you load
people down with burdens they can hardly carry, and you
yourselves will not lift one finger to help them."*
(Luke 11:46 NIV)

If you are waiting for your life to be less complicated before you lend
a hand to someone, that day may never come. In the meantime, life
hurts sometimes, and there are people all around us dealing with loss,
disappointment, hardship, discouragement, and doubt.

The scribes and Pharisees were supposed to know God and make
Him known to others while also helping them follow God's will and
ways. Instead, what Jesus found were religious leaders who added to
God's law, making it burdensome and difficult for others to live out
their faith. Instead of lightening the loads that people were carrying,
they weighed them down even more. Instead of stooping down to lift
someone up, they looked down unsympathetically.

A caring Christian not only encourages and comforts but also
bends down to help carry another's burden when necessary. It's not a
suggestion, it's a command: "Bear one another's burdens, and so fulfill
the law of Christ" (Galatians 6:2). When you're willing to descend
into the muddy waters of another person's troubles and hold that person up, even beginning to lift them out of their personal quagmire,
they will receive desperately needed support, love, and blessings. Not
only that, but you also will be blessed because you're fulfilling God's
command.

*Jesus, give me the willingness and strength to come alongside someone
in need, helping to carry the weight of their burdens as I point them
to You, the One who sustains us and shoulders our heaviest problems.*

**Jesus declares empty religion is that which is
unwilling to bear another's burden.**

Treasure Chest

"For where your treasure is, there your heart will be also."
(Luke 12:34)

We all have things in this life that we treasure. If you are unsure where your treasure is, take a moment to consider what gets the majority of your time, attention, and spending. What you value most is your treasure. Whatever dominates your conversations is what you treasure. How other people might describe you is a good indication of what you treasure.

Sometimes we say that Jesus is our treasure, but our lives can communicate otherwise. We say we want to please God, but we seem to be more concerned with pleasing others or ourselves. We know we should talk with others about Jesus, but it is so much easier to simply keep the subject focused on our hobbies, job, family, or other interests. We know we should tithe, but we would rather spend our money on the next new thing.

What does it mean for us to align our lives with what we say that we treasure? What does it mean to develop a heart for the Lord? Until we gain an understanding of the immense value of encountering God, we never will truly treasure God above all else. Until we make it our regular practice to take the time to discover God's heart and experience the depths of His love, our hearts will seek to find treasure in the wrong places. There is a cost associated with treasuring Jesus above all else. Doing so requires sacrifice and a reprioritization of our time. Jesus knows that living for Him brings us freedom from the grip of misplaced treasures. But living in a Jesus-is-my-treasure sort of way is challenging and requires discipline.

Father, forgive me for sometimes allowing my heart to treasure the wrong things. May my heart be wholly Yours.

Making Jesus your treasure always will be reflected in your in heart's desires.

Ready or Not?

"Let your waist be girded and your lamps burning."
(Luke 12:35)

Are you a planner? Do you try to schedule everything in advance? Do you live according to your daily or weekly agenda? Well, there is something God wants you to plan for and live prepared for: His return. Jesus is coming back, and when He does, He wants people to be ready. Even though no one knows when Jesus will return (see Matthew 24:44), we are still expected to live prepared for that moment.

Heaven belongs to people who prepare for it. Preparation today determines tomorrow's outcomes. The Bible is filled with examples emphasizing the importance of preparation. Nehemiah made preparations to rebuild the wall in Jerusalem (see Nehemiah 2), John the Baptist made preparation for the coming of the Messiah (see Luke 1:76), Jesus is making preparations for believers in heaven (see John 14:3), and God made specific and purposeful plans for humanity's redemption from the beginning. Genesis 3:15 paved the way for John 3:16.

So what does it look like to live prepared for Jesus' return? First, it's living a life that walks by faith, believing what we can't see, trusting what God has said, and obeying His commands. Next, it is living a sanctifying life whereby we die to sin and live unto righteousness, putting away sinful habits and developing Christlikeness. Finally, living ready for the return of Jesus is seeking to glorify God every day, in every situation.

Father, as I seek to live prepared for Jesus's return, enable me to be the person You want me to be and to be live how you want me to live.

Jesus, help me to live every day ready for Your return.

Discerning the Times

"You can discern the face of the sky and of the earth, but how is it you do not discern this time?" (Luke 12:56)

Have you ever looked around at society and thought, "What is going on in the world?" In addition to rampant postmodernism, subjective elevation of tolerance, rejection of absolute truth, and the devaluation of the Bible's authority, there is the societal turmoil of riots, wars, terrorism, and more. These are troublesome times indeed.

Jesus rebuked the spiritual leaders of His generation for a lack of discernment. He blamed them for not recognizing the biblical signs of the momentous time in which they were living. If dark clouds meant rain, then surely all the evidence Jesus put forth about Himself meant that He was God. But the religious leaders rejected the clear signs in front of them and refused to acknowledge the obvious.

We have little control over some of the events that happen around us, but we can choose how we live. The Bible speaks of the importance of discerning the times. Some of King David's men "had understanding of the times, to know what Israel ought to do" (1 Chronicles 12:32). Living in a way that discerns the times around us helps us to know, like David's men, what we ought to do and the direction we ought to take. Discerning the times requires a commitment to studying the Bible, a desire to cultivate communion with God, and a longing for the Holy Spirit to lead us in truth.

God, grant me the knowledge of Your truth and a sensitivity to Your Spirit to live wisely.

Jesus expects us to wisely discern the times in which we live.

Sin and Suffering

"Neither this man nor his parents sinned, but that the works of God should be revealed in him." (John 9:3)

Sickness, disease, disability, and death have affected life since the fall of humanity. We all are touched by those conditions, as they are all part of life in this world. Inevitably the question that follows is why does God allow suffering?

Many believe there is a connection between sin and suffering, and it is true that if there never had been sin, there never would be suffering. In that sense, all suffering *is* the result of sin. But that does not mean all suffering and sickness is the result of specific sin committed by the one who is sick or suffering. Our health or wealth is not necessarily a result of whether we have sinned. Sometimes the righteous prosper, and sometimes the righteous suffer—irrespective of sin. Take the blind man from John 9, for example. This man's blindness was not the result of some sin he committed. Jesus makes that perfectly clear. The purpose of this man's blindness was to reveal the miraculous power of God at work in Jesus. Jesus used this man's disability to demonstrate His divinity. Opening the eyes of this blind man was intended to open the eyes of the spiritually blind.

Suffering provides an opportunity to witness manifestations of God's grace in your life or in the lives of others. Sickness, disease, disability, and death are all invitations to trust God more.

Father God, help me to face challenges in life with my spiritual eyes wide open, because You not only show up in times of suffering and sickness, but You often work through those times.

> **Jesus can use suffering to display God's glory—if we don't turn a blind eye.**

Mud in Your Eye

And He said to him, **"Go, wash in the pool of Siloam."**
(John 9:7)

His heart racing, he recognized the voice he heard speaking to the crowd. It sounded like the man who had been teaching in the temple, Jesus of Nazareth. *Wait, I can hear him coming closer. Is He talking about me?* "Neither this man nor his parents sinned." *Even though I cannot see, He must be standing next to me now, because I can hear Him breathing. Oh my, I think He just put His hand on my shoulder!* "Go, wash in the pool of Siloam."

The blind man was presented with a choice. Would he trust and obey Jesus? After all, this was a rather strange request and even a bit difficult because of the multitudes crowding the narrow streets of Jerusalem. But he decided to obey, and he blindly made his way down to the pool of Siloam without an escort, tripping and bouncing off people as the crowd began to open a path. "Excuse me! I'm so sorry. Forgive me." Stumbling up to the water, the man plunged his mud-covered face below the surface. As the mud washed away, a ray of light penetrated his eyes. Blinking furiously to wipe away the mixture of water and tears, he thought, "I can see!" Then he boldly announced to the watching crowd, "I can see! I can see! I was blind, but now I see!"

Are you willing to go through whatever process God has for you in order to fully embrace the transformation of His healing in your life?

Jesus, help me to cooperate with You as You seek to heal me, help me, and shape me.

> **By participating in the process of our healing, we learn to trust the voice of Jesus and discover the depth of His power.**

Recognizing God's Voice

"The sheep follow him, for they know his voice." (John 10:4)

God wants to talk to you. Sometimes it's hard enough to hear yourself think, no less hear the voice of God. Add to that the fact that Jesus warns in John 10 that His voice isn't the only one contending for the ears of His people. Our ability to recognize God's voice is fundamental for following Him and is critical to our spiritual health and well-being. So how does a person discern the voice of God?

The Bible is where we most often hear God speaking to us today. God will never, ever, speak anything to us that contradicts what He has already said in the Bible. Never. Just because someone says, "God told me this" or "God told me that" doesn't mean that God actually did. Everything must be filtered through the truth of Scripture to discern whether it is, in fact, God's voice. But hearing God's voice involves more than just reading His Word. We must slow down and reflect on what God is saying in His Word as well. Also, the Holy Spirit is God's gift to believers to help guide us in all truth and direct us according to God's Word (see John16:13). Being devoted to God's Word and taking time to be still and silent before Him as you reflect on His Word, allowing the Holy Spirit to guide you in truth, will help you recognize God's voice more clearly. Prayerful consideration of what God has spoken in His Word will allow God to speak more personally into your life.

Jesus, thank you for Your willingness to speak to me. Help me to listen to Your words and follow the guidance You give me in Your Word.

> **Jesus speaking to you is not the result of a mystical experience; it is the result of a personal relationship with Him.**

One Door, One Way

"I am the door. If anyone enters by Me, he will be saved."
(John 10:9)

Life is filled with many choices. Drink coffee or tea, enjoy dark chocolate or milk chocolate, have a salad or a sandwich for lunch, own a dog or a cat. Then there are bigger life choices that can shape the rest of your life, such as whether to go to college, whom to marry, and how to spend your money. Choices can lead you into hardships, and choices can lead you to happiness. When it comes to religion, the world offers choices as well. You can choose Buddhism, Mormonism, Taoism, Universalism—the *-isms* are endless. But nothing is more important than making the right choice when it comes to your eternal destination.

Christianity is not as much about doctrines as it is about the person of Jesus. The "I am" statements of Jesus point to the unique aspects of His identity and purpose. Jesus as *the* door and not *a* door speaks of the exclusivity of Jesus for salvation. Jesus never preached a "whatever works for you" message of salvation. There is, was, and only ever will be one door: Jesus. The message of Jesus as the only way of salvation can be a tough one to swallow in a world where hypertolerance is clearly encouraged. But truth, even hard-to-swallow truth, doesn't make it any less true. Jesus wants to lead people out of that which would rob them of eternal life and into that which brings everlasting life. Jesus is unique, He made unique claims, and He backed up those claims with God-given proof.

Thank you, Jesus, that as I believe and accept You as the door to my salvation, I have gained access to the spiritual blessings you have for me and want to do through me.

To choose Jesus is to choose life.

Life to the Fullest

"I have come that they may have life, and that they may have it more abundantly." (John 10:10)

God wants to do more than give you life after death. He also wants you to enjoy an abundant life here on Earth. But does living an abundant life mean that everyone is in good health, all the bills are paid, the kids are doing great in school, and there's enough money in the bank for a little vacation? Living an abundant life doesn't exclude these things, but it is absolutely more than these things. Living an abundant life is less about what we can get out of life and more about what we give our lives to.

An abundant life comes from giving our lives to Jesus, pursuing holiness, and seeking to be more like Him. The promise of an abundant life comes to us in the context of sheep following their Shepherd, and as we follow Jesus and make choices to trust and obey Him, the more spiritual abundance we will experience in our lives. Living this way allows the Holy Spirit to produce in our lives fruits such as "love, joy, peace, longsuffering, kindness, goodness, faithfulness, gentleness, [and] self-control" (Galatians 5:22–23). The more we listen to Jesus speaking, follow His direction, and allow the Holy Spirit to guide us, the more abundantly these fruits will be produced in our lives and the more blessed we will be. Spiritual change is what reflects our progression toward living an abundant life. The more the fruits of the Spirit are evident in your life, the greater spiritual abundance you will personally experience.

Forgive me, Lord Jesus, for a heart that many times wanders and does not seek You. Help me to start a new walk with You that is not sidetracked but yielded to Your guidance.

The key to living an abundant life is not by trying harder. It is yielding more to Jesus.

The Good Shepherd

"I am the good shepherd." *(John 10:11)*

Sheep need a shepherd. Sheep are very vulnerable animals because they have no sense of direction, are defenseless against predators, can't swim, and are prone to wander. The purpose of a shepherd is singular: to care for the sheep. Shepherds care for their sheep by guiding them and protecting them.

Because sheep are directionless and defenseless wanderers, they need shepherds to guide them to food, water, and shelter. And as long as the sheep listen to the voice of the shepherd and follow, they always will have their needs met. Likewise, if we listen to Jesus's voice and follow Him, we always will have our needs met. Unprotected sheep won't last very long in the wild, so a good shepherd will use his staff to fend off predators, and with the hook he will protect his sheep by pulling them back from danger when they begin to stray. Jesus uses His Word in our lives to defend, protect, and even correct us as His flock, because sometimes protection comes in the form of correction.

Only the Good Shepherd can guide us to the pastures we are all looking for—pastures of freedom, joy, contentment, and virtue. When circumstances tempt you to wander, look to the Good Shepherd to lead you. Jesus knows His sheep, and He knows how to guide us and protect us.

God, show me the areas of my life where I am afraid to follow You. Help me to listen for Your voice and to follow You today. Thank you for faithfully protecting, providing for, and guiding me. You truly are a Good Shepherd.

> **Our souls need the kind of care that only Jesus can provide as the Good Shepherd.**

A Few Good Shepherds

"The hireling flees because he is a hireling and does not care about the sheep." (John 10:13)

Weak churches have weak leaders. Strong churches have strong leaders. The church today needs shepherds who are appointed, called, and gifted by God, not hirelings who approach ministry with a "what's in it for me?" mentality.

Hirelings are bad shepherds who neglect the flock. They allow the sheep to graze in bad pastures and be exposed to life-threatening adversities. They often berate the sheep in order to teach submission rather than lovingly encouraging and biblically correcting the sheep. A hireling abandons the sheep at the first sign of trouble, caring more about self-preservation than selflessly safeguarding the flock.

A good shepherd's main concern is to please God and care for the well-being of the sheep. Good shepherds know the flock, and the flock know them. They lead the flock and don't lord their leadership over the sheep. Good shepherds are examples to follow, not examples to avoid. A good shepherd lays down his life for the sheep rather than running and hiding when adversity comes or the enemy attacks. Good shepherds care more about feeding the flock than entertaining the herd, they care more about the sheep's salvation than their own salary, and they care more about their calling than their comfort. Leaders need to follow the example of the Good Shepherd, and sheep need to run from hirelings.

Jesus, I lift up my church's pastors and elders, and I pray they would always do what is in the best spiritual interest of the sheep entrusted to their care.

> **Jesus calls church leaders to be authentic shepherds.**

Lay It Down

"No one takes it from Me, but I lay it down of Myself. I have power to lay it down, and I have power to take it again. This command I have received from My Father." (John 10:18)

Jesus's life was not taken from Him; He willingly laid it down. Jesus's death on the cross was not a defeat for God; it was the definitive defeat of evil. Jesus died under His own authority, and under His own authority He took up His life again. Christ willingly laid down His life for us (see John 10:15). Judas didn't sell it, Pilate didn't pass judgment on it, and the centurions didn't crucify it. Jesus gave them all permission to take it.

Jesus's willingness did not merely include his voluntary death on the cross. Rather, His entire life was one of willing obedience to God's will. His willingness was His deliberate decision to consistently and continually fulfill the will of the Father who sent Him and submit to the sovereignty of God (see John 6:38).

Salvation is easy for us, because Jesus paid the bill for our sin. But the daily living out of our salvation is not so easy, because it requires a willingness on our part to lay down our lives and give them in surrendered obedience to the will of God, submitting to the sovereignty of God. Just as Jesus willingly made the deliberate decision to consistently and continually fulfill the will of the Father, so too, we must be willing to do the same.

Lord God, make me willing to grow in my attitude of surrender, to lay down my specific dreams, hopes, possessions, habits, or relationships before You so that in them all, I carry out Your will.

Jesus laid down His life for you. Will you lay down your will for Him?

JULY

Rest Assured

"And I give them eternal life, and they shall never perish;
neither shall anyone snatch them out of My hand."
(John 10:28)

Have you ever wondered whether you could lose your salvation? Let me reassure you, God has not saved you so you then have to worry about the security of your salvation. If you trust in Jesus, your eternal destiny is secure. Even though we make mistakes, God assures every true believer that their future is guaranteed and protected.

We must remember that the reason we are saved is not because we deserve it or earn it but because of the redemptive work of Jesus. If grace depends on us, then grace ceases to be grace. God does not give us the gift of salvation only to take His gift back. A faith that saves is a faith that remains. But this confidence is not intended to be used as a get-out-of-hell-free card, which then leads a person to living in reckless disobedience. Rather, it should serve as a comforting reminder that in those moments when we fall short, we are still secure in Him.

If Jesus makes a promise, then rest assured, He is willing and able to keep His promise. If God has not saved us perfectly and permanently, then God is not sovereign. Eternal life is not eternal if you can lose it or if it can be stolen. Our security comes from the One who is able to save us, Jesus, the giver of eternal life and the keeper of it.

Lord God, I know there are many things in life that are uncertain,
but one thing I never need to doubt or worry about is the security of
my salvation. Thank you for helping me to rest assured in the power
and protection of Your mighty grace.

Faith in Jesus means you never need to have
insecurity about your eternity.

God is Greater

"My Father, who has given them to Me, is greater than all."
(John 10:29)

In a world full of ups and downs, it's easy to lose sight of the fact that God is still in control. When you face uncertainties, when the future looks dark, when work has you stressed, or when you're tempted to sin, remember that Jesus is greater than all. When the future looks bright, when you are blessed with success, when you have piles of possessions, and when you are financially secure, remember that Jesus is greater than all.

God is greater than your fears, and God is greater than your feelings. God is greater than your worries, and God is greater than your problems. God is greater than your failures, and God is greater than your shortcomings. God is greater than your enemies, and God is greater than your obstacles. God is greater than your challenges, and God is greater than your limitations. God is greater than your misfortune, and God is greater than your heartache. God is greater than your poverty, and God is greater than your wealth. God is greater than your intellect, and God is greater than your success. God is greater than everything He has created.

We are limited, and God is limitless. We are finite, and God is infinite. Therefore, it is important—no, essential—to know that God is greater than all, because the greatest thing God gives us is Himself. We are not defined by our circumstances, our possessions, our achievements, or our failures. We are defined by our relationship with God, because God is greater than all He has created.

God, thank you that You are stronger than my struggles, and Your promises are more powerful than my problems. My identity is found in You, and You are greater than all.

The greatness of God is experienced through Jesus Christ.

Stoning Jesus

"I have shown you many good works from the Father; for which of them are you going to stone me?" (John 10:32 ESV)

When the subject of Jesus comes up, the conversation often starts out somewhat favorably as people speak of Jesus as a great person or inspirational teacher. Maybe they even will say He was a revolutionary. But the conversation can turn quickly to one of hostility. Why does Jesus cause some people to have such a violent reaction? Perhaps the answer lies in why the Pharisees had such a violent reaction toward Jesus.

Everywhere Jesus went, He attracted huge crowds of people that hung on His every word and watched His every move. He was popular with the people and quickly gained a following. The religious leaders, on the other hand, were losing their grip on their followers as Jesus's teachings and miracles outshined the legalistic entanglements they offered. They were jealous, and when Jesus openly challenged them, they always were left speechless. Jesus was the real deal, and His genuine divinity exposed them as hypocritical counterfeits. But as insidious as jealousy can be, and as real as hypocrisy can taint your view of Jesus, these leaders often tried to stone Jesus for another reason: He exposed sin.

People like Jesus from afar, but when they come face to face with Him, they realize they have a sin problem. At this point people are either persuaded and want to deal with their sin, or they want to pick up stones to throw at Jesus. Which group are you in? Are you willing to allow Jesus to come close and deal with your sin, or are you satisfied keeping Jesus at arm's length?

Jesus, forgive me of my sin and keep me from turning from You when You confront my sin.

We should allow Jesus to lead us to repentance, not rejection.

God's Unbreakable Word

"And the Scripture cannot be broken" (John 10:35)

God's Word is indestructible. It is also inerrant, infallible, and inspired. That means many things to many people, but most importantly, it means that the Bible is always right. There are no ifs, ands, or buts about it. The Bible is undeniably, unconditionally, emphatically true and trustworthy.

In the middle of a discussion with the religious leaders about His divinity and authority, Jesus inserted an assertion about the inerrancy of Scripture. He relied on the infallibility and inerrancy of Scripture to make a point to the Bible experts of His day by using one word from the book of Psalms. In so doing, Jesus affirmed that Scripture is the Word of God and that as the Word of God, it cannot be broken, not even one word of it. If Scripture falters at any point, it can be attacked at every point.

God's Word never can be wrong, ever, about anything. This is one of the most important nonnegotiable truths in Christianity. Practically that means we can have confidence that what we are reading in the Bible is God's Word to humankind. Without the authority and infallibility of Scripture, the Bible is useless, the church is powerless, we are helpless, and the world is hopeless. But because of its authority and infallibility, the Bible is life-giving, life-sustaining, life-guiding, and life-fulfilling.

God, I thank You that the Scriptures are Your inspired revelation and communication of who You are and Your plans and purposes for godly living.

Trusting in Jesus means trusting in the Bible.

The Sufferings of Sickness

"This sickness is not unto death, but for the glory of God, that the Son of God may be glorified through it." (John 11:4)

Sickness is a reality. Millions battle illnesses every day. And yes, even believers get sick and suffer from diseases. We know that sickness and death come from sin—not always personal sin, but always original sin (see Romans 5:12). We also know that God allows illness, but certainly no good can come from the sufferings of sickness, right? Surprisingly, the answer is that God can use the sufferings of sickness for our good and His glory.

God's purpose in allowing sickness is never our destruction. Rather, it's for our instruction. Even though God may not be the cause of our sickness, He can use our sickness. Sometimes it is when we walk through the sufferings of sickness that God speaks the loudest to us. The psalmist understood this when he wrote, "It was good for me to be afflicted so that I might learn your decrees" (Psalm 119:71 NIV). Sickness can help us to trust God more, understand the Scriptures better, and strengthen our faith. In other words, God can use sickness to make us healthier spiritually.

If you are suffering today, let your attention and affections shift away from the things of this world and move toward God. Look to see how your sickness might be "for the glory of God, that the Son of God may be glorified through it" (John 11:4).

God, I know that Your goal is my ultimate good, not always my immediate comfort. I know that You always want what is best for me in light of eternity. When I'm suffering, I will pray for healing, but I also will ask for You to speak to me in my sickness.

Jesus can use sickness for our good and His glory.

Where Was God?

"Lazarus is dead. And I am glad for your sakes that I was not there, that you may believe."
(John 11:14–15)

There's a problem with pain. It makes us question the love of God. For Mary and Martha, the death of Lazarus called the love of God into question. For four days they wrestled and suffered with their brother's death, and for four days they wondered, "Where was God? Why was Jesus late?" Which raises a question: Is it even possible for God to be late?

If you've ever been waiting for someone who has been running late, then you know what it feels like. You keep checking your watch and repeatedly go to the window to see whether they're approaching, all the while asking yourself, "Where are they? What are they doing? What is taking them so long?" The longer you wait, the more your questions turn to frustrations. Jesus wasn't late. God is never late. He is always on time, and Jesus made it to Mary and Martha perfectly on time, according to God's timetable, not theirs.

When devastating circumstances interrupt our lives, even the most faithful among us can wonder, "Where is God?" God is not surprised or offended by our questions, but we must realize that we ask from a limited viewpoint, while God, on the other hand, sees the totality of every situation. And in the case of Lazarus, God wanted to do more than just heal Lazarus; He wanted to raise him from the dead. God sees your circumstances, too, and God cares about you and what you're going through. Be assured that God *is* working, even when it may not seem like it at the moment.

Jesus, I know that Your timing is perfect and that You love me. Help me to remember that sometimes you want to do exceedingly more than I can imagine.

Jesus often wants to change us before He changes our circumstances.

Resurrection Life

"I am the resurrection and the life. He who believes in Me,
though he may die, he shall live." (John 11:25)

Death is not the end of your story, and it was not the end of the story for Mary and Martha, whose brother, Lazarus, had been dead and buried for four days. When Jesus arrived on the scene, He spoke with Martha and confidently told her that Lazarus would live again (see John 11: 23). Martha agreed there would be a future resurrection of the dead (see verse 24), but Jesus was not pointing to some future event, He was pointing to Himself when He said, "I am the resurrection and the life" (verse 25 NKJV).

Jesus identified Himself with resurrection because He is the source and power of resurrection life. Raising the dead is something reserved for God, and Jesus is the One who gives and sustains life (see Colossians 1:16–17). This is more than an essential theological concept, and it is more than dogmatic doctrine. Jesus gives life because Jesus is life. He is the Creator, source, and supplier of all life, and apart from Jesus there is no life.

As God, Jesus made this personal by saying "I am," because resurrection life is found in Him. Jesus is what Lazarus needed for life, He is what Martha needed for life, and He is what every person needs for life. Death was making it hard for Martha to see past her grief and realize that she was speaking to the essence of all life. Sometimes it takes an eye-opening moment for us to truly see God.

Jesus, thank you for being my resurrection and life. Bring Your resur-
rection life to my daily life, filling me with spiritual fullness that only
can come from You, the giver of abundant life.

> **Jesus did not merely claim to be the**
> **resurrection and the life, He proved it.**

What Do You Believe?

"Do you believe this?" (John 11:26)

What you believe means something. What you believe determines what you do, the direction your life goes, and where you spend eternity. As is often the case, what we truly believe is not fully revealed until we face a trial, tragedy, or significant adversity. And as Martha descended into the despair of one of life's darkest experiences, the death of a loved one, Jesus exposed where her belief needed strengthening.

Jesus made it perfectly clear that life is found in Him, both the fullness of life in the here and now and the fruition of life in the hereafter. He not only is the source and power of resurrection life, but also is the source, sustainer, and supplier of all physical and spiritual life. The correlative question is a personal one: Do you believe this?

A solid, Jesus-centered belief will lead to a solid, Jesus-centered life. The depth of our belief in Jesus as the resurrection and the life, in all things and for all things, will determine the strength of our spiritual walk, especially in the hardest moments of life. Our belief is never perfect, and there are times when Jesus needs to expose belief's weaknesses so it might be strengthened. But belief centered on Jesus will find the strength, stability, and support to experience the fullness of life that Jesus promises. Jesus brings resurrection life wherever He goes. Are you allowing Him into every aspect of your life?

Jesus, nothing happens by accident. You are in control. Allow me to see Your hand in the day to day as well as in the incredible. Strengthen my belief when I do not understand your will, because You bring life and light wherever You go.

Belief in Jesus brings fullness and fulfillment to life.

The Day God Cried

Jesus wept. (John 11:35)

Death always brings out deep emotional reactions. Lazarus was dead, and his sister Mary fell at Jesus's feet and wept bitterly. So what did Jesus do? Did He say, "Sister, arise. Don't despair, because your brother is about to come forth from the grave"? No. He was deeply moved in His spirit, and because of the great distress and pain surrounding the sufferings of loss associated with death, Jesus wept. If a picture is worth a thousand words, then the image of God crying is an endless book.

Jesus speaks volumes without saying a word. His weeping says that God weeps with those who weep. His weeping says that God will come alongside you in your time of grief and sorrow. His weeping says this was not the world as He wanted it to be. Death was never supposed to be part of the plan. But sin changed all that. Sin tainted the world. So Jesus wept. His weeping was not disbelief, because He knew in a moment that He would raise Lazarus from the dead. And falling to your knees in tears is not a sign that your faith is falling apart. Deep sorrow is merely a sign of a deep love and deep longing for the day when the consequences of sin are no longer experienced. In that moment, Jesus was living between the pain of loss and the promise of resurrection. Even though we live between the pain and the promise, God enters our grief with us.

Lord, we call upon You in our time of grief and sorrow so that You will give us the strength to bear our sorrows and feel the warmth of Your love and compassion.

Jesus wept so we would know He enters our grief with us.

His Presence in Pain

Jesus wept. (John 11:35)

Sometimes people need a sympathetic ear more than they need a sermon. Sometimes a person in pain needs compassion more than counsel. We are told to "rejoice with those who rejoice, and weep with those who weep" (Romans 12:15), and that is exactly what Jesus demonstrated during the devastation that surrounded the death of Lazarus. Jesus could have spoken to the irrationality of weeping when Lazarus was minutes away from being raised, but He didn't. He was deeply moved to share in the sorrow and grief of death that was profoundly felt in that moment.

Jesus's weeping over the death of Lazarus shows us that even with the certainty of future resurrection, the loss of life still brings pain. And in the deep pain we must seek to understand it in the context of our greater hope. But the pain of death still is pain, and grief still is piercing. Therefore, when someone you know is going through a painful situation, your presence often speaks louder than any words you can offer. There is a time and place for encouraging words, but *when* and *what* to say to someone suffering the anguish of heartache must be Spirit formed and sympathetically presented for the recipient to be soothed from the stinging pain of their suffering.

The example of Jesus weeping alongside the suffering in their time of need should encourage us to be willing to enter into the sorrows of others, because one of the most comforting things we can do for someone is to simply be present with them in their pain.

Jesus, help me to know when to speak to someone in pain and when to weep with them.

Jesus understands our grief and is present with us in our pain.

The Stone of Unbelief

"Take away the stone." *(John 11:39)*

Trusting God takes faith. If you have ever looked at a situation and thought, "God can't do anything here. This situation is dead," then you have come face to face with the stone of unbelief. Obstacles are opportunities for God to work, and until we fully grasp that God can do the impossible, we always will be stuck in a spiritual rut, spinning our wheels, and going nowhere.

Lazarus had been dead for four days, and Jesus was standing in front of his tomb when He said, "Take away the stone." But Martha objected, and with her down-to-earth thinking, she reminded Jesus that moving the stone made no sense and was even a bit ridiculous. Unbelief thinks God doesn't care or isn't capable of changing our dead situation. Unbelief keeps us looking down for human solutions to solve our problems, but faith looks up for God's solution and invites Him to do the extraordinary.

As long as there is a stone of unbelief in the way, you won't see all that God can do in and through your difficult situation. What if Peter never stepped out of the boat when Jesus said, "Come" (Matthew 14:29)? What if the disciples never threw their fishing net on the other side of the boat when Jesus said, "Cast" (John 21:6)? What if the blind man never went to the pool to wash the mud from his eyes when Jesus said, "Go" (John 9:7)? The answer is they would have missed a miracle. Sometimes the stone of unbelief can keep us from seeing the miracles of God.

Jesus, I know miracle power comes from You, but sometimes my lack of faith keeps me from experiencing Your power in my life. Help me in my times of unbelief.

Jesus invites us to take steps of faith so we can witness His power.

The Glory of God

"Did I not say to you that if you would believe you would see the glory of God?" (John 11:40)

What is the glory of God? Trying to put into words what the glory of God includes is like trying to empty the ocean one bucketful at a time. What makes it even more difficult is that the glory of God isn't a thing, and it isn't part of God; it is all of God. At its core, the glory of God is a manifestation of the presence of God, because God's glory is contained in His character. In other words, God is glorious, and everything He does is glorious.

When God shows up, His glory shows up, because His glory is contained in His nature. Whatever God does is a revelation of His glory, because it is a revelation of Himself. We experience the glory of God when we experience the presence of God and when we grow in the knowledge of God. When "the heavens declare the glory of God" (Psalm 19:1), they do so because they highlight aspects of God's nature and character.

The miracles that Jesus performed, like raising Lazarus from the dead, were designed for us to see the glory of God, believe in God, worship God, and glorify Him in our lives. Everything that God is and everything that God does not only reveals His glory, but it only scratches the surface of our ability to comprehend or describe the vastness of His glory. Everything Jesus did was to bring God glory, and our lives should seek to do the same.

God, help me to see Your glory, which is evident everywhere. Help me to cultivate the knowledge of Your glory revealed in Your Word, and help me to share Your glory with the world.

Jesus's greatest desire was to bring God maximum glory.

Does God Hear Me When I Pray?

"And I know that You always hear Me." (John 11:42)

Have you ever felt as though your prayers were going straight to voice mail? *"Hello, this is God. Thanks for calling. I can't take your prayer right now, but if you leave a message, I'll be sure to get back you as soon possible."* I know God is busy holding the universe together and answering the millions of other prayers flooding heaven daily, but how can you be assured your prayers are getting through?

Let's be clear. God hears everything. That means God hears every prayer expressed by every person, every time, everywhere. Nothing slips past God, and nothing goes to some heavenly voice mail. So, the question is not so much whether God hears you when you pray, because He does. The question is whether God is listening with the intention of answering when we pray.

God wants to hear from us. That is clear in the Bible. Prayer is an essential aspect of our relationship with God, but there are things that can hinder our prayers. If we are intentionally turning away from God, God will turn a deaf ear to our prayers (see Proverbs 28:9). If we are praying out of selfishness, God will not pay attention to our misguided requests (James 4:3). If we are praying and doubting what God says, we should not expect to get what we are asking for (see James 1:5–8). However, if we ask according to God's will (see 1 John 5:14), if we ask in faith (see Mark 11:24), and if we abide in His Word (see John 15:7), then we can rest assured that God hears us and will answer our prayers.

Father, continue to refine my prayers so that I am always praying according to Your will.

> **Jesus had full confidence that His prayer was heard by God, because it was fully in the will of God.**

When God Speaks

"Lazarus, come forth!" (John 11:43)

When God speaks, things happen. With a word, the cosmos was created, with a word, light broke the darkness, and with a word, heaven and all its hosts were formed (see Hebrews 11:3; Genesis 1:1, 3; 2:1). What God speaks is accomplished fully, completely, and exactly as He said.

When Jesus speaks, things happen. With a word, those with leprosy experienced healing (see Luke 5:13; 17:14), with a word, the blind found sight (see Luke 18:42), with a word, demons were vanquished (see Matthew 8:16), with a word, a fig tree met destruction (see Mark 11:20–21), and with a word, Lazarus rose from the dead (see John 11:43–44). What Jesus speaks is accomplished fully, completely, and exactly as He said.

God is a speaking God, and He desires to speak to us every day. But the knowledge of God's Word is not the same as personally experiencing His words and allowing them to penetrate our lives. God has given us the opportunity to listen to Him and to learn to hear His voice. As we allow Jesus to speak into our lives, things happen. With a word God can bring light to a dark situation, with a word He can remove spiritual blindness, and with a word He can raise us up to live new lives. Sometimes God allows us to be placed in an impossible situation so that He can speak into it, reminding us of His power and authority while also demonstrating His power to others.

Jesus, I thank You that You desire to speak to me every day. As I seek to hear You today, help me to confirm Your voice through Your Word and by Your Spirit, and apply it to my life personally.

When Jesus speaks into our lives, good things happen.

Loosing the Ties That Bind

"Loose him, and let him go." (John 11:44)

Some people assume that being born again is all that is needed to live a blessed and abundant life. But being made alive spiritually doesn't mean that we are free from past issues. We can be saved but still bound by old habits. We can be spared from death but still need help living.

When Jesus called Lazarus to come out of the grave, he still was bound by his burial clothes. Jesus could have called Lazarus out from the tomb free and clear of any of the remnants of it, but He didn't. Jesus could have unraveled the ties that bound Lazarus in the tomb, but He didn't. Lazarus was a walking miracle, but God was not finished with him yet, and God used others to help Lazarus walk in freedom.

Jesus may call you out from the sepulchre of sin but leave you bound in graveclothes. Sometimes God saves us and immediately delivers us from old habits or bad practices, but there may be some remnants of the grave that we need help to overcome. God can and often recruits the help of others to fully loose us from the ties that bind. Jesus enlisted others to "loose [Lazarus], and let him go."

Sin has lasting effects, and just because we are saved doesn't mean that we can live the Christian life alone. We need the help of community to unravel the restraints of our bad attitudes, selfishness, addictions, temper tantrums, negative words, and complaining mindsets.

God, use me to help others walk in freedom from those ties that bind them, and keep me vulnerable enough to allow others to loosen the graveclothes that hinder my freedom.

Jesus uses others to help us walk in freedom.

A Response to Tragedy

*"Do you suppose that these Galileans were worse sinners than
all other Galileans, because they suffered such things? I tell
you, no; but unless you repent you will all likewise perish."*
(Luke 13:1–5 ESV)

Bad things happen to bad people, bad things happen to good people,
and bad things happen to God-loving people. Every tragedy is not a
sign of God's judgment or punishment. When a catastrophe happens
in our world, it is inevitable that people ask, "Where was God?" We
always seem to question how a good God could allow bad things to
happen.

This question came to Jesus in light of a horrific act of brutality committed during His life. Apparently Pontius Pilate ordered
Galilean worshipers to be massacred, and this senseless bloodthirst-
iness made some people jump to the conclusion that suffering was
related to sinfulness, a belief that goes back at least to the days of Job
(see Job 4:7–8) and still remains today. Yes, it is true that suffering has
its origins in sin, but Jesus makes it clear that we cannot immediately
jump to the condemning conclusion that misfortune or disaster is
related to personal sinfulness. From Jesus's point of view, the people
were asking the wrong question. Instead of wondering why a good
God allowed a tragedy, we should be wondering why a good God
bothers to save sinners. Ultimately tragedy should point us to our
need for God and cause us to turn from sin, because only then can we
avoid the worst tragedy of all: dying apart from God.

*Lord, may tragedies remind me of the urgent need to share the gospel
with those around me. Grant me the courage and character to do so
boldly and compassionately.*

> **Regardless of the cause of a tragedy, Jesus
> wants us to see the urgent need to trust
> in Him.**

The Fruitless Fig Tree

"If it bears fruit next year, fine. If not, then can cut it down."
(Luke 13:9 NIV)

One day God will say enough is enough. Until that day, God is patiently waiting for people to turn to Him and live fruitful lives. Just because God patiently gives people time to do the right thing and live in right relationship with Him, it doesn't mean that He won't eventually deal with sin and their lack of spiritual productivity.

Jesus gives us this parable of the fruitless fig tree for two reasons. The first reason is the good news: God is merciful and forgiving, and He patiently waits for people to turn from sin and to live spiritually fruitful lives. The second reason is the bad news: God's patience has its limits, and God's mercy will one day change to judgment. It is a warning to everyone, because no one wants to be on the receiving end of God's judgment.

There is more good news to be found in this parable, and it is this: God does everything possible to encourage fruitfulness. He will dig around the tree and will fertilize it (see Luke 13:8), because He wants it to grow and be productive. In the same way, God wants us to grow spiritually deep roots so that our lives will be as fruitful as possible. Repentance is evidence of genuine faith in Jesus, and it is the first step required from all who profess faith in His name and seek to live fruitful lives.

God, examine my life and show me the areas I need to dig up and where I need to fertilize so that I can grow deeper, be more productive, and bear more spiritual fruit.

Jesus's patience is long-lasting, but it isn't limitless.

Jesus and Women

"A woman was there who had been crippled by a spirit for eighteen years. . . . When Jesus saw her, he called her forward and said to her, **"Woman, you are set free from your infirmity."** *(Luke 13:11–13 NIV)*

Women matter to Jesus. In a culture and time when women were held in low regard and seen as little more than property, Jesus often shocked His onlookers as He treated women with dignity and respect. Women ate separately, were taught separately, and worshiped separately, but Jesus routinely broke with tradition as He publicly associated with women, spoke with them, welcomed them as followers, and offered forgiveness and healing to women.

As Jesus was teaching in a synagogue on the Sabbath, a woman whose body was severely bent and twisted caught His eye. She had suffered for eighteen long years with this devastating condition. As one who was bent over and unable to lift herself up, she found herself in the company of the One who loves to lift people up. Jesus reached out His hand, touched her (Jewish men did not customarily touch women whom they weren't related to), and declared her free from her infirmity.

Jesus was considerate and caring, and He broke through the oppressive and ugly cultural norms to rescue women from unfair treatment and crippling situations. Each woman's life that intersected with Jesus tells us a different story, but they all reveal the power, love, and compassion that God equally has for all His creation.

Jesus, Your love and compassion extends equally to all people. Help me to love all people as You did.

Jesus challenges us to look beyond culture and lovingly relate to people as He did.

The Right Time to Do Good

"You hypocrites! Does not each of you on the Sabbath untie his ox or his donkey from the manger and lead it away to water it? And ought not this woman, being a daughter of Abraham, whom Satan bound for eighteen years, be loosed from this bond on the Sabbath day?" (Luke 13:14–16 ESV)

Jesus never sinned. Therefore, He never broke the Sabbath, even when He healed on the Sabbath. God gave the law to show His people how to love Him and how to love others (see Exodus 20:1–17). Keeping the Sabbath was intended to refresh you physically from the labors of work and renew your spirit by regularly reminding you that you are made in God's image, you are filled with God's breath, and you inhabit God's world (see Exodus 20:8–11). You are chosen by God, rescued by God, and loved by God, so naturally the Sabbath is important to God. Perhaps that's why it is the longest commandment in the entire Decalogue. Clearly, God is trying to get our attention.

Keeping the law was a sign of devotion to God, but where the Pharisees went wrong was elevating the Sabbath law above the law of love. Jesus exposed their hypocrisy by asking them what they would do if one of their sheep fell into a ditch on the Sabbath. Surely they would "work" to pull it out. Jesus reminds them that a person is much more valuable than a sheep, and therefore He was only doing for a person (one of *His* sheep) what they would do for one of their animals. In other words, it is always the right time to do good for someone.

Father, may I never lose sight of the law of love and doing good for those in need.

Jesus established that it is good to do good, even on the Sabbath.

Spiritual Growth

"To what shall I liken the kingdom of God? It is like leaven, which a woman took and hid in three measures of meal till it was all leavened." (Luke 13:20–21)

The kingdom of God is not like an eruption; it's like fermentation. Yeast is essential when baking bread. Yeast is a tiny living organism that, as it ferments, causes dough to expand. The nature of yeast is to grow and change whatever it comes in contact with. So how is leaven, or yeast, like the kingdom of God?

First, the kingdom of God is the realm where God reigns supreme, and Jesus Christ is King. Yeast is small in size, but after it is mixed into dough, it will spread throughout and cause expansion. In the same way, the kingdom of God started with Jesus, further expanded to His disciples, and has now permeated the world. The kingdom of God changes what it comes in contact with. Also, yeast works from the inside out. Likewise, God first changes the heart of a person, which reveals itself outwardly over time.

Can God use your life to transform the world? Most definitely, but it may not look like some cataclysmic event. Instead, He will use you like yeast, putting you in the middle of the world in which you live. And over time, He will use you to change whatever you come in contact with.

Holy Spirit, I pray that You would permeate every part of my life and change me from the inside out. Use me in the situations around me to cause Your kingdom to shine through. In Jesus's name, amen.

As Jesus reigns in us, He transforms us from the inside out.

The Road Less Traveled

"Strive to enter through the narrow door." (Luke 13:24 ESV)

The Christian life is both challenging and outstanding. Part of what makes Christianity so challenging is that it is countercultural. So if you want to be culturally cool and Christian, you may have a hard time doing both. There is a wide road that is less challenging, more comfortable, easy to navigate, and goes the way of the culture. But it is also a road that leads to ruin (see Matthew 7:13).

Ever since Jesus proclaimed the right way to God, people have tried to widen the entrance gate or even remove the gate altogether. Wide-gate believism leads to wide-gate living, which leads to wide-gate ruin. Wide-gate believism says make your own rules, believe your own truth, Jesus isn't the only way, the Cross is irrelevant, sin is archaic, and truth is subjective. Wide-gate believism never will give you healing, forgiveness, salvation, freedom, and peace. All of those things are only available to us through the narrow gate of Jesus Christ.

Christianity cannot bend to culture. Cultural norms cannot dictate what Christians believe. Yes, the way of Jesus can be difficult at times, and it is uncompromising in its stance that biblical truth should not be tampered with and Jesus is the only way. All are welcome, and God receives all who come to Him, but we must turn from our sin and place our faith in Jesus to enter by way of the narrow gate.

God, You are the way to everlasting life. Direct me in my thoughts and actions so that I will stay on the narrow path and not wander.

Jesus is not one of many ways to God; He is the only way.

Outside Looking In

*"Once the owner of the house gets up and closes the door, you
will stand outside knocking and pleading, 'Sir, open the door
for us.' "But he will answer, 'I don't know you.' "*
(Luke 13:25 NIV)

How tragic it would be to think you are going to heaven, only to
discover that you aren't allowed in. Jesus repeatedly encouraged people to be aware of where they really stand in their relationship with
God. Jesus doesn't want anyone to have any misconceptions about
their salvation. Just because someone goes to church doesn't mean
there is a relationship with God. Just because someone does good for
others doesn't mean there is a relationship with God. And just because
someone had an emotional spiritual experience doesn't mean there is
a relationship with God.

Knowing truth is not the same as living by the truth. It is important to know and understand what the Bible teaches, but it is more
important to live your life in accordance with what the Bible teaches.
A person's faith is not validated by their church attendance or even by
their good deeds. Genuine faith shows itself through Christlike character. Over time, your attitudes and actions will be more reflective of
the nature and character of Jesus. This does not mean you'll never fall
short or make mistakes. But overall, your life will be characterized by
progressive obedience.

No one wants to hear "I don't know you" from God, so to make
sure that God knows us and welcomes us, we need to have an inward
conversion that results in outward obedience.

*Father God, my love for You is shown in my obedience to Your Word.
As I walk in obedience, You will give me peace and assurance that I
am known by You.*

> **Knowing Jesus and being known by Him will
> show itself through obedience.**

Weeping

"In that place there will be weeping and gnashing of teeth."
(Luke 13:28 ESV)

There is no more frightening biblical concept than that of hell. The Bible describes hell as a place of outer darkness, an unquenchable fire, a place of weeping and gnashing of teeth, a place of eternal separation from the blessings of God, a prison, and a place of torment where the worm doesn't die (see Revelation 9:2; Mark 9:48; Luke 13:28). Most of the teachings about hell come to us from Jesus, and despite the various imagery, one thing is certain: hell will be worse than we can imagine.

Understanding that hell is a real place where the wrath of God will be experienced is what makes the grace of God so amazing and wonderful (see Revelation 14:10). God does not want to send anyone to hell (see 2 Peter 3:9). The reality is that hell is reserved for people who have chosen to reject God and His eternal plan and purpose for their lives. When a person chooses to reject the gospel and live separately from God here on Earth, they will live eternally separated from God's blessings. They won't live eternally separated from God, because God's presence is everywhere, even in hell (see Psalm 139:8). But in hell, people will be continually experiencing the judgment of God. The truth about hell should give us a greater appreciation for heaven.

Father, hell makes me grateful for Your grace. May I never lose sight of what I have been saved from, but may I also never speak about hell to anyone without sharing Your love.

> **Jesus didn't avoid the topic of hell, and neither should we. But we should always keep heaven in mind when we're talking about hell.**

Right Side Up

"And indeed there are last who will be first, and there are first who will be last." (Luke 13:30)

Once sin entered the world, people's priorities were turned upside down, but God promises to turn things right side up in His kingdom. After the Fall, selfishness surpassed spirituality, self-seeking surpassed servanthood, and materialism surpassed morality. We have become more focused on our own pursuits than caring for the welfare of others. Ever since sin polluted people's passions, Jesus has been correcting that corruption and turning our understanding right side up.

One needed correction is the idea that a person gets into heaven because of who they are or what they have done. God's gift of eternal life is given equally to all who believe. Success doesn't give you more salvation, and lack of status doesn't give you less standing with God. Prestige plays no part in your salvation. Salvation is possible for all types of people, with no distinction made based on their abilities, works, or social class. Whether someone comes to God as a child or at the end of their life, whether someone is in the spiritual spotlight or not at all, everyone who believes will equally receive the same crown of life.

Position and prestige lead to pride, and pride makes us forget that even though we are to be concerned about our own interests, we also are to be concerned about others (see Philippians 2:4–5). If our spiritual priorities get turned upside down, then God will work to turn them right side up.

God, I am humbled by Your grace, and I am thankful for the equality of grace. Help me to live with right-side-up priorities.

Jesus preached a right-side-up kingdom to help keep our priorities from being upside down.

God Is for Us

"Jerusalem, Jerusalem, the one who kills the prophets and
stones those who are sent to her!" (Luke 13:34)

God loves you, no matter what. He is on your side, and He wants the very best for you, even when you turn your back on Him. God wants you to thrive in every area of your life—physically, mentally, emotionally, financially, and in all your personal relationships. God has spoken to us so that we would benefit from His wisdom and instruction, because God always has our best interests at heart.

Jesus had a deep love for God's people and wanted nothing more than to protect, provide, and guide them. Even though the people had rejected Jesus, He still wanted to rescue them, make them part of His kingdom community, help them grow spiritually, communicate God's love for them, and help them experience the blessings of a relationship with Him. The problem was that Jesus was willing, but the people were not. Jesus offered the safety and protection of shelter under His wings, but the Jews rejected the invitation just as they had done with so many of the messengers sent to them throughout their history.

All too often, we fail to respond to God's love. All too often, we turn God's call to repentance into judgmental finger-pointing. All too often, we allow amusements to monopolize our attention. And all too often, we turn our affections away from the One who loves us the most and has our best interests at heart.

God, help me to be receptive to Your call and responsive to your commands, because I know that what You say and do is done out of Your great love for me.

Jesus loves us too much to leave us alone.

The Strength of Humility

"For whoever exalts himself will be humbled, and he who humbles himself will be exalted." (Luke 14:11)

In today's boastful, social media-saturated age, humility is in short supply. With the daily bombardment of Photoshopped images, big-headed selfies, and self-aggrandizing ravings, it has become harder and harder to find those who are authentically humble. One thing we can be sure of is that Jesus would not be posting a travel selfie from heaven, He wouldn't be tweeting that He was the smartest in the universe, and He wouldn't be bragging about how He turned water into wine.

So how can we live out humility when the temptation to self-promote is so strong? Even if your social media proclivities are not prone to self-puffery, walking humbly in today's society is still challenging. In order for humility to stand a chance in your life, you have to realize that humility is a choice. Being a Christian is all about choosing to follow Christ, and the example of Jesus is one of walking humbly with God. The goal of humility is not that we'd think poorly of ourselves or have low self-esteem. Rather, it is thinking highly of God and rightly relating ourselves to God. The next time you are tempted to self-promote, remember that you're not the center of the universe. God is. And we are completely dependent on Him for our lives and our salvation. Everything is given by God, and nothing is our own, so the One we should be bragging about is Him, not ourselves.

God, I know humility is not something that just happens, but it is something I must chose and must purpose to practice. Work in me as I seek to walk humbly with You.

> **Jesus rejects the prideful and blesses genuine humility.**

Selfless Giving

"When you give a feast, invite the poor, the crippled, the lame, the blind, and you will be blessed, because they cannot repay you." (Luke 14:13–14 ESV)

Living for self is exhausting. It also can lead to a "bah humbug" outlook on life that will steal your joy, close your heart, and make you fearful of losing what you have accumulated. Conversely, selflessly giving (giving where you have no desire or expectation of repayment) liberates your heart, deepens relationships, and reflects the heart of God. But let's not assume that generosity is only for the rich, because it isn't. Generosity is not an issue of wealth; it is an issue of willingness.

Stingy stewards do not honor God. God is looking for His people to demonstrate radical hospitality and extravagant generosity, regardless of their socioeconomic standing. Jesus challenges us to aid, assist, and uphold those who cannot repay us for our care, consideration, and kindness. Doing so leaves the rewards of our actions in the hands of God. The paradox is that in many cases, those who give a bundle to God get a bushel in return. This is not a prosperity message that proclaims, "Give, and God will make you rich." Instead, it is an observation that when you give to God, He gives back to you, and to those who steward well, He makes them stewards of more (see Matthew 25:20–21).

Then, of course, there is the science behind being a good giver. Research shows that giving makes you happier, healthier, socially more connected, and more grateful, and it cultivates giving in others. But generosity doesn't happen without intentional effort.

Father, give me opportunities to bless others from whom I expect nothing in return.

Loving like Jesus always leads you to be more generous.

A Seat at the Table

"A man once gave a great banquet and invited many. And at the time for the banquet he sent his servant to say to those who had been invited, 'Come, for everything is now ready.' But they all alike began to make excuses." (Luke 14:16 ESV)

Running on today's fast-paced treadmill of life, it's easy to feel overlooked, forgotten, or uninvited. If you are like most people, you long to be recognized, hunger to be included, and want to feel part of something greater than yourself. God notices you, you are important to God, you are loved by God, and you are invited to sit at God's table.

The great banquet of Luke 14:16 signifies the kingdom of heaven, and the point Jesus was making is that the symbolic banquet is ready, and He had come to Israel to invite them to have a personal relationship with God. Sadly, many were preoccupied with their own religiosity and legalistic expectations of God and made excuses as to why they were unable or unwilling to accept God's invitation. As a result, God has extended grace to those who were not part of the initial invitation. The inclusion is a fulfillment of prophecy found in Hosea 2:23: "I will say to those called 'Not my people,' 'You are my people'; and they will say, 'You are my God' " (NIV). God has given you and me a personal invitation to have a seat at His table. Will you accept?

God, I know Your banquet is free. It is an invitation by grace, but my acceptance carries responsibility. Help me not to make excuses with Your invitation or with the responsibilities of discipleship.

Jesus wants a relationship with us more than we want a relationship with Him.

Really, Jesus?

"If anyone comes to Me and does not hate his father and mother, wife and children, brothers and sisters, yes, and his own life also, he cannot be My disciple." (Luke 14:26)

Let's be honest. Jesus had some uncomfortable sayings, but one thing we must not do is domesticize the words of Jesus just because they are difficult or uncomfortable. It is clear that Jesus always was more interested in speaking truth than being popular or trendy for the sake of amassing larger crowds (something that pastors should always contemplate). So, does Jesus really want us to hate our families?

Jesus is not demanding that you literally hate your family, but He is using hyperbole to illustrate the steep cost of following Him. Jesus is a good teacher, actually the best that ever lived. As such He challenges the status quo and finds ways to get people to think. Jesus was always clear, concise, and often radical and revolutionary with His teachings. His point here is that if you want to be a Christian, then God must be number one in all circumstances and at all times. We must be willing to give up everything for Jesus. If a person is ever faced with the painful choice of loyalty to family or loyalty to Jesus, the choice always must be Jesus.

By utilizing this extreme language, Jesus is not contradicting the biblical truths concerning love. Rather, He is prioritizing the realities of biblical love. Jesus may call us to leave our fathers and mothers, but He never will call us to stop loving them or our families. But our love for Him must be greater than all other love.

God, I know that the path to true joy is by keeping You first.

Jesus demands that He must come before all other relationships.

The Cost of Love

*"Whoever does not bear his own cross and come after me
cannot be My disciple." (Luke 14:27)*

Are you a serious follower of Jesus, or would you classify yourself as
more of a casual Christian? The harsh reality is there is no Christianity
without the Cross, and there is no Christian who doesn't have their
own cross to bear. Part of God's will for you and me involves a cross.

Carrying your cross involves dying to self and living for God.
This is not some transcendent mysticism, only attainable by the most
puritanically devoted. Nor is it suffering common difficulties, trials,
or diseases. The cross was God's instrument of redemption and a proof
of His love for the world (see John 3:16). Jesus didn't choose the way
of the cross for His own benefit or to gain a deeper relationship with
God. He carried His cross because of His love for others. When we
take up our cross, we take up Christ's love for people. If we encounter
someone without enough food or clothing, to deny ourselves and take
up our cross demands giving up personal time and resources to show
the love of God to someone. Simply talking about faith without visible acts of self-surrender is not authentic discipleship.

Carrying your cross means making crosscentric decisions in a
cross-rejecting culture. It means doing what God wants you to do,
which may not always be what you want to do. It means submitting
your schedule to God's agenda. On the surface it may sound severe,
but as we surrender to God, there is freedom in His sovereignty. As we
die to self, we find life in God, and as we let go of earthly pursuits, we
gain heavenly purpose and perspective.

*God, give me the strength to do more than speak of discipleship but
to actually live out your command to carry my cross through acts of
self-surrender.*

**Jesus carried His cross for the benefit of
others.**

The Cost of Discipleship

"For which of you, desiring to build a tower, does not first sit down and count the cost?" (Luke 14:28 ESV)

The Christian path is littered with abandoned Bibles, empty pews, and the discarded crosses of those who failed to count the cost of discipleship. Making the decision to follow Jesus should not be an impulse decision like buying chocolate at the checkout counter. If you decide to follow Jesus, then you should first count the cost of what it means to be a believer.

Salvation is free, but being a disciple is costly. Counting the cost of discipleship means assessing what we are willing to give up to gain a life with Christ. Counting the cost of discipleship is more than committing to give up this habit or that pastime, although it might include that. It means being ready and willing to give our entire lives to the pursuit of God and the fulfillment of His will. Counting the cost of discipleship means we're ready to love God more than our own lives, and we are willing to love other people as much as we love ourselves. Counting the cost of discipleship means we're willing to hold on to our possessions with a loose grip and not a chokehold.

Although this does not fully encompass the cost of discipleship, it does begin by being ready to commit who we are and what we have to Him. Discipleship is a lifetime of following Jesus and His example, living to please God and not people, and yielding to the leading of God's Holy Spirit.

God, after I have counted the cost of belief, let me live without counting the cost of loving.

Following Jesus is worth the cost of discipleship.

AUGUST

Heaven Throws a Party

"I say to you, there is joy in the presence of the angels of God over one sinner who repents." (Luke 15:10)

There is considerable speculation as to what heaven is like, and the Bible certainly incites our heavenly imaginations with descriptions of multi-winged angelic beings, streets of gold, and a crystal-clear river of life flowing from the throne room of God (see Ezekiel 1:6; Revelation 21:21; Revelation 22:1–2). But what is really going on up there? One thing we know for sure is that heaven is immensely interested in what is going on down here.

Jesus pulled back the spiritual curtain to reveal that heaven throws a party when one person turns from sin and toward God. To repent is more than being sorry for sin, although it includes that. To repent means to undergo a complete change of mind and heart, to turn away from sin's selfishness, and to turn to freedom and forgiveness in Christ. It is true that God has a universe to run, galaxies to uphold, and governments to oversee, and there are many things that bring Him joy. But when just one person joins the family of God, it is so special that all of heaven stops to celebrate. Angels who stand in the glorious, breathtaking presence of God, who see endless, wondrous, heavenly sights, stop, take note, and celebrate when one person becomes a new creation in Christ. God never loses sight of individuals in this enormous world. Every single person matters to God, and they should matter to us. Look for ways to point people to God. After all, heaven is waiting to celebrate.

God, as I have received the blessing of salvation, help me to point others to you in word and deed.

Heaven celebrates when a person turns from sin and self and accepts Jesus as Savior.

The Prodigal Son: Coming to Your Senses

"When he came to his senses, he said . . . 'I will set out and go back to my father and say to him: Father, I have sinned.' "
Luke (15:17–18)

Sin numbs our mind, making it hard but not impossible to come to our senses. We know that sin is wrong, and we want to stop, but we can feel powerless to end the destructive cycle. "*God, how did I get here?*" "*I'll never do it again.*" "*God, can You forgive me?*" Even the apostle Paul cried out, "I do not understand my own actions. For I do not do what I want, but I do the very thing I hate" (Romans 7:15 ESV). For the alcoholic who says, "No more," for the porn addict who says, "That was the last time," and for the angry mom who says, "I won't lose my temper again," there is a way out and a way back to God the Father.

Jesus told of a man who had a reckless son. The son took his inheritance and went out and lived irresponsibly and uninhibited. But eventually the money was gone and so were his freeloading friends. Broke and in desperate need of food, he was forced into shoveling slop. One day the slop-soaked prodigal came to his senses and repented. For this son, his repentance began with a recognition that his bad choices led to his bad situation. He grieved over his mistakes and acknowledged his wrongdoing. However, the son didn't have his act completely together before returning home. He simply came to his senses, walked away from his destructive behavior, and trusted in his father's mercy. If you are sin soaked and ready to come to your senses, then confess your sin, return to God, and allow His mercies to cleanse you and bring restoration in your life.

Father, thank you that You love me unconditionally. Thank you for seeking me out when I go astray.

Jesus waits for us to come to our senses, turn from our sin, and go to Him.

The Prodigal Son: The Father

"And he arose and came to his father. But while he was still a long way off, his father saw him and felt compassion, and ran and embraced him and kissed him." Luke (15:20 ESV)

God hates sin, but He loves sinners. As much as God hates sin because of its destructive effects on us and others, what God hates even more about sin is that it comes between us and Him, hindering the relationship. People often think they have to negotiate for God's love or work hard to earn it, but as the prodigal son demonstrates, God is outrageously generous with His love and lavishly compassionate.

When the wayward son returned home, we might have expected the father to be waiting on the front porch with arms crossed, foot tapping, impatiently listening to his son's speech with an "I told you so" loaded and ready to be fired off. But our God is not an "I told you so" sort of God. No matter what you've done, God loves you. You can always turn to Him, and He will accept you with open arms. That doesn't mean there may not be consequences still to be dealt with because of your sin, but Jesus died on the cross for all of our sins, not some sins. So, no matter what you've done, no matter how big of a mess your life might be, God is waiting for you to come to Him. If you turn your heart toward God, you will discover a continual fountain of grace and love that never runs dry. God is watching and waiting to welcome you into His grace-filled arms, no matter how great the sin, no matter how long the separation. He is ready for restoration and relationship with you. If you need restoration with God, this prayer may help.

Father, forgive me, for I have sinned against You. You are compassionate and gracious, abounding in love. Please refresh me with Your grace and restore my relationship with You.

Jesus accepts us as we are so He can make us all that we can be.

The Prodigal Son: The Older Brother

"All these years I've been slaving for you and never disobeyed your orders. Yet you never gave me even a young goat so I could celebrate with my friends." Luke (15:29 NIV)

It seems as though the prodigals get all the attention. What about the ones who work hard, do what they are told, live responsibly, and obey the law—the ones who don't party all night, get drunk, and get into trouble? Is their responsibility rewarded? That was the attitude of the older brother in Jesus's story of the prodigal son.

In this story the older brother represented the religious leaders who considered themselves righteous and respectable. They faithfully attended synagogue and prided themselves on keeping the law. Outwardly they were living blameless lives, but inwardly they were loveless legalists, appalled that Jesus would be welcoming of sinners. Their self-righteousness and lack of love made them resentful of God's mercy and grace. They felt entitled to God's mercy and grace because of how they had lived.

Do you find yourself resenting God for blessing someone other than you? As long as we act like the older brother and stay angry at the Father's grace, as long as we hold on to a holier-than-thou attitude, we will remain outside of the place where there is joy and blessing. We always should rejoice when God showers people with His grace and mercy, because we all need it.

Father, forgive me for feeling slighted when You shower Your love on someone else. Keep me from having the older brother's attitudes shown in this parable.

> **Jesus loves us because of who He is, not because of what we do (good or bad).**

Managing God's Money

"The master commended the dishonest manager because he had acted shrewdly."
Luke (16:8 NIV)

God cares more about your money than you might think. Jesus had a lot to say about money. In fact, Jesus spoke more about money than about heaven and hell combined. The Bible covers such topics as earning and spending, saving and giving, and investing and even wasting our money.

In the parable of the shrewd manager, Jesus doesn't praise the manager's dishonesty, but He does acknowledge his shrewdness. What is shrewdness? To be shrewd means that you're smart, strategic, and resourceful. Did you know God wants you to be biblically shrewd with your money? Well, He does, because how we handle our money reveals the condition of our hearts. It is important to get a grip on your money without letting your money get a grip on you.

How do you make sure you are properly handling your money? To begin with, don't love your money. You've got to decide whether God is going to be number one in your life or whether money will be, because there can only be one number one. Next, don't trust your money. Money can be gone in a flash (see Proverbs 23:5). If you want security in your life, then the center of your life must be built on something more permanent than money. God and His love for you are permanent, immovable, and unchangeable. Lastly, don't expect money to satisfy. Pursuing money will mess you up and leave you wanting more (see Ecclesiastes 5:10). Instead, work hard at whatever you do, invest wisely, give generously, and trust God to provide.

God, I know You will meet all my needs. I trust in You, and may I never make money my god.

Let Jesus be your Master, not money.

Eternal Investments

"I tell you, use worldly wealth to gain friends for yourselves, so that when it is gone, you will be welcomed into eternal dwellings." (Luke 16:9 NIV)

Integrity grows in the dark. It's when nobody is watching that integrity is solidified. It's in those moments behind the scenes, those unseen, unglamorous daily choices of life when you choose to do the right thing, even though no one will see it. That's when your integrity stands or falls.

Jesus tells an interesting parable here in which a manager is about to be fired for being lazy and wasteful. The manager knows he is about to lose his job, so he decides to negotiate significant discounts with some of his boss's accounts, without the boss's knowledge or permission. He was thinking, "I'll make some business friends and good connections, and maybe they'll hire me later." On the surface it seemed like Jesus was praising this dishonest manager, but He wasn't. Jesus used the manager's shrewdness to make the point that stewardship requires integrity. Like the manager in the story who had to give an account to his boss, we are stewards of God's gifts and talents. One day we will give an account of how we used what God gave us, and the best thing we can do is to use our gifts with eternity in mind.

Earthly investments have a time limit to their enjoyment, but heavenly investments can be enjoyed endlessly and eternally. We should set out to use our resources to do as much good for as many people for as long as possible—for the glory of God and the good of others.

Father God, give me an opportunity today to invest in the life of someone else.

Jesus challenges us to invest more in other people than in our financial future.

The Little Things

"Whoever can be trusted with very little can also be trusted with much, and whoever is dishonest with very little will also be dishonest with much." Luke (16:10 NIV)

Would people describe you as dependable when it comes to completing tasks and serving others? When you ask some people to do something, it's as good as done. You do not have to keep checking in, and you don't have manage their progress. They will simply take care of it. They're dependable. It has been said that the greatest ability is dependability. So how's your dependability?

If you want to do big things for God, it starts by being faithful in the little things. There's a growing sense of entitlement among people today with attitudes that say things like, "I should have that promotion"—without going through the process of earning it. It is a sentiment that believes the *career* path is more important than the *character* path. Why all the fuss about the little jobs? It's because God uses the little jobs to test our integrity and develop our character. The path that God often takes a person, though, is a path filled with determination, diligence, hard work, and attention to detail. Leaders are fashioned in their faithfulness to work hard in the small things. The goal of faithfulness is not that we will work for God, but that God is free to work through us.

Take care of the little things that God places before you, because your faithfulness in the little things will prove you can be trusted to be faithful in the big things when they come.

Dear God, no job is too small or beneath me. Help me to never despise the small tasks, because oftentimes small tasks lead to bigger opportunities.

Jesus develops integrity as we are faithful to complete the little things.

God Sees Everything You Do

"You are those who justify yourselves before men, but God knows your hearts." (Luke 16:15 ESV)

Absolutely nothing is hidden from God. There are no keeping secrets from an all-seeing God. He knows when a bird falls to the ground. He knows the number of hairs on our heads (see Matthew 10:30). He knows what we do and what think. He knows our motives. And He knows our hearts (see 1 Chronicles 28:9). Cain couldn't go far enough outside the Garden of Eden to hide His brother's murdered body from God (see Genesis 4:8–10). David couldn't sweep his secret sin with Bathsheba under the royal carpet (see 2 Samuel 12:12). And Ananias and Sapphira couldn't fool God with their false piousness (see Acts 5:1–11).

The Pharisees were consumed with justifying themselves before men. Outwardly, they did more and went farther than the average Jew, but they were living before men and not before God. True religion is a matter of the heart before God. Jesus was saying that if you are not living openly before God and seeking to please Him with your thoughts, attitudes, and actions, then you are living like a Pharisee. As Christians, we don't live to impress others with how spiritual we are but instead live to please God through genuine obedience.

You may be able to fool some of the people some of the time, but you can never fool God any of the time. So live to please God and not people.

God, You know me better than I know myself. Search me and show me my wrong thoughts and attitudes. Give me a pure heart so that I will live for Your glory, not for my own.

What Jesus thinks about you matters most.

Living with a Scarlet D

"Everyone who divorces his wife and marries another commits adultery, and he who marries a woman divorced from her husband commits adultery." (Luke 16:18 ESV)

The elephant in the sanctuary is that divorce happens, even to Christian couples. It is true that God hates divorce (see Malachi 2:16), but He does not hate the divorced. If you have been divorced, you are not a leper, and you don't need to feel like you're walking around church with a scarlet D stitched on your clothes. With a teaching as matter-of-fact as this one from Jesus, it can seem as though divorce is never allowed and always wrong. While it's true that divorce is always the result of sin, divorce itself is not always a sin.

Divorce is complicated, messy, and sad, and its consequences last a lifetime. The reality is that not every Christian divorce and remarriage is a biblically sound decision. God allows divorce in the instance of sexual immorality or adultery. If your spouse is, or was, unfaithful, then you have the right to divorce. However, it is not God's ideal, and you are not commanded to make that choice. But God has made allowance for it. The apostle Paul shared another allowance in which divorce is permissible: a Christian married to an unbeliever is free to remarry if the unbeliever wants out of the marriage (see 1 Corinthians 7:10–16).

Divorce is emotional and can influence our ability to make biblically based decisions. So seek the wise counsel of a trusted, spiritually mature believer who will lovingly, clearly, and accurately speak God's uncompromising truth to you if divorce is being considered.

God, help me to choose to love, even when I may be facing difficult marital situations.

> **Jesus upholds the sanctity of marriage and reminds us that it should not be dissolved on a whim.**

Happily, Ever After?

"The time came when the beggar died and the angels carried him to Abraham's side. The rich man also died and was buried. In Hades, where he was in torment, he looked up and saw Abraham far away, with Lazarus by his side."
(Luke 16:22–23 NIV)

Everyone loves a story with a happy ending—the rags-to-riches, hero-saves-the-day, guy-gets-the-girl kind of stories. Jesus told a story that has both a rags-to-riches ending and a riches-to-rags ending. It is a story that speaks about the reality of heaven and hell. Most people believe in heaven and feel they will go there after they die, but not as many people believe in a literal hell. Perhaps it comes from this desire for life to have a storybook ending. But the reality is that not everything ends with happily ever after.

Hell is not an idea, a figment of the imagination, or the setting for a horror movie. It is a gruesome reality that awaits those who refuse to let God rule their lives. To deny the permanence of hell is impossible without also removing the permanence of heaven. Each is a reality, and each has ultimate finality. That can be a hard pill to swallow, but the finality of hell should cause everyone to stop and think about their lives and the decisions they're making, because they have eternal results.

We cannot fully appreciate the sweetness of God's grace until we understand the bitter reality of hell. The only happily-ever-after ending is reserved for those who turn to God and trust in Him in this life.

Father, may I always live worthy of the salvation You freely offer and that I will forever enjoy.

> **Jesus wants us to pay attention to how we live, because the consequences affect where we spend eternity.**

The Bible Is Enough

"If they do not hear Moses and the Prophets, neither will they
be convinced if someone should rise from the dead."
(Luke 16:31 ESV)

If a person will not be changed by the Word of God, then they will not be changed by witnessing a miracle of God. The primary purpose of miracles in the Bible was not for them to become substitutes for God's Word but to support the authority of it.

The rich man in Jesus's parable was in his eternal predicament due to his neglect of God's Word. Jesus made it clear that anyone who does not respond to the Word of God will not be convinced, even if they were to witness a miracle. This parable portrays our human desire for the remarkable, the dramatic, or the miraculous to occur. People often remark, "Why doesn't God just speak audibly to us? Why doesn't He just show us a sign? Then I would believe." But we need to remember how many people saw Jesus turn water into wine, feed the five thousand, and raise Lazarus from the dead, and still they walked away without believing in Him. Only a few followed in the end. A life that is not moved by the Word of God will not be moved by a miracle of God. Just ask Pharaoh.

The Bible alone has all the things necessary for a proper understanding of who God is, what He has done, and what He has yet do. It answers who we are, how we are to live, and how we enter into a saving relationship with God.

God, I thank You that Your Word is all-sufficient for me to learn about You and live a life that glorifies you.

> **Jesus reminds us that the Word of God is all-sufficient for salvation.**

Watch Yourself!

"Things that cause people to stumble are bound to come, but woe to anyone through whom they come. It would be better for them to be thrown into the sea with a millstone tied around their neck than to cause one of these little ones to stumble. So, watch yourselves." (Luke 17:1–3 NIV)

One of the biggest mistakes we make in life is forgetting how much our actions affect the people around us. Every day we make decisions, but how often do we stop and ask ourselves, "How will this decision impact those around me?" or "Will this choice hurt someone else?" It is terrible when we stumble, but it is far more serious when we cause someone else to stumble.

Jesus's language is extreme. His warning is heartfelt, but His message is clear: actions have consequences, and we should not cause another person to sin or stumble in their faith. God sees this as a horrendous thing. God wants us to be aware of how we are living, because our lives impact others. Everything you say and do has an effect on someone else. So with such a warning, we must look for ways to avoid being the cause of someone else's sin.

It starts by being careful how we live. The more we keep ourselves away from sin, the less likely we will be to cause someone else to sin. Mature people limit their freedom for the benefit of others, not because they are afraid of what other people think, but because they are motivated by love.

Oh Lord, may I be an encouragement to others in their walk with You and not a cause for stumbling. In Jesus's name.

Whatever we do, wherever we go, whatever we say, we make an impression of who Jesus is by what we say and how we act.

The Role of Rebuking

"If your brother sins against you, rebuke him." (Luke 17:3)

Healthy relationships are built on love (see Proverbs 17:17). This means there may be times when love demands that we speak up. Among the least enjoyable, yet significantly beneficial, relationship responsibilities of those who love the Lord is the task of confronting someone who has hurt us or who is doing something wrong. You may be the only one who cares enough to point out what everyone else sees but what no one chooses to address.

The Bible includes reminders that urge us to care for, warn, and help others maintain a wholesome walk with God. When you expose sin and call for repentance, know that not everyone will be eager to receive correction. So keep your aim to build up the other person in their faith. Resist the natural, sinful impulse to guilt trip or tear down. Instead, seek to make loving correction through encouragement. The Bible tells us to "encourage one another and build one another up," and "do not rebuke an older man, but encourage him as you would a father, younger men as brothers" (1 Thessalonians 5:11 NIV; 1 Timothy 5:1 ESV). Every speaking-the-truth-in-love conversation should begin and end on a positive note. And if a brother or sister in Jesus goes through the uncomfortable awkwardness of having an unpleasant conversation that brings correction into our lives, we should be gracious and thankful for their demonstration of love.

God, I ask for the grace, humility, and love to gently speak the truth when You lead me to take steps of confrontation. Equally, may I be gracious and humble if I am lovingly confronted.

> **We need to always ask Jesus to help us when loving rebukes are necessary.**

No Grudges Allowed

"If your brother sins against you, rebuke him; and if he repents, forgive him." (Luke 17:3)

Unfortunately, most of us have all been hurt by someone. We have been the recipients of thoughtless or hurtful words. We have felt the pain from the selfish action of others. And whenever the subject of forgiveness comes up, so do the memories of those heartaches and hurts. It's easy to trick ourselves into believing that by holding on to a grudge, we will teach the other person a lesson. But the truth is that refusing to forgive only hurts us. Forgiveness is not about the other person. Forgiveness is all about us.

God calls us to be forgiving. As a matter of fact, forgiveness for the Christian is not optional. We are to forgive others because God has forgiven us. You never will forgive someone more than God forgives you. So as gracious recipients of forgiveness, we are to be gracious givers of forgiveness.

Is there someone you are having a hard time forgiving? First, realize that forgiveness is a process. It doesn't happen overnight. Forgiveness is a choice that begins by letting go of feelings to retaliate or punish the other person (see Romans 12:19). Forgiveness accepts that no one is perfect, and we all have faults (see Colossians 3:13). Finally, forgiveness remembers how we have been forgiven by God of countless offenses, countless times, and therefore we should be more quick to extend forgiveness to others.

Father, I don't want to be bitter or hold a grudge. Help me to experience freedom by releasing my hurts and extending grace to others because of the grace You extend to me daily.

Jesus reminds us that we cannot afford to hold on to unforgiveness.

Faith Builders

The apostles said to the Lord, "Increase our faith!" And the Lord said, "If you had faith like a grain of mustard seed, you could say to this mulberry tree, 'Be uprooted and planted in the sea,' and it would obey you." (Luke 17:5–6 ESV)

Nothing is impossible for the one whose faith is strong in the Lord. But as powerful as God is, He moves in response to our faith.

It is important to understand there is saving faith, and there is working faith. Saving faith, at its core, is believing that Jesus is Lord and that He paid the penalty for our sin. Working faith, at its core, are the actions involved in living out our faith. The size of our faith is less important than the object it is placed in. Jesus's example about faith in Luke 17:5–6 is less about actually uprooting a mulberry tree and more about the fact that God will give you the power to accomplish what you could not do in your own strength, if you simply have faith.

So what do you do if you're feeling like the apostles and think your faith could use a boost? The key to tapping into your faith begins by intentionally seeking God's plans over your own plans for life. It's all a matter of priorities. Keep God and His plans for your life your first priority. Next, pray, but pray like you mean it. Pray like God is in the room. Stop praying predictable, monotonous, lip service prayers and really pray. Also, be purposeful when you're reading your Bible. Slow down, take notes, and highlight. Do more to help experience what you are reading, because the more the Bible is in your heart and mind, the more you will be a living demonstration of faith.

God, as I ask You to increase my faith, I know I must also keep You first in all things.

> **The strength of our faith is not found in its size but in the person of Jesus Christ.**

Faith and Duty

"We have only done what was our duty." (Luke 17:10 ESV)

Everything I am, everything I have, and everything I ever hope to be, I owe to Jesus. I am forever indebted to Jesus for all He has done for me, but even if I served Him perfectly for the rest of my life, I never would deserve my salvation. I don't serve God because He is laying some heavenly guilt trip on me, and I don't serve God because He is forcing me to do so. I serve God because I love Him and because it is what I was created to do.

When we do good and when we help others, we are merely living as we were created to live. When we resist sin and when we forgive others, we are merely living as we were created to live. When we are faithful, generous, and compassionate, we are merely living as we were created to live. The trap we can fall into is thinking that when we've done something good, when we've forgiven that person who hurt us, when we've been generous with our time or money, or when we didn't give in to that temptation, we deserve some sort of special recognition from God.

In the parable in Luke 17:7–10, Jesus is explaining there is no special pat on the back waiting for us because we simply did what we were created to do. God has done everything for us, and He has blessed us with every spiritual blessing in the heavens in Christ (see Ephesians 1:3). So our service and obedience is merely living as we were created to live. Our lives have value and our service to God has purpose, but we live for God because we love Him.

Father, it is my life's attitude to freely, fully, willingly, and lovingly live for You because You saved me, You sanctify me, and You supply my every need. The least I can do is give my life back to You.

> I serve Jesus because my love and loyalty are expressed through obedience, not obligation.

Attitude of Gratitude

"Were not ten cleansed? Where are the nine? Was no one
found to return and give praise to God except this foreigner?"
(Luke 17:17–18 ESV)

Gratitude has its benefits. Grateful people are happier people. They experience better sleep and have healthier hearts and fewer aches and pains. Grateful people tend to have a positive outlook on life. Grateful people tend to see what they do have rather than what they do not have. And like a muscle, the more you exercise gratitude, the stronger it grows.

Jesus healed ten people with leprosy. He completely, supernaturally, and wonderfully changed ten lives. Ten people had the same life-changing experience, but only one came back to say thank you. Where were the other nine? How could they so quickly take the grace of God for granted? It can be easy to judge the lack of gratitude in the nine others, but how many times has God done something for you, and you forgot to circle back and thank Him?

Beyond the physical benefits to gratitude, there are also some spiritual benefits. Gratitude glorifies God and is an important part of our worship. It opens our spiritual eyes to see the blessings of God and draws us closer to Him. Gratitude is a cure for anxiety (see Philippians 4:6) and leads to contentment, and "godliness with contentment is great gain" (1 Timothy 6:6 ESV). Gratitude reaffirms our need for God and is a great testimony to others of what God has done in our lives.

Jesus, forgive me for not saying thank you as often as I should. I want to be like the one who returned to express gratitude. Thank you for saving me, forgiving me, and providing for my needs each day.

Regularly saying thank you to Jesus has both physical and spiritual benefits.

Great Expectations

"For indeed, the kingdom of God is within you." *(Luke 17:21)*

God's plans are greater than my expectations. Expectations can be good, but unfortunately, our expectations also can be unrealistic. Expectations shape your beliefs, and unrealistic expectations can rob you of joy, lead to disappointment, and even blind you to the truth.

When Jesus came to Earth, the Jews were expecting the Messiah to come and elevate the Jewish nation to a place of prominence and power. Instead of receiving the message of repentance and salvation that Jesus came to proclaim, they rejected Him because He wasn't what they expected. Jesus told the Pharisees their expectations were wrong and that He was the embodiment of the kingdom of God. Sometimes we have our minds so fixed on what we're expecting that we can't see the truth right in front of us. Jesus was the fulfillment of all the prophecies, but because He didn't look like what they were expecting, they rejected Him.

There are bound to be times when God doesn't work as we expect Him to. But God can do what He wants, when He wants, and however He wants. If God doesn't meet our expectations, the problem is with our expectations, not with God's answer to our prayers. Let's expect His goodness, His faithfulness, His provision, and His perfect timing. Let's expect Him to work all things together for our good, and then let's step back and allow Him to do exactly that.

God, help me to release my expectations to Your perfect will. You are loving, gracious, and kind. You know all things, and You are always on time. Even when my expectations are unmet, everything that comes from You is perfect and good.

Jesus is all-knowing and all-loving. Expect Him to do what is best.

Is the End Near?

"And as it was in the days of Noah, so it will be also in the days of the Son of Man." (Luke 17:26)

Society is in a downward spiral. If we look at the deteriorating moral values in our world, the abortion, pornography, drug addiction, child abuse, shootings, human trafficking, and the terrorism that plague our world, we are left wondering, "Is the end near?"

Jesus's disciples asked Him the very same questions. Jesus said the time of His return would resemble the days of Noah. So how was it in the days of Noah? Genesis 6:5 says, "The LORD saw that the wickedness of man was great in the earth, and that every intention of the thoughts of his heart was only evil continually" (Genesis 6:5 ESV). The people in Noah's day didn't think they were doing anything wrong. They thought Noah was crazy, and they didn't give God a second thought. That is, until it started raining. Waiting until it rains to buy an umbrella isn't smart, and in the same way, putting God off and thinking everything is just fine isn't smart, either.

Before the rain came, Noah lived for God and did what God called him to do, despite the scoffers who mocked his faithfulness, obedience, preparations, and message of righteousness. This is how people will be acting prior to the return of Jesus, and it is how people are acting now. People didn't believe Jesus the first time, and people don't believe Him in our time. The end may be near, or it may still be way in the future, but our part is to be ready, to be faithful, to be obedient, to be prepared, and to proclaim God's message, no matter the day or hour.

Heavenly Father, help me to live every day in light of Your Son's return. The day of the flood began like any other, and so too will be the day of His coming.

We should be living in constant readiness for Jesus' return.

Looking Ahead

"Remember Lot's wife." (Luke 17:32)

Learning from the past is commendable, but living in the past is counterproductive. Before God destroyed the city of Sodom, He sent two angels to rescue Lot and his family from the coming annihilation. Their instructions were clear: "Do not look behind you nor stay anywhere in the plain. Escape to the mountains, lest you be destroyed. . . . But his wife looked back behind him, and she became a pillar of salt" (Genesis 19:17, 26). Why was looking back such a horrible sin, causing the judgment of God to fall upon Lot's wife? Doesn't that seem a little harsh? After all, wasn't it just a quick glance?

Unfortunately for Lot's wife, it wasn't just a look. It was in direct disobedience to God's instructions, and disobedience never leads to blessing. What was so important to Lot's wife that it led her to disobey God? Honestly, it doesn't matter. There may have been pleasures she enjoyed, privileges she relished, or even power she possessed, but the point is that something in Sodom caused her to have a lingering desire to stay there.

We need to remember that faith is always pointed toward the future, and faith always has to do with the truths and events that have yet to materialize in our lives. If we let the past outweigh our confidence in the future, then we will get stuck in a spiritual rut. We need to stop living in the rearview mirror and keep moving forward on the road that God has ahead of us. As Paul wrote, "Forgetting the past and looking forward to what lies ahead, I press on" (Philippians 3:13–14 NLT).

God, keep me from becoming too attached to this world, and keep me from lingering on things that prevent me from walking closely and obediently with You.

Keep moving forward on the path Jesus has for you.

Good God

"No one is good except God alone." (Luke 18:19 ESV)

All of us *occasionally* do good. But none of us *always* do good. That's because according to Jesus, no one is good except God alone. Those who think of themselves as pretty good people ought to consider how Jesus nullifies all such thinking when He points to the standard for good, which is God.

As Jesus walked along with His disciples, a man came to Him and asked, "Good Teacher, what shall I do to inherit eternal life?" (Luke 18:18). Jesus responded, "Why do you call Me good? No one is good except God alone" (verse 19). Jesus's reply was not a denial of His deity but an opportunity for the man to confess his faith in Jesus. It's as if Jesus were saying, "If you are going to call me 'good,' then let it be because you acknowledge My divinity, not because you think that by calling me good, you can get something from Me. I am good because I am God."

God is the only One who can rightfully be called good. But what does *good* really mean? It means that God has no evil in Him. It means that His motives and methods are always pure. It means that He always does what is right. It means that His purposes and plans are always perfect. The ultimate proof of God's goodness is seen in His plan of salvation. The goodness of God is more than one facet of His glorious nature; it is the overall summation of His character. You cannot have goodness without God, and you cannot have God without goodness.

Jesus, You are good, and You are my example of what goodness should look like in my life. Fill me with Your goodness, and let my life be an example of Your goodness.

Jesus is the standard for goodness.

Sell Everything?

"One thing you still lack. Sell all that you have and distribute to the poor, and you will have treasure in heaven; and come, follow me." (Luke 18:22 ESV)

Why do Christians get so uncomfortable when God talks about money and possessions? Is it because there are passages like this, which talk about giving all you have to the poor? We know we should give to God, but does God really want us to give away *everything* we own to follow Him?

When the rich young ruler came to Jesus, he came with a seeker's heart and a desire to live an upright life. He even boasted that he had kept the Ten Commandments all his life. Though Jesus recognized his sincerity, He also saw there was something holding the young man back. By asking the rich young ruler to give away his possessions, Jesus wasn't setting a precedent for every Christian to follow. Vows of poverty are not prerequisites for the Christian life. Jesus wanted to demonstrate that money and possessions, just like power and influence, can become distractions that prevent a person from truly following God.

This command was given to one rich man, not to every rich man, but the principle behind it applies to all of us. We should carefully consider what we hold on to, and if something has priority in our lives over God, then we need to be willing to let it go for Him. Secondly, Jesus definitely speaks to how our resources should be used to help those in need. The heart of worship is valuing Jesus above everything. Outward acts only show how much we value Jesus.

God, may my heart's desire be to lay up treasures in heaven, where my joys will last forever.

Love Jesus principally, share sacrificially.

The Real Problem with Riches

"How difficult it is for those who have wealth to enter the kingdom of God! For it is easier for a camel to go through the eye of a needle than for a rich person to enter the kingdom of God." (Luke 18:24–25 ESV)

God doesn't condemn riches or wealth, but He does love to use money as a litmus test to expose what is important to people. The Bible gives many warnings about the dangers that come with money. More money won't make you any happier than you already are, because if you are unable to find contentment with what you have now, you won't be content with more.

God doesn't have a problem with your having money. Abraham was blessed with an abundance, Job had great riches, and Joseph of Arimathea was wealthy, and these were all faithful men. So why did Jesus speak so much about money? It's because there is a fundamental link between our spiritual lives and how we think about and handle money. The problem with wealth is not in having it. It is how we get it. It is how we use it. And it is how we view it.

God doesn't say that rich people can't be saved. Our salvation and sanctification are not tied to our bank accounts. But with wealth comes the temptation to find security in our savings and not in the Savior. Keeping money in the proper perspective always means worshiping God more than gaining wealth.

God, You are bigger than my finances. You know my monetary situation, and You are the God of all resources. Give me what I need, and may I find my contentment in You and nowhere else.

The greatest wealth comes to those who find their contentment in Jesus, not their money.

The Work of Salvation

"What is impossible with man is possible with God."
(Luke 18:27 ESV)

Salvation was God's idea, planned by God before time began, provided by God at immeasurable cost, and offered by God as a free gift to all. A person cannot save themselves, because no one in and of themselves seeks God, and no one in and of themselves qualifies for salvation (see Romans 3:9, 11). God saves, God sustains, and God sanctifies.

With God, all things are possible is not a good luck charm or a blanket promise that guarantees our success in whatever we do. Yes, God is all-powerful, but this does not give us the right to claim His power for whatever we want. God acts according to His will, not ours.

Jesus's point is clear: from beginning to end, salvation is from God and is based on the finished work of Jesus and not the work of human effort. The great, the good, and the rich won't gain salvation because they are great, good, or rich. Salvation is a sovereign, supernatural work of our great God. Salvation is beyond purchase, and it cannot be hijacked by human determination. It is beyond all human engineering employed through religion, morality, good works, or individual striving. But what is impossible with man is possible with God. Both rich and poor come to God the same way, by trusting completely in Jesus, and Jesus alone, for their salvation. Salvation is, and always will be, impossible with man but possible with God.

God, I am thankful that salvation is supplied and sustained by You.
You have made a way where there was no way on my own.

**Salvation is impossible apart from Jesus, but
with Jesus it is possible for all.**

What's in It for Me?

"Truly, I say to you, there is no one who has left house or wife or brothers or parents or children, for the sake of the kingdom of God, who will not receive many times more in this time, and in the age to come eternal life." (Luke 18:29–30 ESV)

My service to God does not obligate Him to bless me. I serve God not to get something from Him but because it is a privilege to serve Him. Our motivation in serving God should be authentic, pure, and genuine. We love God and serve Him because He is God, not because of the gracious things He does for us or for the rewards He promises to us. That said, God does not expect us to forget or be ignorant of the gracious future promises that await us.

When Jesus asked the rich young ruler to sell everything, give it to the poor, and then come follow Him, the rich young ruler went away sad, because he had great wealth. Peter then spoke up and said, "See, we have left all and followed You" (Luke 18:28). Jesus responded with loving reassurance that we always will get more than we ever give up for God.

It is a wondrous truth that if we love God, obey His Word, and serve Him faithfully, there will be eternal rewards for each of us in His kingdom. But there are also blessings to be had in this life. As we give our lives to God daily, we become more like Jesus, strengthen our faith, experience God's peace and presence in our lives, build relationships with others, become less focused on ourselves, and further God's kingdom. That doesn't sound like much of a hardship if you ask me.

God, You have done so much for me. The fact that You reward me for my faithfulness is a blessing that is hard to understand. Thank you for Your goodness to me.

You always will get more than you ever give up for Jesus.

Leaving and Cleaving

*" 'For this reason a man shall leave his father and mother and
be joined to his wife, and the two shall become one flesh.' "*
(Matthew 19:4–6)

The first step to a successful marriage involves leaving and cleaving.
Marriage creates a new reality and a new community. And at the heart
of what it means to leave father and mother and cleave to each other is
the creation of a new allegiance. This means that after God, your new
priority and commitment is to your spouse, not your mom or dad.
No matter how much you love mom's cooking, no matter how much
you enjoy dad's bad jokes, your spouse takes priority.

Leaving is a two-way street. It is not only the couple who needs
to leave, but the parents also need to release their children into their
new relationship. That is why marriage services include the question,
"Who gives this bride in marriage?" The primary responsibility of a
husband is to his wife. The primary responsibility of a wife is to her
husband. Yes, you still honor your parents, but there's a leaving that
must take place. Letting go can be hard for both parents and children,
but it is essential for marriages to thrive.

Leaving without cleaving is also insufficient. When forced to
choose between your career, your family, your friends or your spouse,
if you do not choose your spouse, you have not fully understood what
it means to cleave. Cleaving doesn't mean that you are stuck together;
it means that you are sticking together, no matter what.

*Father, help me to experience all You have for me in my marriage by
Your grace and through my commitment to my spouse.*

> **Jesus emphasizes the importance of aligning
> intimately and uniting purposefully with your
> spouse.**

Single and Satisfied

"Some decide not to get married for kingdom reasons."
(Matthew 19:12 MSG)

Marriage might be for most, but that doesn't mean it is for everyone. Singleness can be holy, joyful, and satisfying if that is your calling. While marriage may bring joy, help, and companionship, it also multiplies your distractions, because you are concerned about another person's well-being and happiness. Marriage is a high calling and a good calling, but some may decide to ditch the marriage vows and choose to be single for the Savior.

The call of being single is often a temporary call that comes with the opportunity to learn, grow, seek, and exclusively pursue the call that God has on your life. It's a season to seize every opportunity that God gives you, easily and spontaneously. Singleness is not about your being single, it is about God. Single Christians are Christians first, and that calling is intended to say something about God, His supreme sufficiency in your life, and your desire to serve Him wholeheartedly.

Your marital status does not change God's desire to work in and through your life. God wants to use you right where you are, whether you are married or single. Knowing whether God is calling you to a season of singleness is like knowing His will in anything else. It requires persistent prayer and purposeful reflection, as God's will often becomes clear over time. Our identity is not found in our marital status; it is permanently established in our union with Christ. Jesus is to be, now and forever, the driving, shaping, and controlling force in the Christian's life.

Jesus, I know my love and devotion to You come first and must remain first, whether I am married or single.

> **Whether you are married or single, your purpose is to glorify Jesus.**

Jesus Loves Kids

"Let the little children come to me, and do not hinder them,
for the kingdom of heaven belongs to such as these."
(Matthew 19:14 NIV)

Time is precious, life is short, and children grow up fast. No parent wants to look back and have any regrets or "if only" thoughts about raising their children. When it comes to children, God makes it clear: children are not irrelevant or insignificant, and eternal life is available to all, even little ones.

Jesus was leaving Galilee for a final time and heading to Jerusalem. After tackling some tough questions from the religious leaders, some children were brought to Jesus, perhaps by their parents, to be blessed by Him. Jesus's well-intentioned security team body blocked the parents and tried to turn the children away. But compassionate Jesus did not cast the children aside. Instead He called them closer and blessed them.

Jesus wants us to have a compassionate attitude toward children and do all we can to lead them to faith. It's important to help children understand early on what it means to trust Jesus as their Savior, because Jesus wants to bless children as well as adults. We live busy lives in which time is precious and life is short. Be purposeful and invest in the spiritual lives of your children. Never stop bringing children to Jesus. He loves them and wants to bless them.

Father, may the value of children never be lost on me, and may I learn to approach You, Jesus, with the same humble simplicity of a child.

Never stop bringing children to Jesus.

When God Says No

"You don't know what you are asking." (Matthew 20:22 NIV)

No one likes to be told no, but if God gives you a no, are you able to accept His will for that situation? God doesn't leave your prayers unanswered. Sometimes He will answer them with a yes, other times it will be with a no, and still other times it may be with a not now. But every answer is according to His perfect will, whether or not we like it in that moment.

Case in point, Mrs. Zebedee, the wife of a Galilean fisherman and the mother of James and John, who one day asked Jesus to allow her sons to sit on either side of Him in the coming kingdom. Jesus's answer was an unmistakable no that He followed with a loving reprimand.

It is only natural to be disappointed when God answers with a no, but we must never forget that God always has our good and His glory in mind. God never gives us anything accidentally. He always has a plan and a purpose for what He gives and what He prohibits. If something is not for our good or for His glory, the answer will be no. If the timing is wrong, the answer will be no. If the motives are wrong, the answer will be no. If the method is wrong, the answer will be no. If you want God to give you a yes, then it must be God's will, God's way, and in God's time, or the answer will be no. God has a bigger plan, a bigger perspective, and a bigger purpose than we can know and comprehend. We must learn to trust God, knowing that if He says no, His will is best, and there is likely a lesson for us to learn.

God, when You give me a no, help me to be more concerned with what You are trying to show me than with what I am not getting.

Jesus knows better than we do, even when the answer is no.

Serving and Giving

"The Son of Man did not come to be served, but to serve, and to give his life as a ransom for many." (Matthew 20:28 NIV)

God has wired us to be happiest when we serve others and give our lives away. The irony is that we think we will be happiest if we make a name for ourselves. We believe that happiness is tied to position and power, but the way Jesus lays out for His followers is quite different. Jesus would have us live by a different standard, one that exalts Him, not ourselves, one that seeks to follow Him and not the world, and one that serves Him faithfully by doing His will and not our own.

Jesus poured himself out day after day. He gave Himself to the disciples, He gave Himself to the crowds, He gave himself to the sick, He gave Himself to those in need, and on the cross, He gave Himself for the world. Jesus did not come into the world for Himself, He came for us. His death was not for Himself but for us. His resurrection was not for Himself but for us. His ascension was not for Himself but for us. And His return will not be for Himself but for us. Jesus humbled Himself, surrendered His rights, and obeyed God, even to the point of death on the cross. And being His servant begins with the same attitude.

When we realize that Jesus has served us even in our inadequacies, selfishness, and sin, it should motivate us to serve others for His sake and for His glory.

Father, help me to have a servant attitude, even when I may not feel like it. Work on my attitude so that my heart and actions follow.

Serving and giving make us more like Jesus.

Getting a Better Look at Jesus

"Zacchaeus, hurry and come down, for I must stay at your house today." (Luke 19:5 ESV)

"Hey, Jesus is here!" someone yelled. That was all it took for the crowd to instantly form. Everyone stopped what they were doing, because the One who had Galilee all abuzz was passing through their town that day. Then from among the crowd, you could hear the voice, but you couldn't see where it was coming from. "Excuse me! Coming through. Pardon me! Make room, please." The more he pushed, the more the crowd seemed to pull.

"This isn't going to work," he thought. "Ah, there we go." He saw his opportunity. Just over there was the local sycamore tree. Without a second thought, up climbed the rich little man named Zacchaeus, all so that he could get a glimpse of Jesus. Zacchaeus, Jericho's chief tax collector, was despised by the people because he became rich off the backs of his countrymen. Zacchaeus used his position to take as much as he wanted while leaving the people overtaxed and resentful. And because he had the support of the Roman authorities, the people were powerless to stop him. So when Jesus said He was going to have dinner at this man's house, the crowd was stunned. And I suspect that Zacchaeus was too.

Faith doesn't just affect our thoughts and emotions; it produces action. Zacchaeus did not let obstacles (his height, the crowd, and the fact that he was an outcast) stop him from drawing closer to Jesus, and the result was life-changing.

God, help me to always be as eager to see You as Zacchaeus was the day that he climbed the sycamore tree.

Don't let obstacles keep you from Jesus.

SEPTEMBER

Rescue Mission

"For the Son of Man has come to seek and to save that which was lost." (Luke 19:10)

A church that fails to take up the cause of Christ to seek and save the lost will find that it is no longer a growing church. Generally our failures to engage in local evangelism and missions are not because of a lack of love toward others but because of our intense self-centeredness that often leads us to overlook the needs of someone else, especially when it comes to introducing them to Jesus. Somehow we think that if we build it, they will come. People will just drive by and see all the Christian activity going on, and their curiosity will lead them to visit our church. And to some degree, that does happen. But if we are not actively going out and seeking lost people in order to give them the message of salvation, we cannot be surprised if no one is walking through our church doors.

Jesus ate with sinners because He came to save sinners. Wherever Jesus went, He made friends. He didn't make people feel they needed to change to be His friends. Rather, being friends with Jesus changed people forever. Jesus loves sinners, and He loved them enough to go to them and share His message of hope and salvation.

The effort and commitment Jesus applied toward His mission to seek and save the lost should serve as our example to exert a similar amount of effort to seek and save those who are lost without God.

God, send lost people my way, and make me ready to share the gospel with them. Let me also look for the lost among those I know so that I can share the gospel with them.

The world needed Jesus when He came, and it still needs Him today.

Minas and Me

"To everyone who has, more will be given." (Luke 19:26 ESV)

You have two choices as a Christian: either you can use the gifts and talents God has given you for His glory, or you can squander them.

As Jesus approached Jerusalem days before His crucifixion, He detected the crowd's expectation of an imminent establishment of the kingdom of God. Jesus knew very well that God's kingdom was not set to instantly appear. So to prepare His listeners and His followers, He gave them a parable about stewardship (see Luke 19:11–27). In this parable Jesus delivered the key to understanding what our lives in Christ should be about while we wait for God to establish His kingdom. We are here to be wise stewards of all the treasures that Jesus has entrusted to us.

It is easy to assume that only the rich have been given much, but the reality is that we all have been given much (see 1 Corinthians 4:7). We have been given abundant grace, the Word of God, and the gifts of the Holy Spirit. And as 1 Peter 4:10 says, "Each of you should use whatever gift you have received to serve others, as faithful stewards of God's grace in its various forms" (NIV). If we are blessed with talents, wealth, knowledge, time, and the like, it is expected that we use these to glorify God and benefit others.

As we prepare ourselves for life in God's coming kingdom, we are to be using the gifts God has given us to bless others in the meantime. And for those who are faithful in using what God has given them for His glory, more will be added.

God, I do not want to squander what You have so generously and graciously given to me.

> **Jesus holds us responsible to use what we have been given for His glory.**

The Aroma of Worship

"Let her alone; she has kept this for the day of My burial. For the poor you have with you always, but Me you do not have always." (John 12:7–8)

It was a few days before Passover, and despite the warrant that was out for Jesus's arrest, He made a stop at the house of His close friends in Bethany, on His way to Jerusalem. Martha was busy serving, as she liked to do, and Lazarus was reclining at the table with Jesus, very much alive. Then Mary came to the table carrying an alabaster flask filled with an expensive perfume worth a year's wages. Unexpectedly and unreservedly, in an act of extravagant worship, she broke the flask and poured out the fragrant oil on Jesus's head and feet. Then she unbound her hair, and with great courage and humility, knelt down and wiped Jesus's feet with her precious hair. Mary wasn't a wealthy woman. The alabaster flask containing such a costly perfume represented her savings, but she lovingly and willingly gave all she had to Jesus for His glory. She expressed the depth of her love and devotion to Him by a costly sacrifice.

Our approach and attitude toward worship reveals our estimation of God. The purpose of worship is to elevate Jesus. Mary's anointing of Jesus reminds us that Jesus is worthy of our best and our all. Mary understood the uniqueness of Jesus's identity, and with loving adoration, she determined to respond accordingly. We should never hesitate to give God our best and our all, because even though our sacrifices may not always be understood by everyone, our worship is always worth the cost.

Jesus, may I never hold back expressing my love for You. Let my worship always be genuine and always motivated by my love for You.

The purpose of worship is the exaltation of Jesus.

Breaking God's Heart

As he approached Jerusalem and saw the city, he wept over it and said, "If you, even you, had only known on this day what would bring you peace—but now it is hidden from your eyes.
(Luke 19:41–42)

As the crowds were cheering, Christ was weeping. As praises were lifted up toward the heavens, the purest of tears fell down on a cynical Earth. On this profound and prophetic day before the King of humanity prepared to ride into His Holy City, He stopped and wept. Why did Jesus weep when He looked over Jerusalem?

Being God, Jesus knew the crowd that was crying out, "Hosanna!" soon would be shouting, "Crucify Him!" He knew that betrayal, denial, conspiracy, abandonment, and death awaited Him. He knew the destruction of this sacred city was looming, inevitability coming in the not-so-distant future. But it was more than all of these things that broke the heart of God. Unbelief and rejection were at the core of what was breaking His heart that day, and it is at the core of what breaks His heart today. God knows the painful consequences that come to those who shut the doors of their hearts to Him, and His heart is broken every time.

God does not want anyone to be lost. He does not take any pleasure in seeing those who reject Him suffer because of their rejection. God's heart breaks when we fail to faithfully follow Him.

God, help me not to harden my heart, especially against those with whom I disagree or those who disbelieve in the truth. May my heart be broken for what breaks Your heart.

Jesus is a compassionate God, sorrowful and sovereign.

God's Word

"Is it not written . . . ?" (Mark 11:17)

Are you fully trusting in God's Word? Did you know that your spiritual successes and failures are tied to it? The Bible is the ultimate authority, and it is the key to spiritual growth and stability in your life. People grow spiritually not because they are busy at church, but because they are turning to and trusting in God and His Word.

Jesus unequivocally and authoritatively upheld the supremacy of the Word of God. Jesus used the Word of God to resist temptation, to reveal the nature and character of God, to rebuke the misapplication of truth, to pronounce His deity, to proclaim truth, to dispel doubt, and to attack misrepresentation. Jesus made it clear on many occasions that God's Word is necessary, God's Word is sufficient, and God's Word is final.

We act on what we believe, meaning our behavior and attitudes are a reflection of what we believe is true. Jesus consistently and continually emphasized that the Word of God is essential to properly worship God and to properly live for Him. The Bible makes no mistakes. It can be comprehended, it cannot be eliminated, and it needs to be the most important thing in your daily life. It is the most significant thing that you can give yourself to each day. We should never cease from turning to and trusting in God's never-ending instruction to us.

God, the Bible is Your inspired Word. The more I read it, the more I will know it, and the more I know it, the more I will use it. The more I use it, the more useful it is to me.

> **Jesus wants us to fully and completely embrace the authority and usefulness of Scripture.**

The Tables are Turned

"Is it not written: 'My house will be called a house of prayer
for all nations'? But you have made it 'a den of robbers.' "
(Mark 11:17 NIV)

Jesus was fired up! It is possibly the most startling and unsettling scene in the description of Jesus's life when He entered the temple days before His crucifixion and, with virtuous outrage, overturned the merchants' tables and kicked out the profiteers. It is an unusual image of the often-branded gentle Jesus, meek and mild. You can imagine the chaos as coins scattered on the ground and onlookers scrambled to pick up the fallen money, vendors frantically tried to catch their pigeons as feathers filled the air, and money changers quickly closed up shop to avoid their tables from being targeted next. The exploiters were furious, the exploited were applauding, and the disciples were uncomfortable.

It was seemingly out of character for Jesus, who is complex but also consistent. He practiced the kind of behavior that He preached. He told His followers to love their enemies, He praised the peacemakers, and He taught the importance of loving your neighbor. That is why people took notice of this unexpected display. And that is the point. This was not an impulsive temper tantrum. It was a deliberate act with an intentional message. God is angered when worship is exploited.

If you want to anger God, then get in the way of people coming to worship Him. Jesus is zealous for our access to God. He came to rip the veil (see Luke 23:45) and give us an up-close-and-personal relationship with our heavenly Father.

Lord, cleanse my heart of anything that displeases You and hinders
my relationship with You.

Jesus despises anything that hinders access to God.

House of Prayer

" 'My house will be called a house of prayer for all nations.' "
(Mark 11:17 NIV)

If you doubt the importance that God places on prayer, just consider the above statement of Jesus. One thing that is supposed to distinguish Christian churches and Christian people is the priority of prayer. Preaching is important, but Jesus never said, "My house will be called a house of preaching." Worship music is important, but Jesus never said, "My house will be called a house of worship music." Serving is important, but Jesus never said, "My house will be called a house of service." The church should be a place where people are opening their hearts and coming to God in the worship, thanksgiving, and supplication of prayer.

The early church understood the priority of prayer. In fact, there are more than thirty references to prayer in the book of Acts alone, which is more than any other book in the New Testament. Before the church did anything, they prayed. It was second nature for them. The early church did life together. They wept together, ate together, worshiped together, laughed together, shared together, and made sure to pray together. People who are strangers throughout the week are not likely to be intimate in prayer when they gather together. A healthier prayer life will lead to a healthier church.

When the church becomes a house of prayer, it invites the presence and power of the Holy Spirit, it increases the faith of a congregation to believe God for the miraculous, it moves people from seeking their own purposes to seeking God's purposes, and it creates greater intimacy with God.

God, we do many things as the church. Help us to find pleasure in praying together.

Jesus expects the church to be a place where prayer is a priority.

Confidence in Prayer

"Have faith in God. . . . Therefore I say to you, whatever
things you ask when you pray, believe that you receive them,
and you will have them. (Mark 11:22, 24)

God is not a vending machine, and prayer is not the loose change we drop in the coin slot, hoping that God will dispense what we ask for. The heart of prayer is communion with God. All too often we look at God as existing for us rather than realizing we exist for Him. And that perspective can be reflected in the way we pray. It is an amazing privilege we have been given to be able to approach the almighty God in prayer, but we need to be more focused on worship and fellowship with God rather than coming to Him with a grocery list of needs.

God wants to grant our requests, but we make it impossible for Him to do so when we ask for things that contradict His nature and character. We need to continually seek Him and look to the Bible to ensure that our motives line up with His will. We need to realize when Jesus tells us that "whatever things you ask when you pray, believe that you receive them, and you will have them," it is not a license to think that God owes us whatever we ask. We must keep our prayers consistent with the teachings of Scripture and pray in accordance with the will of God. If we ask for something that is not in God's will, we cannot expect to receive it. Belief in prayer is not so much belief in what we ask for, but belief in the One we are asking. We limit God when we pray and don't believe. We need to pray with authority and confidence, but our confidence comes from praying according to His revealed will. God knows what is best for us, and we believe Him to answer us as He sees fit.

Lord, I ask for greater faith so that I may pray with greater confidence
for your greater good.

Jesus reminds us that our confidence in prayer
comes from our faith in God.

Prayer Blocker

"And whenever you stand praying, if you have anything
against anyone, forgive him, that your Father in heaven may
also forgive you your trespasses." (Mark 11:25)

Unforgiveness hinders prayer. If you're someone who has trouble letting things go, if you keep score of rights and wrongs, then you need to know that you will make your life harder than it has to be. If we hold on to unforgiveness, we will create a spiritual blood clot that restricts the free flow of God's grace in our lives, and our prayer life will come to a screeching halt.

The problem with unforgiveness is that it always hurts us more than the person we refuse to forgive. Many people ruin their health and their lives by continually taking the poison of unforgiveness. The most dangerous side effect of holding on to unforgiveness is that it damages our relationship with God. When we realize that we are helping ourselves when we choose to forgive, we can stop swallowing the poison of unforgiveness, and our spiritual lives will be healthier. The God of the universe wants a close, intimate relationship with us so that He can reveal Himself to us, so that He can guide us, and so that He can support our lives.

If unforgiveness is hindering your prayer life and your relationship with God, then begin by making the decision to forgive. If you are truly willing to forgive, depend on the Holy Spirit. God is there to help you through the process.

Father God, bring it to my mind if I am holding on to any unforgiveness. I don't want anything to hinder my prayers and block my relationship with You. So help me to forgive as I have been forgiven.

Forgiving others as Jesus forgives ensures a
healthier prayer life.

The Authority of Jesus

"I also will ask you one question; then answer Me, and I will tell you by what authority I do these things: The baptism of John—was it from heaven or from men? Answer Me." (Mark 11:29–30)

The authority of the Bible hinges on the authority of Jesus. The authority of God has been challenged throughout history, beginning with Satan's rebellion in heaven. The rejection of God's authority is the peak of arrogance and pride. God is holy and just. His Word is true and trustworthy. He does not deceive or speak lies. His commands are for our good and His glory.

So when the religious leaders came to Jesus and asked, "By what authority are You doing these things?" it was a clear assault against His divine authority. Jesus answered their question with another question (see Mark 11:29–30 above), where He implied that anyone who correctly identified the source of John's authority would correctly identify the source of His authority. Their unbelief rested in a failure to perceive the divine authority of the ministries of both John and Jesus. Again and again Jesus revealed Himself as He does now: through His Word and through His power. They simply refused to believe and submit to His authority.

To follow Jesus is to be under His authority. To follow Jesus is to do what He says to do. His authority is for all time, in every place, and in the everydayness of our lives. Are you submitting your life to the authority of Jesus?

Jesus, I know all authority in heaven and on Earth belongs to You. If there is any area of my life that I am not submitting to Your authority, reveal that to me so I may surrender all to You.

Jesus has been given all authority, and His authority is authentic and reliable.

A History of Rejection

"Therefore still having one son, his beloved, he also sent him to them last, saying, 'They will respect my son.' " (Mark 12:6)

We know that Jesus loved teaching in parables, because through these poignant illustrations, He simplified abstract concepts while revealing the hearts of His listeners. But not everyone appreciated what Jesus was revealing in those sometimes piercing stories. A case in point is the parable of the tenants, which infuriated the religious leaders He was addressing.

Jesus saw their rejection of truth as being the same as their ancestors, who killed God's prophets who were sent to correct them and turn their hearts to God. The Jewish leaders had claimed to accept God's message but had a history that proved otherwise. Outwardly, to the people of God, they appeared to be honoring God. But Jesus knew their hearts, and their hearts, in fact, were far from Him. After just verbally sparring with the chief priests and other religious leaders (see Mark 11:27–33), the parable of the tenants was like pouring salt on an open wound. Just in case they didn't fully understand Jesus, He gave a very clear and embarrassing picture of their disobedience.

The parable makes it perfectly clear: If you do not listen to Jesus, you have refused your last hope. Jesus is God's final offer. Nothing else remains when Jesus is refused. No one else will be sent. No further messengers are waiting in heaven. If you reject Jesus, then you reject your last chance at help and hope.

Father God, may I never be too stubborn to receive your correction. May I always willingly accept all that Jesus has to say, even when it goes against my preconceived thoughts.

Jesus is God's final offer of salvation to humanity.

Building on the Cornerstone

"The stone which the builders rejected has become the chief cornerstone." (Mark 12:10–11)

In every stone building, one stone is crucial. It is laid first, and it is there to ensure that the building is square and stable. It is the rock upon which the weight of the entire structure rests. It is the cornerstone. The Bible describes Jesus as the "chief cornerstone" of our faith, a stone upon which the weight of our salvation rests. Isaiah 28:16 says, "So this is what the Sovereign LORD says: 'See, I lay a stone in Zion, a tested stone, a precious cornerstone for a sure foundation' " (NIV).

The very people who should have most welcomed the coming of Jesus rejected Him. It is a warning to all the religiously proud and biblically astute, the well-learned and the self-confident. No amount of religious education can take the place of Jesus. You may know Greek and Hebrew, you may hold a church office, and you may even be well-respected, but nothing takes the place of Jesus, our cornerstone. When the pressures of life bear down on you, there's only one cornerstone capable of handling the weight. It won't be your education, it won't be your position, and it won't be your reputation. There's only one cornerstone you can trust to handle the weight of life's issues. That cornerstone is Jesus. Trust Him with every aspect of your life, and you will find that He never fails. He's not just a rock; He's the cornerstone. Some accept Jesus, and some reject Him. Why do some reject Jesus? Simply put, they want to build something different from what God is building.

Lord Jesus, you are my rock and my foundation. You are the surety for my heart, my home, and the work of my hands. You are my life's chief cornerstone.

> **Either you will build your life on the cornerstone of Jesus, or you will trip over it.**

Paying Taxes: The Ancient IRS

"Render to Caesar the things that are Caesar's, and to God the things that are God's." (Mark 12:17)

God establishes governments. Those who are in positions of power and authority in government have been placed there by God, whether you voted for them or not, and whether you like them or not. God has put government in place (see Romans 13:1).

In another feeble and obvious attempt to entrap Jesus, the religious leaders asked Jesus if it was lawful to pay taxes to Caesar. Since Rome was an immoral government, many Jews felt that it was immoral to pay taxes. So the trap was set. To reject taxes showed Jesus to be a traitor to Caesar, and to support taxes showed Him to be a traitor to His own people. In one succinct sentence (see Mark 12:17 above), Jesus showed that God and Caesar each had legitimate realms of authority with corresponding responsibilities. But if there is a conflict between kingdoms, God is supreme over all human authority. We must never go so far in rendering unto Caesar that we violate our obligation to God, who is sovereign over all.

Jesus changed the subject and moved the debate from the earthly realm to the heavenly realm. Their money had Caesar's image on it, so it belonged to Caesar. But human beings bear the image of God, so we belong to God. That means the business of rendering unto God what is God's involves all creation bringing glory to Him by living according to His Word.

Father, thank You for helping me to see life rightly and for always putting life issues in their proper perspective so that I understand who I am, and to whom I am responsible.

Jesus affirms human government while acknowledging the sovereign authority of God.

Knowing the Word of God

*"Are you not therefore mistaken, because you do not know the
Scriptures nor the power of God? (Mark 12:24)*

How important is the Word of God to you? Everything God does
in the Christian life, He does through the Word of God or the Holy
Spirit. Your attitude and approach toward God's Word will determine
what God will accomplish in your life.

The religious leaders should have known God's Word the best,
but Jesus gave them an embarrassing talking-to when He told them
they were wrong and didn't really know God's Word. Ouch. That had
to hurt. But believers can be just as guilty as the Sadducees, because
it is tempting to read a passage or two out of context, build a theology around it, and ignore the larger truths and teachings of God's
Word. When we don't know God's Word, we lose our grip on truth.
When we lose our grip on truth, we open ourselves up to all sorts of
falsehoods. If we are going to know truth, then we must know Word
of God.

We can avoid many mistakes in life by simply knowing and better
applying the truths in our Bibles. The better we know our Bibles, the
better equipped we will be to identify error and avoid being lead astray
by it. Our greatest goal in this life should be to glorify God and grow
in our knowledge of His Word. The success of your Christian life
largely depends on your devotedness to knowing the Word of God.

*Father, forgive me for the times in my life when I have taken Your
Word for granted. Keep me in Your Word and always hungry to know
You better.*

> **Knowing Jesus better means knowing your
> Bible better.**

Knowing the Power of God

*"Are you not therefore mistaken, because you do not know the
Scriptures nor the power of God? (Mark 12:24)*

There is greater power in God than there is in the entire universe. God
is infinitely great and infinitely powerful. The problem is that God's
power is often misunderstood, because we tend to think of it in terms
of physical strength or as a variety of resources at His disposal. But the
power of God is the intrinsic and inherent ability of the omnipotent
God to carry out His will. The power of God is demonstrated by His
ability to accomplish His will in every situation by any means He
chooses in order to glorify Himself. God's power is centered on His
will and His glory.

When the chief priests, scribes, and elders confronted Jesus,
their first mistake was not knowing the true meaning of the Word
of God. Their second mistake was not knowing the true meaning
of the power of God. Had they understood the true nature and character of the miracle-working God revealed in the Scriptures, they
would not have doubted the power of God or that Jesus was God
personified.

Today there is a tendency to focus on one or the other. Many people focus on knowing the Word of God but fail to embrace the power
of God, which is so necessary for His Word to be properly applied
and obeyed. Others are overwhelmingly concerned with the power
of God but lack the stability that only the Word of God can provide.
This is why we must seek to live in spirit and truth, pursuing both the
knowledge of God's Word and the knowledge of God's power.

*God, I know You work in powerful ways in my daily life through
answered prayer, provision, direction, healing, and hope. May I
never lose sight of Your wonder-working power.*

**Jesus is the embodiment of God's Word and
the personification of God's power.**

Relationships in Heaven

"For when they rise from the dead, they neither marry nor are given in marriage, but are like angels in heaven." (Mark 12:25)

Marriage in heaven won't be the same as marriage on Earth. Of all the Bible verses about marriage, the words "they neither marry nor are given in marriage" from Mark 12:25 are unlikely to be read during a wedding ceremony or hung over the doorpost of your home. Those of us who are blessed with good marriages may be distressed by what Jesus says here, thinking that eternity might be devoid of those special relationships with our loved ones.

While the relationship of marriage is a wonderful and divinely ordained covenant, earthly marriage will be replaced one day by a new heavenly marriage. Marriage on Earth represents the marriage of Jesus to His bride, the church. In Heaven there will only be one marriage in which we all are married to Jesus. Jesus reminds us not to think of heaven as an extension of Earth as we know it. Our relationships to one another will be different in heaven from what we are accustomed to on Earth. Physical laws no longer will apply, and social relationships will take on a new dimension because we all will be in perfect relationship with God. We anticipate by faith what He has promised for the future, but we struggle because we can't begin to imagine the reality of it.

Even though we understand that Jesus meant people won't continue to be married in heaven, it doesn't mean that deep relationships will cease there. We have been created with a desire for companionship, which always has been designed to be fully fulfilled by God. We will worship God together and be one family forever.

Father God, I know my heavenly relationship with You will satisfy my every need.

> **Our relationship with Jesus will surpass all earthly relationships.**

Life After Death

"Have you not read . . . , 'I am the God of Abraham, the God
of Isaac, and the God of Jacob'? He is not the God of the dead,
but the God of the living." (Mark 12:26–27)

You were made to live forever. Death is not a period; it's a comma. Even though your heart will stop beating one day, your life won't be over. You will rise from the dead to live eternally.

The Sadducees didn't believe in the resurrection, and they only accepted the first five books of the Bible, called the Pentateuch. So in order to explain to them that they were wrong about life after death, Jesus quoted from Exodus 3:6. He made the point that God said "I am," not "I was," the God of Abraham, the God of Isaac and the God Jacob, demonstrating that these men of faith were very much alive. In other words, Jesus was affirming that God is the God of the living, and these patriarchs are living because of the immortality of the soul and the reality of a resurrected body. Death does not break our the relationship with God. The patriarchs were dead to the visible world, but they still were alive unto God in the invisible world.

What we hope in for tomorrow always changes how we live today. Who we are today and how we choose to live each day should be directed by what we know is coming tomorrow. The promise of resurrection life is more than a promise of eternal life. It is a promise of living with, and worshiping perfectly, God forever. As Christians we are living for God this side of heaven, and we will be living with God on the other side of this world.

God, help me to live for You today as I wait to live with You forever.

> **Jesus stresses that death changes our**
> **relationship to the world, but it does not**
> **change our relationship to God.**

The Shema

*"The first of all commandments is: Hear, O Israel, the LORD
our God, the LORD is one."* (Mark 12:29)

Your mind is like a muscle. The more you use it. the stronger it
becomes. Our minds include our perceptive and rational thoughts,
ideas, imaginations, and feelings. They control how we reason and
what we believe. To expand our mental capacities for God, we need
to train and renew our minds through disciplined development.
Spiritual disciplines like study, meditation, and memorization of
Scripture—especially long passages of Scripture—will help get us into
the flow of godly living.

In Jesus's day, reciting the Shema meant renewing your relationship with God. This was done regularly, even multiple times a day.
Whenever someone recited the Shema, they celebrated God's grace
and proclaimed their faithfulness to God alone. Life is all about loving and living for God, and the Shema expresses the foundation of
Christian living. We will do our minds and lives a great service to
know and live by the Shema:

"Hear, O Israel: The LORD our God, the LORD is one. Love
the LORD your God with all your heart and with all your soul
and with all your strength. These commandments that I give you
today are to be on your hearts. Impress them on your children.
Talk about them when you sit at home and when you walk along
the road, when you lie down and when you get up. Tie them as
symbols on your hands and bind them on your foreheads. Write
them on the doorframes of your houses and on your gates."
(Deuteronomy 6:4–9 NIV)

*Jesus, help me to live by the principles found in the Shema, for it is a
beautifully simplified summary of living a godly life.*

**Jesus used the Shema to remind us how to live
holy lives.**

Loving God

"And you shall love the Lord your God with all your heart, with all your soul, with all your mind, and with all your strength.' This is the first commandment. (Mark 12:30)

The essence of true worship is the love of God. Knowing God includes believing Him, trusting Him, and worshiping Him. Simply put, it is loving Him. When Jesus states loving God as the greatest command, it is not only to become the defining force for how we feel about God in our *hearts*, but it also should stimulate our desire for Him in our *souls*. It should inspire the thoughts of our *minds* toward God and become the driving force that gives *strength* to our obedience. Loving God motivates every decision we make and empowers us to live lives that please Him.

Loving God with all your heart begins in the deepest part of your being and often is expressed when you're talking about God, because "out of the abundance of the heart [the] mouth speaks" (Luke 6:45) . Loving God with all your soul is the overflow of your emotions and often is expressed when you're kindhearted. Loving God with all your mind, the seat of our intellect and will, often is expressed when you're intentional in your pursuit of knowing God. And finally, loving God with all your strength happens as you're doing—when you're exerting physical energy pursuing and serving God.

God, You designed us to be loving worshipers, to love You with all our hearts, souls, minds, and strength. Empower me by Your Spirit to grow to love You with such an all-encompassing love.

Jesus calls us to love God completely.

Loving Others

"And the second, like it, is this: 'You shall love your neighbor as yourself.' There is no other commandment greater than these." (Mark 12:31)

It is just a fact: Some people are hard to get along with, no matter how hard you might try. Some people even seem to enjoy being difficult. Maybe it's the "get off my lawn!" individual, or the micromanaging boss, or the inconsiderate, loud-music neighbor. No one said that loving your neighbor would be easy, but it is necessary.

To begin with, we must not limit our neighbor to those who live next to us. Our neighbor, according to Jesus, includes anyone and everyone we have the opportunity to meet along life's journey. In other words, our neighbor is everyone. But did you catch what He said? (See Mark 12:31 above.) We are not only to love others, but we are to love others in the same way we love ourselves. Now that is a tall order. What Jesus was saying is that we need to think about others as much as we think about ourselves. He means that we should remember the needs of others like we remember our own needs. We should be seeking the happiness, goodness, peace, and security of others as much as we seek those things in our own lives. Loving others means wanting what is best for them, caring about what happens to them, and actively using the gifts and influence God has given us to make a godly impact in the lives of others. It is impossible to love God and hate others but loving others they way God wants requires His help.

Dear God, I know that my love for others is a reflection of my love for You. So fill me with a supernatural love for others so that I never do wrong toward my neighbors.

Jesus loves people, and we *must* love others too.

All You Need is Love

"There is no other commandment greater than these."
(Mark 12:31)

We are not governed by rules but by love. Loving relationships are important to God, and a loving relationship with God enables us to have loving relationships with others. As we pursue our relationship with God in wholehearted devotion, the overflow of God's love in our lives will spill over into the lives of others. It must always be God first and people second, because we cannot give to others if we are spiritually bankrupt. God always must come first in our lives.

Love is to be such a dominant aspect in the life of a Christian that a Christian can actually be recognized by the quality of his or her love. Jesus said, "By this all will know that you are My disciples, if you love one for another" (John 13:35). But God wouldn't tell you to love others if He wasn't going to help you do that.

Love is learned! That means the more we see it in action and the more we practice loving others, the better we will become at it. The best way to learn how to love God and love others is by looking at Jesus. As we follow His life, we see what perfect love for God looks like and how perfect love for others is expressed as we give God all our energy, passion, and zeal. Only by loving God supremely will we be able to genuinely love others. And as we truly love others, we demonstrate that we love God supremely. No wonder Jesus said, "There is no other commandment greater than these."

Jesus, fill me with Your love. Teach me and enable me to love God and to love others as You showed me through Your life.

Jesus makes love the most important thing in life.

David's Riddle

"David himself calls Him 'Lord'; how is He then his Son?"
(Mark 12:37)

I love riddles. For example, what gets wet while it is drying? Jesus sometimes chose to communicate through unconventional means. For some of His listeners, it may have even felt as though He was giving them a riddle or puzzle to solve.

The Jewish leaders were looking for someone like David to appear as a patriotic political leader, one chosen by God, anointed by God, and a natural descendant of David's. So one day while Jesus was teaching in the temple, He asked the million-dollar question, a question about the Messiah's identity. Jesus, quoting from Psalm 110, said that David himself said by the Holy Spirit, "The LORD said to my Lord, 'Sit at My right hand, till I make Your enemies Your footstool' " (verse 1). He raised the question of how the Christ is both Son and Lord. I wonder if any of the people arguing that night managed to figure it out. This riddle is only solvable if you know that Jesus, the Messiah, is both God and man—human and divine. As a man, He is David's son; as God, He is David's Lord.

It is a riddle for the natural mind. Its solution only can be supplied by the Spirit of God opening the eyes of our hearts to see the truth of the Messiah, who is both the Son of David, and the Son of God, fully God and fully man. Tragically, what Jesus said will remain a riddle to the natural, unbelieving mind, because this incredible truth only can be solved and understood by grace through faith. (By the way, if you've been trying to figure out the riddle in the first paragraph, the answer is a towel.)

Jesus, the incarnation is a deep mystery, but it is also leads me to worship You greatly.

> **Jesus is more than the Son of David. He's the Son of Man.**

Watch Out for Fakes

"Beware of the scribes, who desire to go around in long robes, love greetings in the marketplaces, the best seats in the synagogues, and the best places at feasts, who devour widows' houses, and for a pretense make long prayers. These will receive greater condemnation." (Mark 12:38–40)

Warning! Danger! Attention! When we see words like these on signs, it causes us to stop, take notice, and proceed with caution. When Jesus uses an attention-grabbing word like *beware*, everyone should stop, take notice, and proceed with caution.

Religious fakes, professional charlatans, frauds, hucksters, and scam artists use their religious position for their own financial gain. We are not talking about hardworking pastors or honest Christian ministries. Rather, we are talking about hypocrites who see religion as a way to make a buck and who intentionally prey on unsuspecting people. Unfortunately, this is nothing new. Jesus draws our attention to scribes, who were guilty of devouring widows' houses. Jesus warned that things are not always as they appear. The scribes were highly respected religious leaders in the first century, and many of them took advantage of that respect for their own selfish gain. They used sacred religious practices to line their pockets and receive special treatment. But those respectable exteriors hid hypocrisy and deceit.

Beware of pretend piety and religious showmanship. It's better to have less with a humble heart than more with a prideful heart. No one is perfect, but let's not pretend to be holier than we are.

God, guard my heart and protect me from outward piety and shameless self-advancement.

Jesus wants us to have nothing to do with religious fakers.

Two Mites

"Truly I tell you, this poor widow has put more into the treasury than all the others. They all gave out of their wealth; but she, out of her poverty, put in everything—all she had to live on." (Mark 12:43–44 NIV)

Little things can make a big difference with God. A few stones and a sling can drop a giant, a couple of sardines and a crust of bread can feed a multitude, a walking stick can part an ocean, and a few cents from a poor widow can do more than thousands from the well-to-do.

One day a widow walked into the temple court, unnoticed by the crowd but seen by God. In her poverty, loneliness, and helplessness, she went faithfully to the temple to worship God and present her meager offering. Among the loud, resonating clanks heard from the heavy-hitter givers, her coins fell silently and unheard by the crowd. But her small offering made a big noise with God. Jesus, seeing what this simple widow did, seized the moment to highlight the true nature of giving to God. According to Jesus, she gave more than anyone else, even though she gave the least.

The reason this poor widow gave more is not because of the quantity she gave but because of the proportion she gave. Where others gave from their overflow, she gave of her sustenance. God sees all we do, even when it might seem small and insignificant. Never underestimate the impact that little things can have when they're placed in the hands of a big God.

Dear God, I know my giving is not measured by the amount I give but by my willingness to give sacrificially. Help me to let go of my selfishness and love You with sacrificial generosity.

Jesus sees what is often overlooked by others.

Deception

"Take heed that no one deceives you. For many will come in My name, saying, 'I am the Christ,' and will deceive many."
(Matthew 24:4–5)

Not everything you think and feel is true. We all can have intellectual blind spots. Everyone is open to error. No one is free from fault. Limited knowledge and a sinful nature leave us vulnerable to misunderstand, misread, misquote, and misjudge reality.

With so many voices and opinions vying for our attention, it can be challenging at times for anyone to separate fact from fiction. Throughout the Scriptures, we are warned against the dangers of deception, not only in the end times but also in our day-to-day lives. Deception happens when you get swept away by a wrong idea, but you're convinced that it is truth. That's what Paul warned Timothy about when he said that people will reject the truth and chase after myths (see 2 Timothy 4:3–4 NIV).

So how do we protect against deceptive philosophies, false Christs, erroneous arguments, and intellectual blind spots? We have to start with God. God is the standard of truth. Our best defense against deception is the personal and regular study of the Bible. We can choose to base our decisions on what we think, on what other people think, or on what God thinks. Hold fast to the truth of God so that no one leads you astray.

God, I pray that You would give me discernment and wisdom so that I will be on guard against those who might try to deceive.

> **If you are disconnected from Jesus, you are open to deception.**

Signs of the Times

"And you will hear of wars and rumors of wars. See that you are not troubled; for all these things must come to pass, but the end is not yet. . . . All these are the beginning of sorrows."
(Matthew 24:6, 8)

How is the world going to end? The Bible is not silent when it comes to the end times, that is, what will take place on Earth shortly before Jesus returns. The world is a chaotic place, and there will be tumultuous events that will precede Jesus's return. These turbulent convulsions have been divinely permitted as part of God's eschatological schedule for this world.

War is brutal business. But even with the obvious cruelties of war, history proves our obsession with warmongering. Jesus warned us that war always would be with us, and, in fact, it even would increase as time went on. He also made it clear that these things *must* take place, but the end is not right now. The presence of war, famine, false teachers, natural disasters, and pandemics does not mean the end is upon us but merely that these things are the beginning of the end. Jesus said that the frequency and intensity of these events will increase until finally God brings everything to an end.

We won't understand everything about the end times, and that's okay. Jesus isn't trying to confuse us or discourage us but to give us comfort in knowing that even as bad as these painful realities are, believers do not need to be worried. God is in control and has a sovereign plan for the world.

Father God, regardless of when You return, pour out Your protection, wisdom, boldness and power so that I may be engaged in the world, living out and sharing the gospel.

> **The timing of the end is unclear, but Jesus's return and victory is certain.**

Enduring Faith

"And because lawlessness will abound, the love of many will grow cold. But he who endures to the end shall be saved."
(Matthew 24:12–13)

The Christian life isn't easy. Some mistakenly assume that once they become part of God's family, their struggles will be over. But once pressures mount and difficulties surface, they can lose heart and give up. Our faith is not proven by how we begin but by how we finish. Perseverance is the evidence of genuine faith. Belief involves more than just a momentary decision; it involves a life of following God and living according to His Word, regardless of the difficulties we face.

Jesus told His disciples to be on guard for what awaited them. He didn't want them to be surprised by the many trials and tribulations that were ahead of them. As much as Jesus was warning the first-century disciples of the unique trials awaiting them, His admonition also applies to us today. We do not know all the events and trials that will precede the turbulent end times that lead to the return of Jesus, but we do know that we are called to be faithful until the end as we wait.

As Christians, we are able to endure because of the power of the Holy Spirit at work in us. Perseverance does not save us; it is a demonstration of the genuineness of our salvation. Our continued perseverance to follow God and live for Him will ensure our ability to endure until the end.

Jesus, renew my strength and let my faith be an enduring faith, unshakable, immovable, and steadfastly focused on You each and every day.

Intimacy with Jesus provides the power to endure.

The Beginning of the End

"Therefore when you see the 'abomination of desolation,'
spoken of by Daniel the prophet, standing in the holy place . . ."
(Matthew 24:15)

If you were to put ten theologians in a room and ask them to list some of the most difficult Bible passages to understand, it wouldn't take long for them all to list Matthew 24:15.

The abomination of desolation is a prophetic event found in the book of Daniel (see 12:11) that Jesus refers to here, though it has some historical fulfillments. Antiochus IV Epiphanes, who ruled Palestine from 175–164 BC, treated Israel with such violence and contempt that they rebelled against him. When he came to suppress the rebellion, his forces entered the temple, stopped the regular sacrifices, set up an idol, and offered blasphemous sacrifices of swine on the altar. This was an abomination of desolation. But there is also a future fulfillment when daily sacrifices will be offered in Jerusalem and then cut off and replaced by some sort of blasphemous display. This prophecy of Jesus is significant, because it represents an important time marker signaling the nearness of the final return of Jesus Christ.

Regardless of how you view the totality of end times prophecies playing out, one thing is shared: how we should live in light of the coming return of Jesus. We should carefully watch the events of the world and their relationship to biblical prophecy, wait patiently and expectantly for Jesus's certain return, walk worthy of our calling, and work for the Lord while there is still time.

Jesus, although I may not understand everything about how the end times will play out, I know that how I live in light of Your return is what matters most.

Jesus gives us a visible sign that will start the beginning of the end.

The Worst is Yet to Come

"For then there will be great tribulation, such as has not been since the beginning of the world until this time, no, nor ever shall be." (Matthew 24:21)

The world will get immeasurably worse before it gets immeasurably better. The horrors of the Holocaust will pale in comparison to what is coming. There is a time that is fast approaching when there will be unparalleled devastation, unequalled suffering, unrivaled brutality, and unmatched deception. I wish this were an exaggeration, but it's not. The dangers Jesus warned of are things His church has faced from the beginning: deceiving teachers, persecution, and disasters. But what Jesus was saying here is that all of these will increase and intensify as His return draws near.

Why would God allow such a horrific time to exist? One purpose for the Great Tribulation will be to lead people, especially His chosen nation of Israel, to repentance. Jesus Christ gives us warnings to encourage us to get right with Him and to live out His life-transforming message. Jesus's warnings also encourage us to endure difficulties and remain faithful as His witnesses in the face of whatever tribulations we might face. Hardships should not make us bitter; they should make us better.

We do not know the day or the hour of His return, but we do know that those who are watching and waiting for Jesus to come back will be living rightly. No matter what is happening here on Earth, God wants us to keep our eyes on the heavens.

Jesus, I know that because of You, I am ultimately a victor over the trials in life. I know that nothing in this world can separate me from Your unwavering love. Please give me the strength to endure whatever trials come my way.

Jesus gives warnings to encourage us to live rightly.

Lightning Crashes

"For as the lightning comes from the east and flashes to the west, so also will the coming of the Son of Man be. For wherever the carcass is, there the eagles will be gathered together." (Matthew 24:27–28)

The second coming of Jesus Christ will be globally unmistakable. His appearing will be sudden, visible, dramatic, glorious, and universal. Just as certain as He came, He certainly will come again. When Jesus came the first time, it was a quiet and unassuming arrival. When Jesus comes the second time, it will be cataclysmic and conquering. For those who belong to Christ, His coming will be a marvelous deliverance from a horrible period of time, but for those who have opposed Him, it will be a day of reckoning.

Most of us think of the here and now rather than the then and there. But we should encourage one another with the knowledge of Jesus's return (see 1 Thessalonians 4:18). The hope of His return steadies our souls and enables us to face all sorts of hardships and persecutions, because we know that at the return of Jesus, the presence of the curse finally will be removed. He will establish His holy kingdom, where there will be spiritual blessings and no evil. Even though we do not know when Christ is coming back, we can have confidence that He will return, and we can purpose to live in the here and now with our minds anticipating His then-and-there coming.

God, although it might be hard to wrap my mind around the reality of Jesus's Second Coming, it is true. I want to live every day as though it were my last. I want to work diligently, anticipating Christ's return.

Find hope in the fact that Jesus is coming back!

OCTOBER

Angels

"And He will send His angels with a great sound of a trumpet." (Matthew 24:31)

Few things capture the imagination like angels. Their stories in the Bible read like the science fiction imaginations of Hollywood, but they are far more than fiction fodder. Despite popular depictions, angels do not ride puffy white clouds, slide down rainbows, come with twinkly music, play harps, or resemble babies with apple cheeks. Angels are spiritual beings created by God to serve Him and act as His messengers.

Angels are mentioned more than three hundred times in the Bible. We see them ministering to Jesus in the desert. They showed up at the Resurrection and the Ascension, and the book of Revelation is full of them, with repeated reminders not to worship them. They are vast in number (see Revelations 5:11), they are marked with incredible strength (according to 2 Kings 19:35, one angel in one night slayed 185,000 members of the Assyrian army), and they work tirelessly to protect and serve God's people (see Hebrews 1:14). One of the most spectacular angelic events the world will ever see will be when heaven is emptied and all the angels come with Jesus to gather up the believers to meet with the Son of God.

It is true that God works in mysterious ways, and the unseen world of angels certainly qualifies as mysterious and intriguing. But even with all the mystery that surrounds these amazing beings, and even though they should not be the focus of our attention, one thing is clear: they are great examples of obedient servants and faithful worshipers. And one day we will be gathered together to worship and serve God communally and harmoniously.

God, I am thankful for your special messengers and guardians and how they help us on Earth.

One day Jesus will come with all the heavenly hosts.

Election

***"And He will send His angels with a great sound of a trumpet,
and they will gather together His elect from the four winds,
from one end of heaven to the other." (Matthew 24:31)***

If you are looking for a theological fight, then just bring up the subject of election. Few topics have sparked more debate throughout church history than the subject of election. The doctrine of election is still a misunderstood and mismanaged truth among many of God's people, because after all the doctrinal dust settles, most debates have only caused more division and less unity.

Let's face it. Some things in the Bible are just hard to understand. But here is what you should know about the subject of election. The Bible teaches both the election of God and the choice of humankind. Throughout the Bible, two truths have run parallel: God is in absolute and complete control of the universe, and people are responsible for the choices they make. God's sovereignty and people's responsibility seem opposite and irreconcilable truths, and from our limited perspective, they are. Divine sovereignty and human responsibility are integral and inseparable parts of salvation, though only God knows how they operate together. They are two equivalent truths that run side by side, only uniting at the throne of God.

God's sovereignty is not the enemy of our responsibility. No one has completely solved this mystery, so let's seek to share the common ground of love and remember that God has a plan for our lives, and the choice is ours as to whether or not we'll live according to His will.

God, Your sovereignty is never weakened by my choices. Even though I may not fully understand how there is no conflict between Your sovereignty and my freedom, I rest in Your ability to allow them to coexist.

> **God is sovereign, we are responsible, and one day Jesus will come for His chosen people.**

Ready for His Return?

"But of that day and hour no one knows, not even the angels of heaven, but My Father only. . . . Therefore you also be ready, for the Son of Man is coming at an hour you do not expect." (Matthew 24:36, 44)

Jesus is coming again. Personally and visibly, He is coming back. Are you ready to meet Jesus when He returns? Even though we do not know the day or the hour of His return, one thing is certain: Jesus expects us to be living in a state of readiness.

Readiness for the return of Jesus is less about looking for Him to appear in the sky tomorrow and more about living to glorify Him today. Readiness starts by being right with God. If there is something in your life that has come between you and God, the time to deal with it is today. Do not put off till tomorrow what you need to fix today. Readiness also means serving Jesus now. Remember that while we are waiting for Jesus to return, God is still working in the world today, and He has work for you and me to do (see Ephesians 2:10). Lastly, readiness means that you are actively and continually cultivating your spiritual life so that you are sensitive to God's leading and the opportunities He provides to serve Him and show His love to others while you await His return. In other words, stay close to Jesus and "continue in him, so that when he appears we may be confident and unashamed before him at his coming" (1 John 2:28 NIV). Stay close to Jesus by reading His Word, spending time in prayer, and continuing to be in community with God's people. Think less about *getting* ready and more about *living* ready.

God, prepare me for what You are preparing for me. May I not only wait expectantly for Jesus but also live purposefully until He comes again.

> **Jesus could come at any time. Therefore, we should be ready all the time.**

The Dangers of Laziness

"You wicked, lazy servant!" (Mathew 25:26 NIV)

Do you do as little as possible, as slowly as possible, and with as little effort as possible? Is your motto, "I'll get around to it" or "Why do today what I can put off until tomorrow"? We all have periods of time when we feel less energetic and struggle to find motivation. Sure, sometimes we feel like enjoying a lazy summer afternoon. At other times we just need a break to recharge and refocus. Neither of those are bad, but we all are capable of becoming lazy if we are not careful.

Laziness is a common problem in the workplace, in school, and even in relationships, and the Bible is unmistakably clear that laziness is a sin. We were created to work—not to be workaholics but to faithfully complete the work God has given us to do, and to do good works for the glory of God. For the believer, there is no such thing as secular work. Every task is to be a sacred reflection of our commitment to honor God in all we do. Therefore, all laziness is a form of spiritual laziness. Remember, the Bible tells us, "Whatever you do, work at it with all your heart, as working for the Lord. . . . It is the Lord Christ you are serving" (Colossians 3:23–24 NIV).

We also need to guard against becoming lazy with our faith. When we take our faith for granted, pray halfheartedly, stop reading the Bible, or stop spending time with God, we are being lazy with our faith. Laziness is not overcome with busyness; we combat laziness by being spiritually proactive. Stop making excuses, start moving in the right direction, don't let your feelings dictate your spiritual productivity, ask God for help, and get started today!

Jesus, destroy every form of laziness that might keep me from being productive in all areas of my life.

Jesus will say "well done" to those who don't give in to laziness.

Blessed to be a Blessing

"For to everyone who has, more will be given, and he will have abundance; but from him who does not have, even what he has will be taken away." (Matthew 25:29)

God wants to bless your life, and He wants you to be a blessing in others' lives. God has built into every believer spiritual gifts, passions, unique abilities, personality traits, and talents. This is what makes you uniquely you and qualified to accomplish what God has for *you* to do. In other words, God has given you everything you need to do what He has called you to do and be the person He has called you to be. But God gave you all these things to benefit others, not just yourself.

It is not acceptable merely to put all God's gifts aside and ignore them. The actions God takes toward a person depend on the actions that person takes toward God (see James 4:8). You have been created to worship and serve God, and the more you put into growing and serving Him, the more God will bless you with so that you can be an even greater blessing to even more people. The less you use what God has given you, the less you will see God work in and through your life.

We all have been given much (see 1 Corinthians 4:7), and "each of [us] should use whatever gift [we] have received to serve others, as faithful stewards of God's grace" (1 Peter 4:10 NIV). We should ask God for wisdom on how to use the resources He has given us for His purposes so that He may be glorified. And remember, God rewards each person according to what they have done with what He has given them. Are you using your gifts for the benefit and blessing of others?

Lord, help me to be faithful and to use the gifts, talents, and abilities that You have given me to assist and benefit others.

Jesus encourages the generous giving of ourselves to others.

Did Hell Move?

"Depart from Me, you cursed, into the everlasting fire prepared for the devil and his angels." (Matthew 25:41)

Hell has fallen on hard times. It seems as though hell has boarded up its windows and placed a "for sale" sign out front. The idea of eternal punishment and the wrath of God seem to be forgotten and untouched teachings today. Who wants to hear a message about wrath, punishment, and anguish? Most of us would rather hear about the love, grace, and mercy of God. It seems as though more and more people look at faith as nothing more than fire insurance. They are like the little girl who prayed, "Lord, make me good—not too good, but just good enough not to get a spanking."

When we come to God to receive salvation, we must accept what He is saving us from. Jesus described hell as an eternal fire, prepared for the Devil and his helpers. But just as hell was prepared for Satan and his agents of evil who rebelled and rejected God, it is also a place reserved for anyone who chooses to rebel and reject God. If you look to Jesus just to make you feel better about your sin and ease your conscience, but you continually live for yourself, then you are exploiting His grace and missing the point of salvation.

Hell is a painful reality, and therefore it is understandable why we do not like to talk about it. However, we need to understand the reality of hell so that people might understand how much they need the good news of the gospel. Neglecting the reality of hell weakens the seriousness of God's view of sin. God loves you, He encourages you to accept His grace, and He doesn't want anyone to experience the reality of hell.

God, you have given me the way to heaven. I choose to follow You and be where You are.

Heaven is the only place where you will eternally experience the love of Jesus.

Timing Is Everything

"The hour has come that the Son of Man should be glorified."
(John 12:23)

Our days are numbered, and we all have an appointment with death (see Hebrews 9:27). That is not intended to be overly dramatic or unnecessarily morbid, but it is the truth. When we come to that appointed time, what matters most is not the wealth we've accumulated, how high up the corporate ladder we climbed, or what neighborhood we lived in. What will matter most is this: Did you give your life to Jesus? And did your life reflect that choice by living out His will for you?

Jesus knew His days were numbered. He knew He was on His Father's timetable, and while He was fulfilling God's will and doing God's work, He was protected until His appointed time. The religious leaders who sought to kill Jesus would not be permitted to seize Him until God allowed it. Until that time, Jesus would accomplish all the work God set out for Him to do, culminating in His final work on the cross when He would then say, "It is finished!" (John 19:30).

God has appointed and foreordained works for us to accomplish (see Ephesians 2:10), and our dedication to fulfill all that God has for us should be our primary purpose in life. And rest assured, we are completely protected until the work that God has for us is done, because He always will protect us and give us what is best.

God, help me to make a choice as to whether I will live my life for myself or lay hold of the hope, the glory, and the realization that lies beyond it and live fully submitted to Your will, realizing that my life is to be lived on Your schedule.

> **Like Jesus, we should continue to fulfill God's purpose for our lives until our appointed time.**

Dying to Live

"Most assuredly, I say to you, unless a grain of wheat falls into the ground and dies, it remains alone; but if it dies, it produces much grain." (John 12:24)

One of God's spiritual realities is that life comes from death. Take the seed, for example. God designed the seed's cycle of life and death in such a way that a plant cannot live and bear fruit unless a seed dies and is buried in the ground. Then the seed can spring forth with the promise of bearing fruit.

Jesus's life was lived in anticipation of His death. Throughout Jesus's life, He was careful to keep His crucifixion a secret. During His first miracle of turning water into wine, Jesus said, "My hour has not yet come" (John 2:4), and He repeated that to the disciples on more than one occasion (see John 7:30; 8:20). But then His hour arrived, and Jesus helped to explain the purpose of His death by comparing His life to a seed, which must first die to bear fruit. As 1 Corinthians 15:36 reminds us, "What you sow does not come to life unless it dies" (esv). In a similar way, we would not have eternal life unless Jesus first died for our sins.

This cycle of death and rebirth is part of God's plan for our rescue, because without the sacrificial death, burial, and resurrection of Jesus Christ, there would be no hope and no true life. It is, however, an example for us to follow. May we imitate Jesus, willingly dying to self so that through such a death, we may bear much fruit.

Jesus, thank you that You were willing to die to bring life. Teach me to take up my cross daily so that I, too, might bear fruit.

The life Jesus lived qualified Him for the death He died; His resurrection enables us to die to ourselves and bear lasting fruit unto life.

Following Jesus

"If anyone serves Me, let him follow Me; and where I am, there My servant will be also." (John 12:26)

Following Jesus is hard. Sometimes it can even feel like life gets harder the closer we get to Jesus. God calls us to live out His standards no matter what anyone else says. And let's be honest. That can be very difficult at times. Every step closer to God that we take, every time we do what's right over what's easy, and every choice we make to serve God rather than ourselves is a decision rooted in obedience, submission, and self-denial.

We are not saved by our service to God, but we are saved so that we might serve God. If we are going to accept salvation from Jesus, then we must be willing to accept that we are called to serve Jesus. Although no amount of self-sacrifice merits our salvation, no genuine service occurs without self-sacrifice. Jesus yielded His will all the time, in every situation, to the Father, and He was obedient even to death. That means when we serve Jesus and follow in submission and obedience, it often involves death. Only in Christianity does abundant life come by dying to ourselves. Our death in Christ is a death to our old selves, our old ways, and our sinful living.

Believers, we need to hold the same viewpoint as Jesus, living out the reality and the paradox that through death there is life.

Jesus, help me to faithfully follow You, emptying myself of my own plans and serving You through a self-giving, self-sacrificing, self-denying death that brings true life.

Jesus's sacrificial life for us means that we are to sacrificially live for Him.

God Honors Those Who Honor Him

"If anyone serves Me, him My Father will honor." (John 12:26)

Our response toward God will determine God's response toward us. Many people say they believe in God, but when it comes down to priorities, God is not number one. Few people honor anyone higher than themselves. God is not pleased if we worship Him at church but not at our workplace. It is not honoring to God to praise Him when we are with other Christians but ignore Him the rest of the time. God expects us to honor Him completely with our words, with our actions, and in all areas of our lives, always.

Fundamentally, when we honor God a few things happen. We will treat God as better than ourselves, because expressing God's supremacy gives honor to His authority. Honoring God changes us from self-absorbed egotists to people who exalt and elevate God. Honor is so vital that the Bible regularly stresses it. We are to honor God with our income (see Proverbs 3:9), with our bodies (see 1 Corinthians 6:20), and with humility (see Proverbs 15:33). The Bible also stresses what happens when we do not honor God. Romans 1:21 brilliantly depicts what happens when honor for God disappears from a person's life. Failing to honor God negatively affects our reasoning, our thinking becomes dysfunctional, and our hearts become darkened.

Our actions give worth to our words. So let's honor God with our words and our lives, because if we honor God, God also will honor us.

God, if I choose to live for myself, then I am honoring myself over You. Taking the focus off myself and instead placing it on You is the simplest way to start honoring You.

Honoring Jesus always pleases God.

Walking Shoes

"I have come as a light into the world, that whoever believes in Me should not abide in darkness." (John 12:46)

Walking has quite a few health benefits. Done regularly, it can be the key to losing weight, lowering blood pressure and cholesterol, and boosting your memory as well as reducing your risk for heart disease, diabetes, cancer, and more. The Bible describes our lives without Christ as living in darkness. Walking with God and knowing God is walking in the light. The Bible tells us that as Christians, we are "sons of light" (see John 12:36) and therefore should not walk in the darkness any longer.

Truth not only is that which we believe intellectually, but it is also that which we believe practically. We do not believe that God is light if we do not walk in the light. It doesn't mean that we walk perfectly, but it does mean that we walk with the Perfect One and seek His perfection for our lives. Walking in the light is a lifestyle whereby we are living under the direction of God instead of the influence of the world. It means seeing things the way God sees them, sharing His values and standards for life, and responding the way He would have us respond.

Walking with God has quite a few benefits as well. Done daily, it can be the key to losing the weight of sin, lowering the stresses of life, boosting your spiritual defenses, reducing your risk of heart issues, and more.

Thank you, God, for always shining Your light on me and on my life. May Your light always lead me and guide me. Help me walk in the light today and shine Your light on others.

Reflect Jesus by walking in the light.

What Is God Doing?

"What I am doing you do not understand now, but you will know after this." (John 13:7)

There are times when God's ways only make things more confusing. The Bible can serve as a spiritual textbook, complete with indexes referencing every subject imaginable. But what do you do when you can't find the answer to your question? We tend to prefer a God who is accommodating, and when we pray the right kind of prayers and offer willing obedience and suitable sacrifices, we expect God to give us a timely response so that our lives will work the way they're supposed to. But we should not expect to always understand everything God is doing.

You may have a PhD in theology, but you never will fully comprehend God or understand all His ways. God never promised that He would fill us in on all His plans. But we can be sure that God always does have a plan. Ultimately, whatever God is doing is for our good and His glory. God knows what He is doing. We are never promised all the answers, but trusting Jesus in the mystery of the unknown is what it truly means to walk by faith. Otherwise, we will live a shallow, cliché Christianity, which offers up quick and often unhelpful answers to the unknown questions we may be facing. We can strongly believe in Jesus and still have unanswered questions. Much of the Christian life is spent trusting Jesus now and understanding His plans later.

Jesus, I know that You don't always explain to me why You are doing something. Help me to trust even when I am tempted to object because I am unaware of Your purposes.

It is more important to trust Jesus than it is to always understand what He is doing.

Washed by Jesus

"If I do not wash you, you have no part with Me." (John 13:8)

There is a myth that says we must clean up our acts before we can come to God. The truth is that we can come to God with the good, the bad, and the ugly of our lives, because God promises to make us completely clean (Psalm 51:7). Once we have been cleansed from our past, present, and future sins through Jesus Christ, we have experienced the cleansing of salvation and do not need to be washed again in the spiritual sense. But the lifelong process of sanctification is one of washing ourselves from the filth of sin that we experience as we walk through the world.

Jesus explained to Peter that without cleansing, there is no fellowship with God. Jesus moved from the physical illustration of washing feet to the spiritual truth of washing the inner person. Jesus often spoke of spiritual truths in physical terms. God has rigid requirements for those who want to enjoy fellowship with Him. Unless Jesus cleanses us from our sin, we cannot share in intimate fellowship with Him. All cleansing in the spiritual realm can only come from Jesus, and the only way anyone can be clean is if they are washed by Jesus (see Titus 3:5).

It doesn't matter what we have done, how shameful we have behaved, or how many times we have made the same mistakes, because Jesus' cleansing is complete and permanent. Are you willing to let Jesus wash away your sins so that you can enjoy intimate fellowship with God?

Dear God, please wash me thoroughly from my iniquity and cleanse me from my sin. Forgive me for where I have missed the mark. Cleanse me spiritually so that I can be pure in Your eyes and have fellowship with You, now and forever.

Only Jesus can make you clean.

Clean Living in a Dirty World

"He who is bathed needs only to wash his feet, but is completely clean; and you are clean, but not all of you."
(John 13:10)

Living the Christian life isn't easy. We live in an unclean world that is full of all kinds of dirt, unbelief, anxiety, and evil. As we live out our daily lives, some of the impurities and negativities from this world rub off on us. Some of what we watch on television may leave an imprint on our minds, some of the people we hang out with may influence our behavior, and some of the conversations we have may affect our attitudes. So how do we cleanse ourselves from the spiritual dirt that we pick up?

Jesus made it clear that positionally we are clean once we trust Him for our salvation. That's called justification. But practically as we go through this life, we are going to get dirty from walking in the world and will need regular cleansing. First John 1:9 gives us the first step in washing away the dirt: "If we confess our sins, He is faithful and just to forgive us our sins and to cleanse us from all unrighteousness." We are going to get a little dirty as we live in this world, but we don't need to live in the mud. If we confess our sin, if we are sorry for it and turn from it, then God will be faithful to cleanse us. Then, just as fresh water cleanses our bodies, the "washing of water by the word" cleanses our souls (Ephesians 5:26). The Word of God purifies our thoughts, scrubs our motives, and cleans our consciences as we take it in and obey its truths.

God, cleanse me, and I will be forgiven. Wash me, and I will be clean. Give me purity of mind, body, and soul.

Jesus uses confession and the Word of God like soap and water to cleanse us.

Watch and Learn

"If I then, your Lord and Teacher, have washed your feet, you also ought to wash one another's feet. For I have given you an example, that you should do as I have done to you."
(John 13:14–15)

Hands that created the universe washed dirty feet. Fingers that painted the picturesque sky were muddied after they cleansed soiled feet. The roads and backstreets of Jerusalem were like winding dirt trails. Therefore, it was the custom of the day for a slave to wash the feet of guests as they arrived. With no servant present and no disciple offering to do the job, Jesus's kneeling to wash the disciple's feet was one of the most profound pictures of servanthood and humility the world ever has seen.

Jesus did more than talk about being a servant; He lived it. Jesus did more than wash feet that night; He left an unequaled example for us to follow. Jesus didn't establish another sacrament for us to follow by calling His disciples to wash feet, but He did set the standard to find ways to humble ourselves in service to others. Obeying this mandate in humility is not natural for us. Sure, there are times when we like to help others, but service that involves self-sacrifice is difficult to live out.

We are to follow this example of love and humility with a willingness to meet the needs of others, to put others before ourselves, to resist being puffed up with pride, and to stand ready to serve others.

Heavenly Father, give me a heart like the heart of Jesus, a heart more ready to serve than be served.

We serve Jesus when we serve others.

Just Do It

"If you know these things, blessed are you if you do them."
(John 13:17)

Knowing is not the same as doing. The biggest challenge in the Christian life is bridging the gap between knowing what to do and doing what we know to do. It's easier to read and listen to God's Word than to obey it. We have endless resources at our fingertips that will teach us and expand our knowledge and understanding of God, but we need to do more than talk the talk of our faith. We need to walk the walk of our faith.

Jesus not only encourages us to live out what we know to be true, but He also declares that as we live out His commands, we will find happiness. When we live lives that are committed to the actions of doing what God's Word instructs us to do, there is blessing. That blessing includes God's favor and His presence in our lives. It is no surprise that the brother of Jesus, someone who saw Jesus up close and personal, who saw God talk the talk and walk the walk, exhorts us to be "be doers of the word, and not hearers only, deceiving yourselves" (James 1:22).

The Bible provides us with the knowledge we need to live a blessed life, but the way to blessing requires action. We can't just listen to God's Word, we must do what it says, because the blessing does not come from knowing, it comes from doing. In other words, don't merely talk about compassion; lend a hand. Don't simply teach about generosity; give. Don't just agree with what Jesus says; do it.

God, may I always grow in the knowledge of You, but may that knowledge always be followed with a life of action.

> **We know Jesus is changing our lives when do what He says.**

The Pain of Betrayal

"Most assuredly, I say to you, one of you will betray Me."
(John 13:21)

Betrayal is one of the worst things a person can do to another person. When someone you have loved and trusted breaks your trust, it can feel as though the floor has dropped out from under you, and you begin to question everything you once believed to be true. Betrayal can shatter your self-esteem, make it hard to trust others, and cause you to doubt yourself. But don't forget that God understands betrayal because it happened to Him. And He can help you get through it.

What Judas Iscariot did to Jesus was appallingly unfair. There is no indication that Jesus ever mistreated Judas. There is no evidence that Judas ever was left out, neglected, or treated unfairly by Jesus in any way. During the Last Supper, when Jesus told the disciples that one of them at the table would betray Him, they didn't immediately react by collectively pointing their fingers at Judas. The fact of the matter is none of the disciples knew who the betrayer was (see John 13:24–25).

Jesus understands what it's like to be betrayed. He experienced physical wounds, and He experienced the emotional pain that comes from the betrayal of a close friend. There is no denying that betrayal hurts, but we should not let it ruin our lives. Surrender betrayal over to God before anxiety, bitterness, anger, or a desire for revenge take hold of your heart. The enemy wants us flounder in the pain of betrayal, but God wants us to forgive, receive His healing, and move forward with His plans and purposes for our lives.

Jesus, I thank You that You are there for me when I am hurting. Help me let go of my hurts and forgive others, even when trust has been broken, so that I may move forward with You.

People may betray you, but Jesus never will.

The Eleventh Commandment

"A new commandment I give to you, that you love one another;
as I have loved you, that you also love one another."
(John 13:34)

Love is not optional. If you follow Jesus, you must live a life of love. It is not a sacred suggestion or some good, heavenly advice. It is a command. Love was the foundation of Jesus's life and the very reason He came to the world (see John 3:16). So what makes this command to love new?

The command to love is not new in time, because God always has been a God of love. It is only new in expression. The command to love is new in that we are to love as He has loved us. It does not erase any earlier commands to love; it only adds to the expression of love and expands the spiritual depth of its significance. What does loving as He has loved us look like? His love was large and incredibly patient. His love was gentle and consistently kind. His love refused to be jealous. His love did not brag, traffic in shame or disrespect, and it did not selfishly seek its own honor but lived for the glory of the Father. His love was not easily irritated or quick to take offense. His love joyfully celebrated honesty and humility, and it found no delight in what is wrong. His love was and is a safe place that never stops believing and never gives up (see 1 Corinthians 13:4–7). His love was unconditional and sacrificial. He never stops loving, and neither should we.

Jesus, fill my heart with Your love. Help me love as abundantly and as
completely as You have loved me. Help me to show the same patience,
tolerance, kindness, and caring to others that You have shown me.

Living like Jesus means loving like Jesus.

The Mark of Love

"By this all will know that you are My disciples, if you have love for one another." (John 13:35)

When the world hears the word *Christian*, arguably the word *love* doesn't come to mind. Mahatma Gandhi famously said, "I like your Christ. I do not like your Christians. Your Christians are so unlike your Christ." People can look at Christians and think we are hyper-judgmental, hypercritical, bad at being friends with non-Christians, narrow-minded, and uptight. And let's be honest. There is some truth to those opinions, unfortunately.

Jesus loved people. He loved thieves, prostitutes, tax collectors, diseased people, poor people, children, and His followers. He loved people who were devoted to Him and those who were different from Him. He even loved difficult and dangerous people. Jesus makes this kind of love the mark of genuine discipleship. It is to be the evidence and confirmation by which people can know that we are His followers. It is a love that begins with our fellow believers and is most clearly seen by how we love one another and have genuine community with each other. But this love doesn't end there. It extends outwardly to include the responsibility we have to love our neighbor as ourselves.

Christians have not always presented a pretty picture to the world of what loving others should look like. Too often we have failed to show the beauty of Jesus and the holiness of God by not rightly expressing love. It is love that will prove to the world that we are the real deal and that we are His followers. So let's start loving one another the way God expects us to.

Jesus, may I be a loving representative of Your love and mercy to the world around me.

Jesus makes love the mark of His followers.

When the Rooster Crows

"Most assuredly, I say to you, the rooster shall not crow till you have denied Me three times." (John 13:38)

Jesus is the source for our forgiveness and freedom, not our shame. If we are more concerned about what others think, then there will be times when we will be tempted to keep our faith quiet. It doesn't matter how biblically perceptive you are, how gifted you are, or how educated you are, because if you lack courage, you will keep quiet when you should speak up for Jesus. Courage says, "I will live the way God wants me to live, and I will speak the way God wants me to speak, no matter what the consequences might be."

Poor Peter. The most shameful moment of his life, denying Jesus, is preserved in Scripture for all to see. Before that shameful moment, Peter vowed that he would defend and even die for Jesus. But in a moment of weakness, he faltered. You can be sure that it wasn't the eyes of the onlookers that broke Peter's heart that night. Instead, it was the look in Jesus's eyes that certainly crushed Peter's spirit and brought tears of guilt and shame to the surface.

Peter feared the ridicule that might come from being associated with Jesus, and if we are honest with ourselves, we can fear the same thing. Many of us chicken out, hesitate to speak up, and even hope that no one's looking when we ask God to bless our food when we're in public. If someone else's opinion matters more to you than God's opinion, it will be a struggle to stand for Jesus. But if you keep your focus on God, He will give you the strength to stand so that you won't be ashamed when the roosters crow.

God, may I never be ashamed of You. Give me the courage to always stand up for You.

> **You should never be ashamed to stand for Jesus. He was not ashamed to die for you.**

The Cure for Troubled Hearts

"Let not your heart be troubled; you believe in God, believe also in Me. (John 14:1)

Troubles stalk us like a pack of hungry wolves. Worry lingers like an unwanted house guest. Hard things happen. Life can feel unbalanced, uncertain, unfair and untidy. We all experience days when we feel down, anxious, exhausted, or discouraged. Even the most optimistic among us have moments of uncertainty.

After the Last Supper and before His difficult journey to the cross, Jesus gives the disciples the bad news. It was a decisive and dramatic moment for the disciples, because Jesus had made it very clear that He would be leaving them. The idea of Jesus leaving was unbearable. They had left everything to follow Him, and now He was going away. What would happen to them? As the stunning news began to sink in, the disciples' insecurity and anxiety skyrocketed. Seeking to calm their spirits, Jesus told the disciples not to let their hearts be troubled.

Is your heart troubled today? Believe in God and place complete confidence in Jesus. Believe Jesus for who He is and what He says He provides for us. Believe in heaven and that heaven is your home. Believe that Jesus will take you there. And believe that Jesus will be there for you. Believe that Jesus has and is the answer for your troubles, and believe that He is the supplier of your every need.

Jesus, I confess that I often allow problems into my heart rather than trusting You for the solutions. Forgive me when I lack trust in You. Help me to believe You and trust You more.

Believing in Jesus brings peace to a troubled heart.

What Will Heaven Will Be Like?

"In My Father's house are many mansions; if it were not so, I would have told you. I go to prepare a place for you."
(John 14:2)

Everything you believe about heaven may be wrong. When Jesus taught about heaven, He never said it would be a distant land filled with puffy clouds, plush bathrobes, and harp music. Also, heaven will not be a never-ending church service in the sky, where we sing one hymn after another for all of eternity. And the icing on the misconception cake is that every Christian will receive a set of keys to their very own luxury estate when they arrive at the pearly gates. *Wait, what?* Now before you scream "Heresy!" and burn this book, keep reading.

The night before Jesus was crucified, He told His disciples that He would be leaving them, and they could not follow Him. To give them some encouragement, Jesus said He was going to prepare a place for them in His Father's house. The idea here is not so much that Jesus needed to go and sweep up in heaven and put some finishing touches on our heavenly homes. Instead, the emphasis is on the fact that Jesus would be preparing a place for us by going to the cross. The preparation was His crucifixion. Jesus was about to be make a way for people to inherit eternal life and spend eternity in the presence of God.

Whatever heaven, the new heaven, and the new earth ultimately will look like, heaven will be a place of glorious life, joy inexpressible, limitless peace, pure love, and beauty beyond description. And the greatest thing of all is that it will be the residence of God's presence.

God, I long for the day when I will experience the closeness and the perfection of eternity in Your presence.

Jesus prepared a place for us by paying for our sins.

One Way

"I am the way, the truth, and the life. No one comes to the Father except through Me." (John 14:6)

Jesus refuses to be politically correct. In our pluralistic society, the message of the exclusivity of Christ often is considered an offensive one. But that should not be surprising, because much of Western culture believes that all roads lead to God and that all you need to do is just be good or sincere. Jesus is not willing to compromise the truth for the sake of acceptance. Despite what some may say, all roads do not lead to God. There is no substitute for Jesus, no work-around, and no alternative path of salvation. Jesus is the one and only way to God.

He alone is how we come to God. He alone is the truth. He alone is the source of life. Without the way, there is no reaching God. Without the truth, there is no knowing God. Without the life, there is no living for God. Without faith in Jesus, there is no forgiveness of sins, there is no hope beyond the grave, and there is no home prepared for us in heaven.

We must be courageous when it comes to this truth. We must not recoil when we're challenged, and we must not hesitate from telling others that Jesus is the only way, even if it means that we are slighted by others or even rejected. To deny this truth or lessen it is to deny or lessen the authority of Scripture. Jesus as the only way is both exclusive and inclusive. He is both the only way to God and available to all who believe.

Jesus, I believe You are the only way of salvation. May I always uphold that truth while also showing others that You have made a way for all who believe.

Salvation is found in none other than Jesus alone.

Truth

"I am the way, the truth, and the life. No one comes to the
Father except through Me." (John 14:6)

Truth is not a collection of doctrines; truth is Jesus Christ. It's not
a creed or even a book. Jesus does not just tell us truths about God;
He is the ultimate expression of God. The thing about truth is that
it doesn't require belief to be true. For example, I'm typing this on a
gray MacBook. If you are reading this and doubt that my computer is
gray, that doesn't change the fact that it is still gray. Your belief in that
statement doesn't change the truth of it.

Seeing truth primarily as the dynamic, living person of Jesus will
change how you relate to truth, how you apply truth, and how truth
is lived out in your life. That means you can never know the truth of
your circumstances unless you first accept truth from Jesus. If we want
to know truth, then we must seek to know Jesus and approach truth
through a personal relationship with Him. We do that by spending
time with Him, by talking to Him, by listening to Him, and by sharing our lives with Him. The way we get to know others is the way we
get to know truth. Truth is not something we need to search for; it is
someone that we must follow.

As followers of Jesus, we are to walk in the truth (see 3 John 1:3),
love the truth, believe the truth (see 2 Thessalonians 2:10–12), and
speak the truth in love (see Ephesians 4:32).

God, I thank You for the gift of truth and that I can know and
experience truth. I will always be restless until I find my rest in Your
truth.

Truth has a name, and it is Jesus.

What Does God Look Like?

"Have I been with you so long, and yet you have not known Me, Philip? He who has seen Me has seen the Father."
(John 14:9)

Most people struggle to imagine God. There is no description that fully explains what God looks like. The Bible gives us glimpses of who God is by revealing facets of His character such as His love, compassion, power, and creativity. God is holy, perfect, and blameless. God is self-sufficient and self-sustaining. Although we cannot see God, the Bible teaches us that we can know Him personally.

Philip wanted to see God, so Jesus essentially told him, "Look at Me, Philip, and you will see the Father." We are not left to ourselves to figure out what God looks like, because He has revealed Himself in Jesus. Knowing God is not a guessing game. We need only to look to Jesus in order to see God the Father. To see Jesus is to see God (see Colossians 1:15). Jesus went on to tell Philip that if he needed proof, then he could look at His words and His works (see verse 10). In other words, "My words prove that I am in the Father, and the Father is in me, because what I speak is truth. And My works prove the same thing, because only God can do what I have done."

We must understand that Jesus did not come simply to demonstrate what God looks like, or even how God works. He came so that we can live in right relationship with God. When you look to Jesus, you not only will see God, but you will see how much God loves you and wants to be a part of your life.

Jesus, help people see You as I live out my daily life.

If you want to see God, then look to Jesus.

Loving Obedience

"If you love Me, keep My commandments." (*John 14:15*)

Don't be afraid to obey God. As Christians we know we should obey God, but often when God tells us to do something, we respond by saying, "Okay, I'll think about it." Our love for God shows itself in our willingness to live for God. The Bible is full of life instructions and commands, and God expects us to obey them fully. God's commands are not served up buffet style, where we pick and choose the instructions we want to follow and leave the ones we don't like. Partial obedience is disobedience.

God measures our love by our obedience. But if you find yourself struggling to obey, remember this: If you follow God's directions, you'll be blessed (see Proverbs 16:20). Doing what God says is the way to experience lasting joy and happiness (see John 15:10–11). This doesn't mean you will have fewer problems in life, but it does mean you will have fuller joy in life. God's commands are designed to protect us and guide us to His best for our lives. Simply put, life just works better when we obey God.

When you love God, you naturally will want to do what He says. So instead of trying harder to obey, perhaps we should focus on loving Jesus more, because the more we love Him, the easier it will be to hear His voice and to follow His instructions for living. Want a good rule of thumb? Listen to God, obey immediately, and watch His perfect plan unfold in your life.

Jesus, my love for You comes before my obedience to You, but my obedience comes because of my love for You. Grow my love for You so that I will obey more.

We prove our love for Jesus by obeying Him.

Getting to Know the Holy Spirit

"I will pray the Father, and He will give you another Helper,
that He may abide with you forever . . . for He dwells with you
and will be in you." (John 14:16–17)

The Holy Spirit is God, the Holy Spirit is a person, and the Holy Spirit lives in every Christian. The moment that we believe in Jesus as Lord and Savior, the Holy Spirit comes to live in us. Our bodies become homes for the Holy Spirit (see 1 Corinthians 3:16), and the Holy Spirit helps us live the Christian life.

Before Jesus died on the cross for our sins, He promised that after He left, His Spirit would be sent to live inside every Christian. God's Spirit has been given to us so that we can know who God is and know how to live for Him. It is the Holy Spirit who draws us to Jesus, and it is the Holy Spirit who convicts us of our need for Christ. The Holy Spirit is our Helper who often will speak to us in our minds. He will lead us by making an impression upon our hearts to say something, do something, or think something according to God's will, and He will take spiritual truth and make it understandable to us. The Holy Spirit never will speak anything to us or lead us in a direction that doesn't align with Scripture. If what we are considering conflicts with anything in the Bible, then it is not from the Spirit of God.

Life is not always going to be a smooth ride, but we always will have the Holy Spirit with us to help us navigate this life and live in a way that pleases God.

God, teach me and guide me by Your Spirit, that I may live a God-honoring life. Help me to always be sensitive to the Spirit's leading, and strengthen me to follow where You lead.

Jesus promised the Holy Spirit to help us live godly lives.

The Work of the Spirit

"But the Helper, the Holy Spirit, whom the Father will send in My name, He will teach you all things, and bring to your remembrance all things that I said to you." (John 14:26)

If someone asked you exactly what the Holy Spirit does, how would you answer? To start with, the Holy Spirit is the presence of God in us who helps us to daily live out the purposes of God. As believers, we have been given the Holy Spirit as our Helper, Teacher, and the guarantee of eternal life with God. Through Him we have direct access to our heavenly Father. His presence, guidance, and wisdom help us to live an abundant life here on Earth. And although His work within us takes a lifetime, He is there so we don't have to struggle through life in our own strength.

The Holy Spirit is actively working in the world today to accomplish the plans and purposes of God. Our first meeting with the Holy Spirit is when He convicts us of our sin and shows us our need for Jesus (see John 16:8). After believing and being filled with the Spirit (see 1 Corinthians 3:16), we are taught by the Spirit (see John 14:26), we are conformed into the image of Jesus by the Spirit (see 2 Corinthians 3:18), we are empowered by the Spirit to display godly attributes (see Galatians 5:22), and we are given gifts so we can serve God and others (see 1 Corinthians 12:7–11). When we are weak and don't know what to do or how to pray, the Spirit helps us to pray and even pleads to God on our behalf (see Romans 8:26). The Holy Spirit is God's amazing gift of Himself to every believer, and the more we allow God's Spirit to work in us, the more we will serve God faithfully and live devoted to God's will for our lives.

Holy Spirit, lead me, guide me, teach me, and help me live a life that honors God.

The Holy Spirit is the One who carries on the work of Jesus in the world today.

The Peace of God

"Peace I leave with you, My peace I give to you; not as the world gives do I give to you." (John 14:27)

Can we really experience personal peace? We often try to find peace from the ordinary stresses of life, such as a long workday or a family drama, by doing things like watching a television series, eating, listening to music, reading a book, or even exercising. But the peace we find from these activities is only temporary. Peace is not the result of trying harder to obtain it; it is a gift we receive from God.

Jesus promised to give us peace, but we must be willing to accept it. Accepting God's peace doesn't mean that our lives will be trouble free and filled with sunshine and rainbows. It means that even when our world seems to be falling apart, we can still have the peace of God ruling in our lives (see Colossians 3:15). Shortly before Jesus's death, He prepared His disciples for the stress and anxiety they would experience because of His absence by saying that His peace would strengthen and sustain them through it all.

The peace that the world gives depends mostly on circumstances. When there are no problems, life is good, and we feel at peace. But when problems arise, life is not so good and our peace evaporates. The peace that Jesus gives is far different. It does not depend on circumstances but overflows in our lives, even during times of trouble, disappointment, confusion, and anxiety. And the way to receive this peace is by giving every situation over to God in prayer and allowing His peace to fight off those feelings of fear and anxiety (see Philippians 4:6–7).

God, help me to receive the peace You give, a peace in my mind, body, soul, and spirit.

Where Jesus is, His peace is present.

The Purpose of Pruning

"Every branch in Me that does not bear fruit He takes away; and every branch that bears fruit He prunes, that it may bear more fruit." (John 15:2)

People don't like to be directed, corrected, or generally told what to do. People want to be left alone to do what they want, how they want, when they want, and the way they want. People don't want anyone, including God, to tell them what's wrong with the way they're living. Pruning is when you selectively remove unwanted or withered branches from a tree to improve the tree's structure and promote healthy new growth. Pruning is good for roses, vines, and trees, but most people do not like it when God takes the spiritual pruning shears to their lives.

God is the master gardener. He knows when and how much of our lives need to be pruned so that we grow fuller and healthier. God prunes us because He loves us, and that means all of us will, at times, experience being cut back. God will prune away our sinful habits, misplaced priorities, and mistaken views so that we do not grow out of control. He cuts us back to strengthen us so that we might produce fruit, better fruit, and much fruit. God may be pruning you right now. God is cutting away those things that keep you from healthy growth and fruitfulness. Even though pruning is always uncomfortable, it's working to make you better.

Thank you, God, for the times of pruning in my life when You lovingly cut back wild branches so that I can bear more fruit. Even though pruning is uncomfortable, Your pruning prepares me for something better in my life.

Jesus is glorified when we bear fruit.

The Abiding Life

Abide in Me, and I in you. As the branch cannot bear fruit of itself, unless it abides in the vine, neither can you, unless you abide in Me. (John 15:4)

Have you ever walked by a garden and heard the fruit groaning or the vegetables grunting? I hope not! That's because fruits and vegetables don't strain and strive to grow. They simply abide in order to flourish. Every Christian I know wants to live a productive life for Jesus, and the key to succeeding is not found in striving but by abiding in Him.

Would you like to be more loving, more joyful, and more at peace? Would you like to be more faithful, gentler, and have more self-control? You only will be able to bear this fruit in your life if you are joined to Jesus. Having this connection to Jesus will allow Him to provide you with the essential nutrients for a healthy life. A branch is dependent on the vine and gets its life and power from the vine, not the other way around. Without the vine, the branch is useless, lifeless, and powerless. Likewise, we are completely dependent on Jesus if we want to produce spiritual fruit, because apart from Him, we can do nothing (see John 15:5). As we are joined to Jesus, His Word is to fill our minds, guide our actions, and transform our behaviors. Abiding is a lifelong process whereby we keep trusting in Jesus, keep depending on Jesus, and never stop believing in His teaching.

Jesus, help to me always be leaning on You, resting in You, and pouring my heart out to You. May I keep Your words continually before me so they will rule my conduct and behavior.

Staying connected to Jesus is the key to being spiritually productive.

NOVEMBER

Fruitfulness and Faithfulness

"I am the vine, you are the branches. He who abides in Me,
and I in him, bears much fruit; for without Me you can do
nothing." (John 15:5)

Fruitfulness is God's work. Faithfulness is ours. We must resist the temptation to view fruitfulness like successfulness. Success says, "If I just put in the effort, I will see the results." Faithfulness, however, will produce fruitfulness but not necessarily successfulness.

So much of the Christian life is about faithfulness—our willingness to be committed to God's ways, His Word, His mission, and His gospel. Faithfulness is not about the quantity of fruit but about the quality of fruit that is produced. Faithfulness is about trusting God alone to produce spiritual results. Fruitfulness is always a product of God's timing and always according to His supply, which results in some seeing a hundredfold harvest, others a sixtyfold harvest, and still others a thirtyfold harvest (see Matthew 13:8). We must be faithful and content to do our part. And whether we plant like Paul or water like Apollos, we must remember that God gives the increase (see 1 Corinthians 3:6–7).

Fruitfulness is becoming like Jesus (see Galatians 5:22–23) and helping others become like Jesus too. It is the work of God in the lives of people. It begins with the saving work of Jesus in us and then grows as God sovereignly produces godly character in us. As we abide in Jesus and He abides in us, our lives naturally will be fruitful. As we make our home in Jesus the same way that a branch finds its home in the vine, we will produce organically and abundantly for God.

God, help me to stay faithful to You so that through my faithfulness,
You can work in and through me to produce a blessed harvest.

Faithfulness to Jesus will produce fruitfulness
to God.

The Connected Life

*"I am the vine, you are the branches. He who abides in Me,
and I in him, bears much fruit; for without Me you can do
nothing." (John 15:5)*

With Jesus, everything is possible. Without Jesus, nothing is possible.
Apart from Christ, we cannot, with our physical abilities, produce
anything of spiritual consequence. We were designed to depend on
God, and our complete dependence on Him for *everything* is how we
can produce *anything* of value for Him. We need to recognize the fact
that if we do not depend on Jesus, there can be no real, long-lasting,
and abiding spiritual productivity in our lives. Jesus makes it clear
that it is not our activity that produces fruit. Rather, it is through our
enduring relationship with Him that we will be spiritually productive.

Jesus warned His disciples that if they attempted to live the
Christian life apart from an intimate relationship with Him, they'd
discover that they would be unable to produce significant spiritual
results. You can be very busy for God, but your busyness is not what
produces fruit. You must be spiritually connected to Jesus and walking in the Spirit to be spiritually productive. Bearing fruit is the result
of obedience to the Word of God and yielding to the Holy Spirit.

What a relief to know that we do not have to live a restless lifestyle filled with endless religious activity to bear fruit. Instead, we can
enjoy a connected relationship with Jesus. As we abide in Him and He
abides in us, He will do the work of bearing fruit.

*God, help me to fulfill Your purposes for which I was created. Work
through me like a branch to a vine so that I will bear much fruit.*

**Jesus will help us fulfill His purposes and
produce lasting fruit as we abide in Him.**

God's Word in Me

"If you abide in Me, and My words abide in you, you will ask what you desire, and it shall be done for you." (John 15:7)

Has anyone ever taught you how to abide in God's Word? Has anyone told you how to come to the Bible in such a way that it promotes a thriving relationship with Jesus? It is one thing to listen to the words of Jesus, but it is quite another for the words of Jesus to abide in you. For the words of Jesus to abide in us, we must relate to the Bible so that we have meaningful encounters with Jesus and our lives are progressively transformed by Him. We must do more than squeeze Jesus into our busy lives. He must become the reason we live.

If we are honest with ourselves, we would admit that studying the Bible can sometimes feel burdensome, difficult, confusing, and unexciting. But the Bible is the place where we meet God, and it is through our meeting God that we grow spiritually. Abiding in God's Word, therefore, is a state of being constantly fed and formed by Him. It is a lifelong process by which we study God's Word, contemplate it, wrestle with it, take it to heart, and put it into practice. It means that we are committed to communion with God, and we seek to connect our minds with God so that our lives will be transformed by God. It means purposefully planning to spend time with Jesus, resolving to read the Bible intentionally, and deciding to review truth so we can remember it. It means keeping Jesus ever before us so that we can live for Him daily.

Jesus, when I lack the motivation to be purposeful in Your Word, motivate me by Your Spirit to seek You and commune with You so that what I pray for is in accordance with Your will.

Abiding in Jesus is the formation of spiritual habits that produce spiritual growth.

Unshakable, Untakable Joy

"These things I have spoken to you, that My joy may remain in you, and that your joy may be full." (John 15:11)

God is less interested in what brings us happiness and more interested in what brings us joy. God does not want to give us a shallow happiness that dissolves like cotton candy, He wants us to have lasting contentment, confidence, and hope that only comes from Him. We never will find joy if what we are really searching for is happiness. If we are looking for circumstances to bring us joy, or if we say, "I'll be happy when . . . ," then we are setting ourselves up for disappointment. Joy does not come from our circumstances; joy is found in God.

Jesus didn't say to His disciples, "Don't worry, be happy." Rather, He told them they could have the same joy that He had—a divine joy, a joy that comes from a deep and unwavering relationship with the Father, a joy that is grounded so firmly in a relationship with God that no change in circumstances could ever shake it, change it, or take it away, a joy so fixed that it could endure crucifixion (see Hebrews 12:2).

Jesus wants His joy to be our joy. He doesn't just want us to have joy, but He also wants us to have an unshakable, untakable joy, the very joy He experienced—a joy that is constant in turmoil and that conquers all circumstances.

Father God, fill my heart with Your abiding joy, and enable me to walk through all the difficulties of life by the power of Your Holy Spirit and with Your joy abiding in me.

Jesus wants His joy to be our joy.

Fullness of Joy

"These things I have spoken to you, that My joy may remain in you, and that your joy may be full." (John 15:11)

Joy is a choice. Fullness of joy is a lifestyle. It is a sad and disappointing experience when you encounter Christians who have the joy of the Lord in their hearts but wear scowls on their faces. Every Christian can experience a profound fullness of joy, a joy that no circumstance of life can cast out, a joy that is steadfast in sorrow (John 16:20), triumphant in tribulation (2 Corinthians 7:4), and lasting in losses (Hebrews 10:34). Sound appealing?

The Bible tells us that in order to experience joy, there is one necessary ingredient, and that is the presence of Jesus. Jesus not only promised to give His disciples joy, but He said they would receive *His* joy. Jesus is the source of our joy, and He's the sustainer of it, but we also need to cultivate joy if we want to experience the fullness of it. Throughout the Bible, joy is commanded. So we could say, then, if we are not joyful Christians, we are breaking a command.

Let's get real for a moment. If you want to cultivate joyfulness, then stop comparing yourself to other people, complaining about your circumstances, trying to control every situation, and criticizing others. Instead, start practicing thankfulness and start trusting God, even when things are beyond your control. Start choosing to rejoice in God and not your circumstances, because that will allow you to be able live out God's command to rejoice always (see Philippians 4:4).

Jesus, help me to make rejoicing in You a habit. Keep me from letting my feelings take over, especially when circumstances are challenging.

> **We will experience fullness of joy when our love for Jesus is greater than all other emotions.**

Greater Love

"Greater love has no one than this, than to lay down one's life for his friends. You are My friends if you do whatever I command you." (John 15:13–14)

Love is a decision to put what is best for others before yourself. Jesus does not ask me to die for Him, and for that matter, He doesn't ask me to die for you, even though the implication may be there. What He does ask is that I lay down my life for others. I once saw John 15:13 as having a willingness to die for someone else, and that is part of it. But let's be realistic. How often is that a real-life decision? What I've since come to realize is that I can and must lay down my life daily for others *as I live.* I must let love rule my life in such a way that my life is to be lived for the benefit of others before it is to be lived for my benefit. I must do this as Jesus did it for me, expecting nothing in return.

Salvation was easy for us because Jesus did the work. But living out our salvation is harder as we do the works that demonstrate our salvation. We can lay down our lives for others in many ways, some small and some big. It begins by fostering an attitude of deep concern for the well-being of others. When we do this, we will begin to discover countless ways to lay our lives down for those around us. Small acts of kindness, words of affirmation, a listening ear, or help with a to-do list are a few of the small ways we can make the decision to put others first. Greater acts may include courageous forgiveness, giving when it appears undeserved, and going out of our way when we do not have the time.

Jesus, help me to serve, care for, and love others with the kind of great love You demonstrated by laying down Your life for me.

Greater love for others is possible as I walk in the power of Jesus's love for me.

F-R-I-E-N-D-S

"No longer do I call you servants, for a servant does not know what his master is doing; but I have called you friends, for all things that I heard from My Father I have made known to you." (John 15:15)

You were created to be friends with God. We live in a world where technology has made cultivating relationships easier but also shallower. Some people have thousands of social media "friends" but know only a fraction of them personally. God has sent you a personal friendship request in the person of Jesus. And unlike many of our social media friends, Jesus is a friend that draws near in our suffering, remains committed in our stumbling, knows us better than we know ourselves, and loves us more deeply than anyone else ever could and ever will.

Friendship with God means that He knows our hearts and shares His heart with us. Jesus began calling His disciples friends rather than servants because He revealed to them all that His Father told Him. Jesus wants to share with us everything He knows about God. Jesus, in His desire for us to have intimacy with God, draws us into a closer relationship, a friendship, so that we might discover what life with God really means.

Jesus is the model of friendship. He gave everything to His friends—His knowledge of God and even His own life. In Jesus we see what makes a good friend, and that is someone who loves without limits. Because Jesus has transformed our understanding of true friendship, He makes it possible for us to exemplify friendship to the world around us.

Jesus, may I be a friend to others as You are a friend to me.

Jesus is a treasured friend.

Lasting Fruit

"You did not choose Me, but I chose you and appointed you that you should go and bear fruit, and that your fruit should remain." (John 15:16)

We have within us a deep desire to live a fruitful life. Most people want to live in such a way that their life makes a difference in this world. When we die, we will leave behind possessions, wealth, influence, relationships, education, careers, and so forth. The only things that have lasting value are the things that are eternal. When we pass from this life, we will be required to give an account of the life that we lived. Jesus revealed that the sum of our life's work will be determined by the fruit that remains.

Most of what we do won't last. No one will remember much of what we did or said after we die. People won't care where we went on vacation, what books we read, or how many selfies we took. Nothing you do is more important than helping people determine the destiny of their lives. William James is credited with saying, "The greatest use of your life is to invest it in something that will outlast it." If you spend your life giving it away for the sake of the gospel, you will have lived a life that truly made a difference.

God created us to know, love, and glorify Him and to produce lasting fruit. Everything else in life is secondary. There are two ways we can choose to respond to that: either we will choose to invest our lives in that which outlasts our lives, or we can choose to live lives that are without eternal purpose.

Father God, living a life that makes a difference is accomplished through an abiding dependence on Jesus to produce lasting fruit through my life. Help me to abide in Him.

Jesus wants our lives to produce fruit that will last.

Hated by the World

"Because you are not of the world, but I chose you out of the world, therefore the world hates you." (John 15:19)

Don't be surprised if you are hated for living a godly life. This doesn't mean that every person will hate you for everything you do, but it does mean there will be instances and individuals who will hate you because you belong to Jesus. There are people who hate Jesus and everything He stands for. They despise His teachings, they dismiss His authority, and they discard His deity. And if you follow Jesus and stand up for what the Bible teaches, then you will be hated at times as well.

A. W. Tozer pointed out, "To be right with God has often meant to be in trouble with men."[11] Yet, in today's culture of trying to get the most likes, the most views, and the most followers on social media, many believers have become more interested in gaining cultural acceptance and approval than in dealing with the hate sure to come when we love Jesus more than we love the world.

No one wants to be hated. No one wants to experience the ridicule or insult of others. The world tells us that our opinions must conform to the values of the age, and if they don't, then we are judgmental, close-minded, and extremists, and we should be "canceled," or silenced. Christian, you must expect to be hated today for the same reason Jesus was hated. Your goodness reveals their badness. Your truth exposes their error. Your life convicts them of their guilt, and it shows them whom God expects them to be and how He wants them to live.

God, it is not my desire to provoke people to hatred. Prepare me for those times when living a godly life unavoidably produces hatred from the world.

The world hated Jesus, and it will hate those who live like Jesus.

The Persecuted Church

"If they persecuted Me, they will also persecute you."
(John 15:20)

For some, following Jesus costs them everything. More Christians have died for their faith in the last century than in all prior centuries combined since the time of Jesus. Persecution is on the rise in many parts of the world, where believers are being insulted, isolated, humiliated, discriminated against, arrested, beaten, mutilated, tortured, burned, or killed for their faith. While some Christians around the world are experiencing such brutal treatment, it is important for each of us to ask, "What can I do to strengthen the worldwide church?"

The Bible tells us to continue to remember those in prison as though we were with them, and those who are mistreated as though we ourselves were suffering alongside them (see Hebrew 13:3; 1 Corinthians 12:26). Certainly that may move some to raise their voices against these injustices (see Isaiah 1:17) or to write letters to their elected officials concerning human rights violations. Others may decide to partner with Christian ministries that provide support for those who are facing these horrific circumstances.

While considering those options or others, there is something we can all do *today*: Pray! Just imagine if you were the one suffering for your faith. You would be so grateful for the Christians who were lifting you up in prayer. We must take up the responsibility of praying for believers who are being persecuted. This is exactly how the early church responded when Peter was in prison. They prayed earnestly to God for him (see Acts 12:5).

God, I pray for those suffering around the world for their faith in Jesus. Give them courage to face whatever mistreatment the enemy of the Cross assails them with.

> **We are one body in Jesus. When one of us suffers, we all suffer.**

Aloneness

"Indeed the hour is coming, yes, has now come, that you will be scattered, each to his own, and will leave Me alone. And yet I am not alone, because the Father is with Me."
(John 16:31–32)

Are you feeling alone today, like no one cares? Have friends abandoned you? Many godly people in the Bible have felt alone. Consider how Job felt during his troubles (see Job 6:14–15), how Joseph felt when his family rejected him (see Genesis 37:23–28), or how the apostle Paul felt when he wrote, "Everyone abandoned me" (2 Timothy 4:16 NLT). If you are feeling alone today, God understands. But He also would tell you that you're not alone.

Jesus knows what it's like to be abandoned and alone in a human sense. Jesus lived in the presence of God and stayed connected to God, even though He was frequently alone and often without real earthly companionship. Jesus understood God's love to be always present, and therefore He was able to say when others turned away, "I am not alone, because the Father is with me" (John 16:32). Jesus always was aware of God's presence and actively stayed connected to the Father. Therefore, He never was truly alone.

When we feel alone, it's often the result of not having the presence of mind to remember that we have the presence of God with us. When we have the right mindset, we can accept His comfort, His companionship, and His strengthening. If you are feeling alone, break the habit of feeling that God is absent (because He is very much present), and make the effort to get connected.

God, I thank You that You never abandon me. You are always there, and Your presence brings comfort and peace. Use me to come alongside others who may also feel alone.

When we, like Jesus, are aware of God's presence, we will realize that we're never alone.

Overcomer

"Be of good cheer, I have overcome the world." (John 16:33)

In this world you will have trouble—trouble at work, trouble at school, trouble at home, and trouble in your family. You will experience trouble, because that's just the way this world is. We have all gone through times of personal stress, deep sorrow, times of uncertainty, and trying circumstances. Sometimes those moments cause us to question what God is up to in our lives and even ask why God is allowing us to go through such a troubling situation.

If you are facing hardship or adversity, the first step is to remember that Jesus warned us that we would face troubles. Although the warning doesn't promise deliverance from hardship or release from adversity, it does provide encouragement. Our confidence doesn't come from our circumstances or even from an understanding of those circumstances. Our confidence comes from knowing the One who is greater than our circumstances. In the middle of troubles, we can be of good cheer, not because life is easy but because Jesus has overcome the troubles of the world.

Don't let trouble discourage you. Jesus has overcome the troubles of the world and the troublesome Devil. And because Jesus is with you, He is your help, your strength, your joy, your peace, your hope, and your victory.

Jesus, I no longer want to stumble along under the weight of my troubles. I know I can rise above them because You rose from the dead.

**Take heart, because Jesus overcame the world.
And one day we will too.**

Glory to God

*"Father, the hour has come. Glorify Your Son, that Your Son
also may glorify You." (John 17:1)*

God's glory is the highest good. To glorify is to make much of something, and we were created to make much of God. We are never more who we were created to be than when we are bringing glory to God with our lives, reflecting His glory to the world around us, and proclaiming His glory to others.

Jesus spent His entire life glorifying God the Father. He lived a perfect life that perfectly glorified God. He laid aside His preincarnate glory in heaven to come to Earth and rescue and restore humanity's relationship to God. And as Jesus faced the cross, He prayed that through His sacrifice, even more glory would go to God the Father. He prayed that the preincarnate glory He had with God the Father before the world began would be returned to Him, and that through His glorification, it would do nothing less than bring more glory to the Father.

Our lives should be passionately devoted to bringing God glory. We were created for God's glory and to bring God glory in everything we do (see Isaiah 43:7; 1 Corinthians 10:31). When we seek to experience God's presence in our lives, we will in turn seek to glorify God with our lives. We will glorify God by giving thanks, by serving others, by sharing the gospel, and by using our spiritual gifts. In other words, we will seek to make much of God in everything we do.

God, help me to live every day to bring You glory. May my thoughts, words, and actions faithfully represent You and always make much of You.

When Jesus is glorified, God the Father is glorified.

Knowing God

"And this is eternal life, that they may know You, the only true God, and Jesus Christ whom You have sent." (John 17:3)

Eternal life is not a destination; it is a relationship. The goal of existence is to know God, and the essence of eternal life is wrapped up in knowing God and knowing Jesus Christ personally. Our ability to know God comes from God's will to make Himself known. Yes, God is infinitely greater than we are, and we cannot fully comprehend Him. However God has willed that we know Him. Christianity is about a relationship with God, and eternal life is about experientially knowing God presently and eternally.

Jesus describes eternal life as not simply knowing about God but being intimately connected with Him. Pursuing theological knowledge is not wrong, but pursing knowledge for the sake having all the answers is allowing knowledge to puff us up, and that knowledge does not lead to spiritual health (see 1 Corinthians 8:1). Knowing God is more than an intellectual pursuit. It is a practical pursuit of God that brings real life change. We should seek to know God so that we can be led by Him and so that our lives will glorify Him.

Nothing compares with getting to know God. God has made a way for us to know Him, and the Bible is the place to go for that. It is there you will see what God is like, you will discover what His will is, what His plans and purposes are, and how we can live lives that He honors and that honor Him.

I just want to know You more and to love You better. Help me to know You more and to grow closer to You with every passing day.

Knowing God means knowing Jesus.

When God Prays

*"I pray for them. . . . I do not pray for these alone, but also
for those who will believe in Me through their word."*
(John 17:9, 20)

Jesus is not selfish when it comes to prayer. It's easy to say, "I'll pray for you," but it can be hard to follow through when the busyness of life bears down. That is, until you remember that when Jesus was only hours away from dying on the cross, the culmination of God's redemptive mission, He still took the time to pray for His disciples and even for us.

Jesus could have prayed the prayer in John 17 privately, but He wanted all His followers to hear it and learn from it. So what did God pray for when He prayed for His followers? Relationships. God is all about relationships, and He wants us to relate properly to Him (see John 17:13, 17, 23), to relate properly to one another (see verses 4, 21), and to relate properly to the nonbelieving world (see verses 15, 17).

I love it when people pray for me. It is encouraging and empowering. I can tell the difference when I am prayed for and when I am not. It's one thing to have people pray for you, but it is quite another to know that God is praying for us. The Bible tells us that Jesus "always lives to make intercession" (Hebrews 7:25). Scottish minister Robert Murray M'Cheyne said, "If I could hear Christ praying for me in the next room, I would not fear a million enemies. Yet distance makes no difference; He is praying for me!"[12]

The next time you pray for someone else, remember how Jesus prayed for you.

God help me to pray for spiritual blessings according to Your will for others, because then they are guaranteed to find a "yes" and "amen" (2 Corinthians 1:20).

Be encouraged today. Jesus is praying for you.

Isolation versus Insulation

"I do not pray that You should take them out of the world,
but that You should keep them from the evil one." (John 17:15)

Our pursuit of holiness often tempts us to isolate. God isn't interested in our isolating or hiding ourselves away like hermits in some holy bunker. Rather, He wants us to live courageously on life's front lines. Jesus prayed that as we fight this spiritual war, we won't become casualties or prisoners of it.

God loves people—so much so that He sent Jesus into the world to point the way to God and make a way to Him. We should not be shocked, then, that Jesus calls us to join Him in connecting with people and conveying God's message of hope to them. We are called to live in the world but not live like the world. And as we walk in this world, Jesus is our advocate who is praying for us to be protected and kept safe from the ruler of this world.

Christians are not called to live apart from our culture but to influence our culture for Christ. There is a purpose for our presence in the world. There is a plan for our involvement in relationships. If we remove ourselves from worldly relationships, then we are removing the influence Jesus wants us to have in those relationships. There is work for us to do. There are people we need to love and serve, and we have God's good news to share. That is the reason Jesus prayed that we would be insulated from evil rather than isolated from it.

Father, furnish me with Your invincible strength against the enemy,
that I may not be overwhelmed by evil but have the strength to
endure in this world.

> **Jesus wants us to be in the world, influencing**
> **relationships for Him.**

Whateverism

"Sanctify them by Your truth, Your word is truth."
(John 17:17)

What has happened to truth? Truth seems to have switched from relativism to whateverism. We live in a world that responds to truth with a "whatever works for you" attitude. Believe what you want to believe. Do what works best for you. Live for whatever brings you happiness. But just make sure that whatever you decide to do doesn't hurt someone else along the way. And of course, don't tell anyone else that what they believe is wrong. The only absolute is there are no absolutes.

Truth is not subjective whateverism. Truth is not relative. Truth is not based on popular opinion, feelings, or emotions. Truth is theological, because truth cannot be explained, understood, or defined apart from God. Since God is the source of truth, trying to define truth apart from God is destined to be a train wreck. The moment you remove God as the source of truth, all discussions about truth become nonsense. Jesus makes it clear: God's Word is where to go if a person wants to understand truth, and it is also where the transformative power of truth resides.

Truth is powerful, and truth brings life. When we have a standard for truth, it gives us a way to explain and understand what happens in the world around us and provides a basis for making decisions that lead to living godly lives. Truth blesses and uplifts. Truth makes us grow, fills us with love, and makes us walk and talk like Jesus.

God, You are truth, and what You say is truth. Your truth guides me, keeps me, protects me, and strengthens me. Help me to learn truth, love truth, share truth, and live truth.

Jesus affirms that God's Word is truth.

United We Stand

"That they all may be one, as You, Father, are in Me, and I in You; that they also may be one in Us, that the world may believe that You sent Me." (John 17:21)

Unity matters to God. Profoundly so. It was one of the last things Jesus prayed before going to the cross. Jesus prayed that the unity of His followers would be equal to the oneness He had with the Father. He prayed this because unity encourages belief. Our oneness was designed to be a way to prove to the world that Jesus is God.

If unity is tied to belief, then it stands to reason that the more unity there is among believers, the more people would be won to Christ. It also means that division among Christians openly contradicts God's will, repels the world, and damages the gospel. This is not unity at all costs, because unity still needs to be regulated by truth. But it is a unity that stops dividing over ridiculous nonessential issues.

How can we promote unity among believers and within our churches? We need to build up more and tear down less. We need to recognize that every person is important to God. We need to focus on what matters and relax when it comes to matters of opinion and preference. We need to be forgiving of others. If God can tolerate our mistakes and forgive us, then shouldn't we be able to tolerate the mistakes of others by forgiving them? If God loves us with our faults and failures, then we need to work at loving others with all their imperfections as well. This is the way to a unity that the world will notice and inquire about.

Father God, keep me united with my fellow believers, and help me to remember that we are one body, in one Spirit with one Lord, in one faith, and sharing one hope.

Jesus wants us to live intentionally for unity among the community of believers.

The Cup of Suffering

"O My Father, if it is possible, let this cup pass from Me; nevertheless, not as I will, but as You will." (Matthew 26:39)

Jesus came to this earth to die for our sins. That was His purpose and His mission. Yet when the time came to face His death for our sakes, did He pray to avoid it? Did Jesus get cold feet? Was He having second thoughts about God's redemptive plan? Absolutely not!

It's impossible to believe that perfect love would hesitate when faced with sacrifice. That idea runs contrary to the love that Jesus taught and lived. The Jesus we see in the Bible would not waver to give His life for another, no matter the cost. Certainly there was a part of the humanity of Jesus that sought to avoid the physical torture that was looming, but His request for this cup to pass was not a cry to sidestep execution.

Christ's humanity is different than ours because His humanity is never mixed with the weakness of sin. So Jesus is not questioning God's wisdom or God's will when He prays here. Instead, the anguish that caused God in human form to sweat great drops of blood was the spiritual pain and anguish that was looming. The One who knew no sin was going to become sin (see 2 Corinthians 5:21). Jesus was sinless, perfect, and holy, and He was about to become everything God hated. As Jesus looked into the cup of suffering that night, He saw the judgment and wrath of God, which were about to be poured out on Him. Such spiritual agony was distressing, but Jesus faithfully remained committed to do the will of God, no matter the cost.

Heavenly Father, I never will face anything that compares to what Jesus had to endure. But I do know that as I pray, You will give me the strength to face whatever I am called to endure.

The prayers of Jesus are always dependent on the will of God.

Your Will Be Done

"Not as I will, but as you will." (Matthew 26:39 ESV)

The object of prayer is not to get God to do what we want but for us to do what God wants.

Part of the purpose of prayer is connecting with God, and part of connecting with God involves seeking His will and saying, "I want to do what You want me to do." You can look at doing God's will as either *having to* do what God wants or *getting to* do what God wants. One involves an attitude that says, "I'll do it, but I won't like it," while the other says, "I'll do it because I trust God, and He knows best."

There are times when a crisis hits and we pray for God to change our circumstances. And sometimes He will. There are people who have prayed, and their situation turned around by the grace and power of God. But when we pray, "Lord, get me out of this situation," we need to be aware that God may be saying, "Let Me into your situation." God may change your circumstances, but more often He wants to change us instead. Never be afraid to let God overrule your prayers, because His plans are always best.

The example of Jesus encourages us to pray freely and boldly, asking God for whatever is on our hearts. But we must be fully surrendered and submitted to God's plans, even when they may be at odds with our personal will.

God, I pray for Your will to be done in my life and in this world. I pray for Your way to rule in my heart and my head. I'm not in control, God. You are. Even though at times Your plans may be hard to admit and accept, I want to always do what You want me to do.

Jesus teaches us that we need to always be submitted to God's will.

Watch and Pray

"What! Could you not watch with Me one hour? Watch and pray, lest you enter into temptation." (Matthew 26:40–41)

Temptation strikes when we are most vulnerable. When we neglect certain areas of our spiritual lives such as prayer, we can become drowsy and let our guard down, making ourselves easy targets for the enemy (see 1 Peter 5:8). We always will be spiritually weak when we lack the determination to pray.

Jesus doesn't get more practical than "watch and pray, lest you enter into temptation" (Matthew 26:41). Jesus had a simple request for Peter, James, and John in the Garden of Gethsemane, and that was to watch and pray. But they were sleeping instead of praying. Their physical environment overshadowed their ability and desire to obey God. They let their physical limitations restrict the spiritual power they had access to.

We all know our weaknesses. We all know the situations in which we are most vulnerable. Watch out for those! Stress. Late nights. Exhaustion. Social media. Certain social situations. Jesus's remedy against such weaknesses is to watch and pray. Watch out for whatever gives Satan a foothold in your life. Pay attention, and be on the lookout for anything that might hinder your walk with God. And pray, because prayer invites God into your life situation. Prayer requires our persistence and perseverance, because our natural wills, the world, and Satan, will do everything to stop us from watching and praying.

Father, help me to stay watchful over my spiritual life and be on guard for those things that might cause me to stumble.

Jesus is clear: watchful prayer will overcome temptation.

The Flesh and the Spirit

"The spirit indeed is willing, but the flesh is weak."
(Matthew 26:41)

We are at war. We battle our flesh. And although we are Christians, we still struggle against our own appetites and cravings that seek to express themselves in our thoughts, words, and actions.

We want to do what is right, but we struggle under the weakness of the flesh to always do so (Galatians 5:17–18).

Jesus had asked His disciples to "watch and pray," and each time He came back, the disciples were asleep. If there ever was a critical time for Jesus's closest friends to be in prayer, this was it. Surely they could have sensed the intensity in Jesus's voice and the urgency of His demeanor. And surely they could have found the strength to pray for one hour. But they failed not once, but three times. They were willing to be with Jesus, but they did not consider the power of their flesh to overpower their commitment to Christ. They did not understand their own weakness.

Our spirits are ready to do what God wants, but our bodies can be uncooperative. When our strength fails, it will leave us confessing the same old struggles without ever mastering them. Bringing our physical desires under the control of the Holy Spirit is the key to accomplishing what Jesus asks us to do. As we walk by the Spirit, we will not carry out the desires of the flesh (see Galatians 5:16). We must realize that we can't live the Christian life through human effort. If we want to live by the Spirit, we must allow God's Spirit to strengthen ours.

Lord, help me to follow You today instead of letting my flesh lead my decisions. Give me the grace and strength to overcome fleshly desires by yielding to Your Spirit.

Jesus invites me to be strengthened by prayer and the Holy Spirit.

What Went Wrong?

"Friend, do what you came to do." (Matthew 26:50 ESV)

Of all the names to call Judas Iscariot, *friend* would not have been first on my list. It is easy for us to dismiss Judas as a traitor and cast him aside, but there are some lessons we can learn from the apostate whom Jesus called friend.

Judas walked with Jesus for three years. He gave up everything like the other disciples did to follow Jesus. He saw the greatest life ever lived. He witnessed countless miracles. He was there when Jesus fed the five thousand, and he even passed out the wonder bread and miracle fish with his own two hands that amazing day. When Jesus raised Lazarus from the dead, Judas was there as a witness. When Jesus taught the Sermon on the Mount, Judas was there to listen to the greatest sermon ever preached. He saw Jesus's compassion, he observed His forgiveness, and he heard the warnings that Jesus gave to the religious leaders. Judas saw the evidence. He heard the truth. He walked alongside God. He could not have been in a better environment for genuine spiritual transformation, yet he still walked away from Jesus. When Jesus called him friend, perhaps it was a last-chance, compassionate offer for Judas to repent and be forgiven.

Judas had religion but no relationship. He heard truth, but he never embraced it. He believed in God, but he didn't have faith in God. The words of life never changed him. Sometimes even the best of environments won't soften a hard heart, and no one is immune to the destructive power of secret sin. A small sin can lead anyone to a big downfall.

God, keep me from being close to Jesus but not in relationship with Him. May I always deal with my sins and let Jesus into my situations so there is no damage to our relationship.

Walking away from Jesus is the worst decision a person can make.

Two Swords

"Put your sword in its place, for all who take the sword will perish by the sword." (Matthew 26:52)

The night was chaotic. The scene was scary. Judas betrayed Jesus with a kiss as an armed detachment began to surround the Son of God. Peter was thinking, "No one is touching my Jesus," so he drew his sword and took a fisherman's swing in the direction of the armed guards. Luckily for Malchus, Peter was both untrained with a sword and impetuous, or else he may have lost more than his right ear that night (see John 18:10).

Jesus turned to Peter and told him to put his sword away. Violence begets violence, and the kingdom of God is spiritual and will not be initiated or advanced by physical force or worldly techniques. There is no place in the work of God for the sword, unless that sword is the sword of the Spirit (see Ephesians 6:17). Unlike physical swords designed to cut and kill, the sword of the Spirit is designed only to cut away at the inner person to bring healing, hope, and new life.

As followers of Jesus, we have been given the Word of God, or the sword of the Spirit, to wield its blade in the face of evil. It is the source of the truth by which we attack lies, error, and everything that runs contrary to the truth (2 Corinthians 10:5 NIV). We do not need to shrink back when evil comes against us, but we do not fight violence with violence. We do not brandish the steel sword. Our weapon is the sword of the Spirit.

God, help me to use the spiritual weaponry that You provide to come against all that stands in opposition to the gospel, because we do not fight against flesh and blood (Ephesians 6:12).

> **Jesus never used earthly methods to solve spiritual problems.**

Who Killed Jesus?

Jesus answered, **"You could have no power at all against Me unless it had been given you from above."** *(John 19:11)*

The nineteenth-century preacher Octavius Winslow asked, "Who delivered up Jesus to die? Not Judas, for money; not Pilate, for fear; not the Jews, for envy—but the Father, for love!"[13] Even though the Jews and the Romans played a role in putting Jesus on the cross, God was the one who had already planned His Son's death as an atonement for our sin from before He created the universe.

The Father's plan for the crucifixion of His Son was motivated by His love for us, and it was required by His justice. The grisliest spectacle of the ancient world was intended to be unspeakably cruel, mercilessly drawn out, inescapably public, and openly verifiable. It was intended to humiliate and terrify. Even before Jesus's birth in Bethlehem, the decision had been made in heaven that God would have to come to Earth and take drastic measures to fix the problem that humanity had gotten itself into with sin. Jesus would come to Earth and go to a cross. Revelation 13:8 says that He is "the Lamb slain from the foundation of the world." Out of the wickedness and cruelty of humanity, God would fulfill His plan to rescue His beloved creation.

The Cross is proof of God's sovereignty and love. The Cross frees us to live as God intended, humbly, joyfully, and lovingly. If you are ever tempted to doubt God's love for you, even for a moment, then take a long, hard look at the Cross.

God, thank you that before the foundation of the world, You laid out Your design to love us, redeem us, shower us with grace, and make us holy through Christ's death on the cross.

God ordained the murder of Jesus so that our redemption could be accomplished.

Extreme Forgiveness

"Father, forgive them, for they do not know what they do."
(Luke 23:34)

It was the sickest, most twisted moment in all human history as man put God to death. But as nails were being driven into the Divine, securing His shredded body to the coarse crossbeam, Jesus practiced what He had preached (see Matthew 5:44). He interceded on behalf of His torturers. Talk about extreme forgiveness!

Jesus had said and done many shocking and miraculous things during His earthly life, but this perhaps was one of the most remarkable. It makes perfect sense that the first words of Jesus from the cross were about forgiveness. After all, that was the main reason for His death. When Jesus said, "Forgive them," no doubt His words were directed at all those responsible for putting Him on the cross that day. But by extension we, because of our sin, also placed Jesus on the cross.

God is about forgiveness, and God loves people. When you put those two together, you get extreme forgiveness. We all need God's forgiveness—forgiveness that is unconditional, that we don't deserve, that we didn't earn, that was offered before we even asked for it, and that was planned from eternity past. We all need God's forgiveness that allows us to let go of sins we are tempted to hold on to, that keeps us from revisiting old sins, and that stops us from beating ourselves up over our failures. Accept God's forgiveness today, and let go of your guilt and condemnation.

Jesus, You freely offer forgiveness to all. By faith I accept Your forgiveness, and I commit to believe Your truth and to live fully and freely in Your grace. In Jesus's name, amen.

Jesus died so that we might be forgiven.

It's Never too Late

"Assuredly, I say to you, today you will be with Me in Paradise." *(Luke 23:43)*

It is never too late for God to forgive someone, and there is no sin too great that God cannot forgive. As Jesus hung on the cross, He was mocked by religious leaders and Roman soldiers. One of the two criminals being crucified alongside Jesus even added his own measure of insult to injury being piled upon God. The other criminal, however, sensed that Jesus was being treated unjustly, and after speaking up for Him (see Luke 23:40–41), he cried out, "Lord, remember me when You come into Your kingdom" (verse 42).

If ever there was a deathbed conversion, this was it. A hardened criminal who lived his entire life as a thief and a thug found faith in the final moments of his life as he hung next to God. Jesus can forgive someone who has lived a completely wicked and God-rejecting life if they sincerely place their faith and trust in Him before their final breath. No one is insignificant to God. God writes no one off, and no one is beyond the grace of God. God loves the murderer, the rapist, and the thief, and He wants them all to repent and turn to Him.

The thief on the cross is no excuse for someone to squander their life and postpone their decision of faith, but it is a reminder that while you are still alive, it's never too late to receive forgiveness and salvation from God. If you are tempted to think, "God can't forgive all that I have done," remember the thief on the cross. If you are tempted to think, "There is no way that person ever will come to know God," remember the thief on the cross.

Father God, help me to never give up and to never to stop praying for those who seem the most unlikely to be saved. If the thief could be saved with a dying breath, then anyone can.

In this life, it's never too late to trust in Jesus.

The Great Abandonment

"My God, my God, why have You forsaken Me?" (Mark 15:34)

Sin is so terrible that God cannot ignore it. He cannot let it slide or pretend that it's no big deal. Sin must be dealt with if there's going to be a relationship with God.

It was noon, and Jesus had been on the cross for three agonizing hours. Suddenly, darkness fell as midday became midnight (see Matthew 27:45). Supernatural darkness came across the land as a symbol of God's judgment on sin. God's beloved Son had become our sin, and while experiencing the full brunt of His Father's wrath, Jesus could not keep silent. He cried out, "My God, my God, why have You forsaken me?" (Mark 15:34). There is no possible way we can understand Jesus's suffering as He was being made sin for us. For the first and only time in all eternity, God abandoned God. God's great moment of atonement for humanity also was the moment God abandoned His Son. But once redemption was accomplished, the triune relationship was restored to complete oneness, never to be severed again.

Life is filled with good times and hard times, but no matter how bad life gets, God never will stop loving you, and He never will leave you. When your trust is in God; He never will let you go. "I will never leave you or forsake you" (Hebrews 13:5) is now the promise in which all believers can take comfort. Jesus was forsaken so we never have to be.

Thank you, Father, Son, and Holy Spirit, for your willingness, in those hours of unfathomable darkness, to purchase my salvation and ensure that You'll never turn Your back on me.

We are forgiven because Jesus was forsaken.

Paid in Full

"It is finished!" *(John 19:30)*

God finishes what He begins. When Jesus died on the cross, He bore our griefs, He carried our sorrows, He was wounded for our wrong-doings, He was injured for our iniquities, He was punished for our peace, and He was reproached for our restoration (see Isaiah 53:4–5). The final words of Jesus on the cross were not "I'm finished," as in some defeated, "I'm done for" confession. "It is finished" is a victorious exclamation that what Jesus came to do had been accomplished.

The last words of Jesus on the cross are one word in the original language, a single word with inexhaustible meaning. One word declared that the Old Covenant had ended and the New Covenant had begun. A single word certified that His suffering was finished, His work was completed, and His sacrifice for sin was satisfied.

With a single word, Christianity is separated from every other religion on the planet. All other religions are about what you need to do to be right with God. "It is finished" means that you don't need to do anything to be right with Him, because Jesus has done everything! All you need to do is have faith in Jesus. There's nothing more to be done concerning your salvation. Once and for all, we have been reconciled to God.

Are you trusting in the finished work of Jesus? Are you trying to add to what Jesus has done? God desires that you receive and fully rest in His finished work. You don't have to labor for His righteousness, forgiveness, deliverance, healing, or even His peace (see Matthew 11:28–30).

God, what Jesus did on the cross removed the burden of having to work my way to heaven through self-effort. Because of the debt I could not pay, Jesus paid the debt He did not owe.

> **There is nothing left to do for salvation, because Jesus said, "It is finished!"**

Jesus on the Go

"What kind of conversation is this that you have with one another as you walk?" (Luke 24:17)

Does talking about Jesus make you nervous? Perhaps it would help to see how Jesus talked to other people when He spoke about God. We can learn a few valuable lessons when it comes to reaching friends, neighbors, and loved ones with the gospel by looking at Jesus's interaction with two people He met on the road to Emmaus.

First, Jesus walked with them. Jesus joined them within their activity and within the context of their environment. Most of the conversations Jesus had with people were not in religious settings. Jesus talked with people about spiritual issues in familiar places. He talked to people in the workplace, in their homes, and while going places along the way. Next, Jesus asked them questions. God asks questions to generate engagement, create conversations, and build relationships. The best way to get people to listen to you is to listen to them as you ask them questions that force their introspection. Questions also help you connect with people's thoughts and feelings. Then Jesus utilized the truth of Scripture to deal with their unbelief, because "faith comes by hearing, and hearing by the word of God" (Romans 10:17). The Word of God is always the first and most important witness to the reality and deity of Jesus. Finally, Jesus shared a meal with them for the sake of friendship and to further the relationship (see Luke 24:30).

We don't need to hit people over the head with our Bibles or pressure them to make on-the-spot-decisions. Jesus gave people time to process, and so should we.

Jesus, help me to learn from your example when it comes to speaking to others about You.

Find common ground and connect to people's experiences and emotions as you point them to Jesus.

DECEMBER

Resurrection Joy

"Rejoice." *(Matthew 28:9)*

Two thousand years ago, God raised Jesus from the dead. That is more than a mere historical event. It is more than a theological principle. The Resurrection is the foundation of our faith, the assurance of our freedom from sin, and the basis for our eternal victory. Without the Resurrection, Christ's death would have been nothing more than the mere death of any other person, and there would be no salvation for humankind because a dead God cannot save anyone.

Practically, the Resurrection enables us to live holy and victorious lives, because the same power that raised Jesus from the dead is alive and working in each of us (see Romans 8:11). It also means that God keeps His word, proving that God's Word is true. This means we can trust it, we can use it, and we can build our lives on it. The Resurrection means that God created the universe, because God is in control of the universe and is actively at work in it.

True joy comes from knowing that life is different because Jesus rose from the dead. True joy does not depend on our circumstances. True joy comes from God, and therefore it cannot be affected by what happens around us. The Resurrection liberates lives, uplifts spirits, practically affects holiness, and provides surety for a believer's resurrection. It means that faith is powerful, the gospel is true, and we're saved from sin. I'd say that's reason to rejoice.

God, since death could not hold You and the grave could not keep You, I can always rejoice in the Resurrection, because You are alive, and Your help and hope are available to me.

Without the resurrection of Jesus, the Cross accomplished nothing.

From Demon-Possessed to Devoted Disciple

"Mary." (John 20:16)

Mary's devotion to Jesus put her in the spotlight on a few occasions. One such moment happened three days after Jesus had been placed in the grave. On that early Sunday morning, Mary Magdalene, along with a group of devoted women, met at Jesus' tomb. But as they approached, they noticed the giant stone had been rolled away and the body of Jesus was gone. Mary wept, but when Jesus called her by name, she was filled with joy and immediately hugged her Savior.

Mary Magdalene loved Jesus. After all, He drastically changed her life. Once demon-possessed, Mary had been set free by Jesus from seven evil spirits (see Luke 8:1–3). Mary had known the terrifying power of spiritual enslavement and the exhilarating freedom that came as Jesus saved her and set her free as no one else could. There was no way Mary would forget or forsake her Savior after that. This was made evident by her display of rare courage during the Crucifixion. She never left Jesus. She was the last one to leave the cross and the first one to reach the tomb.

Mary Magdalene didn't have much, but she always gave everything she had to Jesus. She refused to be defined by her past. All that mattered to her was who she had become after meeting Jesus. Jesus turned Mary's life around, and as the result of her faithfulness, she was one of the first people to share the good news of the Resurrection (see John 20:17–18).

Jesus, You have saved me and set me free to live for You. You give my life purpose, and Mary's life reminds me to live faithfully and fully for You.

> **When Jesus calls you by name, everything changes.**

Jesus Helps Our Unbelief

"Reach your finger here and look at My hands; and reach your hand here and put it into My side. Do not be unbelieving but believing." (John 20:27)

December is a time when we decorate our homes, light up our lawns, and enjoy some extra time with our family and friends. We spend time looking for special gifts, decorating cookies, and listening to Christmas music. Naturally during this special time of year, our thoughts turn to people who do not know Jesus. And even though many people are open to hearing about Jesus during the Christmas season, some remain skeptical.

God can work with the person who is looking for facts or wanting proof. He did so for the one we call Doubting Thomas. Doubt isn't always a bad thing. Certainly doubt that is in search of truth is good doubt, because no one comes to Jesus without genuinely contemplating the truth. Many people come down hard on Thomas because of his doubt. But let's not forget that the other disciples only believed when they, too, had seen the evidence. When Thomas eventually did see the evidence, he expressed one of the greatest confessions in history about Jesus when he said, "My Lord and my God!" (see John 20:28).

So if you come across doubters this holiday season, don't give them some used car salesman-style pressured pitch about Jesus. And don't beat them over the head with biblical truth. Do like Jesus did, and let the skeptic come to you with their questions. Also, do your best to compassionately respond to their doubts so they can see Jesus clearly.

God, give me the wisdom to speak compassionate truth to any skeptic I might encounter this holiday season. And God, when I have my own doubts, bring me to a deeper faith in You.

Jesus can turn skepticism into faith.

Get Going

"Go therefore and make disciples of all the nations."
(Matthew 28:19)

The world needs Jesus. And God wants to use you to reach the world around you. When the time drew near for the resurrected Jesus to return to heaven, His followers wondered, "What now?" Jesus told them to take what they knew about Him, go into the world, and share it with others.

God is calling you and me to go to people everywhere. No nation is exempt, and no individual is off-limits. This isn't a polite suggestion. God isn't saying, "Look, I know you're busy, but if you have some time, could you do me a favor . . . ?" This is one of God's non-negotiables. If you are a Christian, God expects you to *go*! And no one can say they don't have the gift of *going*. That's not a thing. All of us are to get up and go.

For some, going means going far and wide across the globe to share the gospel. But it also means sharing while we're going here and there and around town. Wherever we're going and whatever we're doing, we are to be sharing. We are to take what we know about Jesus and make Him known to everyone, everywhere. But don't be a weirdo about it. Offering to baptize people in the break room sink may not be the best way to bring up Jesus at work. Instead, start looking for natural opportunities to communicate God's love to someone, because how will they hear about Jesus unless someone tells them? (See Romans 10:14.) Are you intentionally going out looking for a way to share the gospel?

Jesus, help me to be purposeful about sharing You with other people. Open my eyes to see the opportunities for conversations about You, whether I'm on the go or intentionally going.

When Jesus says go, we need to go.

How Do We Make Disciples?

"Go therefore and make disciples of all the nations."
(Matthew 28:19)

Jesus didn't come to make Christians; He came to make disciples. Therefore, discipleship is an important part of following Jesus. Discipleship is the process of assisting in the spiritual growth and maturity of another believer's faith. It is the process of becoming, and helping others become, more like Jesus. Then, of course, there is the fact that Jesus commands us to actively make disciples.

So how did Jesus make disciples? Jesus chose twelve people, and then He shared life with them as He explained and exemplified spiritual life. Jesus ate with His disciples, walked with them, rode in boats with them, and went to church with them. And in the process of living life, He showed them how to live to please God in the real world and in real-life situations. True discipleship is more than learning truth. It is learning how to put spiritual truth into practice. Jesus connected with people relationally and personally, and He equipped His followers to walk as He walked and live as He lived.

To disciple people as Jesus did, we must live out our faith with others and share our lives with them. We must teach others by word and by example. We are inviting people to follow our example as we follow the example of Christ (see 1 Corinthians 11:1 NIV). To disciple like Jesus, we must be willing to invest our lives in the lives of others and help them obey Jesus and grow in relationship with Him.

God, join me in the process of making disciples, because it is a supernatural work that requires the help of Your Holy Spirit.

All believers are to show others how to follow Jesus.

Experiencing God's Presence

"And lo, I am with you always, even to the end of the age."
(Matthew 28:20)

God promises His presence to His people. But if we are honest, as much as the presence of God sounds wonderful, it also can be little hard to understand and somewhat elusive to experience. We know God's presence is everywhere (see Psalm 139:7), but is there something we need to do to become more aware of His presence in our lives?

Experiencing God's presence is not dependent on our being in a particular place at a particular time. It is not determined by some tingly, goose-bump feeling. Rather, it is only dependent on our determination to stay in close relationship with God. The more time we spend intentionally seeking God, the more aware we will grow of His presence in our lives. Remember when Joshua needed some reassurance after taking over for Moses? God reminded Joshua that all of Moses's accomplishments had been due to His presence with Moses, and the same God who walked with Moses would walk with him (see Joshua 1:5). God was with Joshua, but for Joshua to experience God's presence, he needed to stay connected to God's Word. He needed to mediate on it and put it into practice (see Joshua 1:8–9).

We never will fully experience God's presence in our lives if we are just going through the religious motions. If we allow the ordinary to take priority in our lives, it will keep us from experiencing the presence and power of God. And when we learn to find joy in His presence, we are well on our way to living the abundant life that God desires for us all.

God, I want to know You more and walk more closely with You. I want to experience more of Your power and presence in my life.

> **Jesus made it possible for us to experience God's presence, now and forever.**

Facing Failure

"Come and eat breakfast." (John 21:12)

Have you ever blown it? Perhaps you've messed up and think there is no way God could use you anymore. No doubt Peter had some similar thoughts running though his mind. After all, he had been a leader among the disciples, he had been given the "keys of the kingdom" (see Matthew 16:19), and he even defended Jesus when the soldiers came to arrest Him (see John 18:10). Then Peter, whose name means "rock," was reduced to nothing more than a pebble when he denied Jesus *three* separate times (Luke 22:54–62).

God knew that Peter would fail. He wasn't surprised by it. So when Jesus met up with Peter, He refused to let Peter's failure define him or disqualify him. Failure happens to all of us. The important thing about failure is what happens next. Shame over past failures and sins can haunt and inhibit us and, in many ways, erode our intimacy with God. Not to mention the enemy loves throwing our failures back in our faces. But Jesus responded to Peter by standing on the seashore and inviting him back into fellowship. There was even a bonus: breakfast was included.

When Jesus chose you, He saw all your future failures just as surely as He foresaw Peter's. Your failures do not need to define you or disqualify you. God doesn't see failure as the end. God uses imperfect people. If God only used perfect people, then the Bible would be a very short book. The way back from failure begins by restoring fellowship with God.

God, I admit that sometimes I stumble, and it can be hard to accept and remember there is no condemnation for those in Christ Jesus. (see Romans 8:1). I know You are always ready to receive me back into fellowship.

> **Jesus invites us into fellowship, even after failure.**

"Do You Love Me?"

"Simon, son of Jonah, do you love Me more than these?"
(John 21:15)

Jesus wants you to love Him more than anything else. If you have ever been around someone who really loves Jesus, it is hard to forget them. They approach life with confidence, courage, and joy, unlike most. They hardly seem overtaken by the cares and concerns of this life. They recover from setbacks with a ready-to-go attitude and full of faith. They are passionate about doing the things God has given them to do. They radiate His love everywhere they go and in everything they do. They speak His truth in love. Everything they do springs from their love for God. No one could ever live like that unless they loved Jesus more than anything.

Take Peter for example. He was changed forever that day on the beach with Jesus. Part of Peter's restoration from publicly denying Jesus included publicly affirming his love for Jesus. The question Jesus asked Peter is the same one that He would ask us: Do you love me more than these? It is a question that examines our motives and searches the true intentions of our hearts. It doesn't matter what "these" are, because they may be different for everyone. The heart of the question is this: Do you love Jesus more than anything?

After Peter affirmed his love for Jesus, he became unstoppable. He persevered through trials, he stood tall against opposition, and he boldly proclaimed the gospel. He approached life with confidence, courage, and joy, and he recovered from setbacks full of faith. Peter went on to live a life that showed the world that he loved Jesus more than anything.

Dear God, help me to be the type of person who approaches life with a faith unlike most.

May people see that you love Jesus more than anything.

The Comparison Trap

Peter said to Jesus, "But Lord, what about this man?"
*Jesus said to him, "... **What is that to you? You follow Me.**"*
(John 21:22)

Comparison leads to dissatisfaction and resentment. When others seem to get ahead or are seemingly more blessed than us, we can grow envious. Sometimes we look at others and wonder, "Why has God done good things for them but not for me? Why do I suffer when others don't? Why are things always hard for me?" Comparisons like this can happen in ministry too. But there always will be someone who has more influence, more followers, or just more of whatever we want. Instead of focusing on what we don't have, we need to learn to be content with what we do have.

Comparison is a trap because it is rooted in discontent. Peter needed a reminder about resentment before his ministry for God was to begin. When Jesus told Peter that he would die as a martyr for his faith, Peter's knee-jerk reaction was to ask what would happen to his friend and fellow disciple, John. Peter seemed to think that it would only be fair if John shared the same fate as him. But Jesus told Peter that was none of his concern. It was God's decision how their lives would play out. Peter's responsibility was simple: follow Jesus.

God has His reasons for placing us in different situations. Instead of comparing ourselves to others, we need to learn to be content with the path on which God has us and make following Him our main concern. It is the only way to avoid falling into the comparison trap.

Lord God, I know jealousy and envy do not come from You. Give me
a heart of gratitude for all You have given me and not worry about
how You choose to work in someone else's life.

> **Fixing our eyes on Jesus is the key to glorifying God in any circumstance.**

Our Power Supply

"You shall receive power when the Holy Spirit
has come upon you." (Act 1:8)

No one can live a holy life in their own strength. The power to live as God desires only can be done by the power God supplies. It is reassuring to know that God never calls us to do that which He doesn't empower us to achieve.

When Jesus gave His disciples the task of taking the gospel into the world, they had absolutely no ability to carry out such an extensive mission. The work of God only can be done by the power of God. That's why Jesus told the disciples to wait until the Holy Spirit came upon them and provided them with the power they would need. God's kingdom is spiritual. Therefore, only spiritual power will get spiritual work done. The ordinary people God chose were able to do extraordinary things because the Spirit of God worked in and through their lives.

The power of the Holy Spirit is an absolute necessity if we are going to live the way God calls us to live and do what God calls us to do. The Holy Spirit comes to take residence in believers the moment they confess and believe in Jesus Christ as Lord. From that moment on, they have access to the power and person of God—power that transforms people to think the way God thinks, to love the way God loves, and to see others the way God sees them. It's power that gifts people to serve others, power that brings new life in people, power that produces fruit in our lives, and power that bears witness to Jesus as God.

Dear God, may I live each day relying on the power of Your Holy Spirit, because Your Spirit gives me what I need to live a holy and victorious life.

Jesus makes it clear: the Holy Spirit is the power of God to accomplish the will of God.

Your Christmas Witness

"You shall be witnesses to Me in Jerusalem, and in all Judea and Samaria, and to the end of the earth." (Acts 1:8)

You may only be one person, but one person can make a difference. It takes courage to step out and share your faith. We've all had those feelings when we are talking with a neighbor or sitting next to a stranger and were wondering whether we should try to talk about God with them. It isn't always easy to take that first step and bring God into the conversation.

When Jesus said, "You shall be witnesses to Me in Jerusalem, and in all Judea and Samaria, and to the end of the earth" (Acts 1:8), He was giving us God's strategy for evangelism. The disciples were to start in Jerusalem. In other words, they were to start right where they were. Then they were to move outwardly to nearby Judea and Samaria and then expand even further to reach the rest of the world. God's plan to reach the world starts with you, right where you are.

It can be easy to let what-might-happen thoughts or what-if fears of rejection stop you from taking those conversational first steps of bringing up God with someone. Remember, you don't have to have all the answers, and you don't have to memorize the entire Bible before you can be a witness. A witness simply testifies to what they know, what they have seen, and what they have experienced. You don't have to convince or convict someone, because that's God's job. You just need to be willing to start with what you know, right where you are. Yes, you are only one person, but you can make a difference if you are willing to be a witness.

Jesus, may I be ready and willing to be a witness for You and to share what I believe as I live for You and speak about You to the people around me.

> **Jesus wants us to start witnessing for Him right where we are.**

The Gift of Giving

"It is more blessed to give than to receive." (Acts 20:35)

As a kid, Christmas is all about receiving. You spend hours sizing up the boxes under the tree, and when you find your name on a gift, you go through the investigation process of shaking it carefully and listening for clues, all the while hoping that what you are holding isn't a box of socks or underwear. As you get older, as much as it is nice to receive a thoughtful gift, it is a greater blessing to be the giver.

Our God is a giving God. So it makes sense that when we are givers, we help show others what God is like. Jesus didn't say it isn't a blessing to also receive, because receiving does make us happy. But the world tries to tell us that it is better to be a getter than a giver. Jesus, however, turns the prevailing worldly standard upside down by telling us that we will be more blessed when we are givers. When we begin to realize and appreciate all that we have received from God (see James 1:17), it will turn us into givers.

Giving is at the heart of Christianity (see John 3:16), and it should be an important part of the Christian life. Giving goes beyond what we give financially to include giving of our time and our talents to benefit and encourage others. We can begin by asking ourselves, "How can I help this person?" or "Is there something I can do to bless that person?" When we are thinking as givers, that blesses God and will in turn bring a blessing to us.

God, being a giver will help kill my self-centeredness and remove the love of money. Help me to go beyond the holiday and live each day as a giver.

Jesus is the ultimate example of a giver because He gave everything for us.

DECEMBER 13

One Step at a Time

"Arise and go into Damascus, and there you will be told all things which are appointed for you to do." (Acts 22:10)

God grows us gradually. He prefers to work in our lives little by little and inch by inch. You might be wondering why God has taken this approach, since most of us like to see the big picture. We like to plan ahead, we like to know where we are going, and we like to know how long it's going take to get there.

Although God knows the future, He prefers to direct us one step at time. Elijah was told to go and wait at the river before getting further instructions from God (see 1 Kings 17:2, 8), Philip was told to go to the dessert and await further instructions (see Acts 8:26–40), Paul was told to go to Damascus and await further instructions (see above), and Mary and Joseph were told to go and wait in Egypt before getting further instructions (Matthew 2:13). See a pattern? God won't give you the second step until you have been faithful to take the first one.

This is how our spiritual journey goes most of the time. As much as we would like for God to reveal his "big" plan for our lives, the journey God has us on is made up of obedient, single steps. God knows that our growth needs to be gradual as we learn how to trust in Him more completely, depend on His guidance more assuredly, and develop our faith more securely. It's a gradual process that takes time.

God, I know it takes time to learn and that I need to put into practice what You are showing me today before You will lead me tomorrow. Help me to be obedient to take today's steps of faith.

> **As we take a step of obedience, Jesus will show us what to do next.**

God's Grace

"My grace is sufficient for you, for My strength is made perfect in weakness." (2 Corinthians 12:9)

God's grace is the most important concept for the world to understand, because it is the foundation for all biblical doctrine. Grace is the demonstration of God's love shown to a sinful world. Grace is God's undeserved, unmerited, and unearned compassion and acceptance. It is His kindness to the undeserving and His forgiveness for the unworthy.

Grace is God's best for humanity and humanity's most needed provision. It is God's decision to shower humankind with a love that rescues, restores, and is unrivaled. Grace is getting what we don't deserve, because what we deserve is death with no hope of eternal life as a result of our sin. But God has said, "For by grace you have been saved through faith, and that not of yourselves; it is the gift of God" (Ephesians 2:8). Grace is not earned; it's given. God's grace is always available to us for every problem and every need we face. God's grace never runs out and never changes, because it is limitless and changeless. Grace is God giving us nothing less than Himself.

Grace changes people. Grace grabs you where you are and brings you to where God wants to take you. God's grace frees us from sin, guilt, and shame. God's grace allows us to pursue good works. God's grace enables us to be all that God intends us to be, which is more like Him.

Gracious God, help me to comprehend Your grace more and experience it more in my life. Give me enough grace for today so that I can show grace to others.

God's grace comes to us through Jesus.

The Sufficiency of His Grace

"My grace is sufficient for you, for My strength is made perfect in weakness." (2 Corinthians 12:9)

No one is perfect. We all have weaknesses. But God can use everything for good, and that includes our weaknesses.

When life gets hard or when we face a difficult situation, we usually turn to God and pray that He will ease our hardship or change our situation. That's what the apostle Paul did when he suffered from what he called a "thorn in the flesh" (2 Corinthians 12:7). On three different occasions, Paul asked God to remove it. However, God's final answer to Paul was that the thorn would remain and His grace would be sufficient. God used Paul in amazing and powerful ways, but He also allowed an affliction to remain in Paul's life so that He would stay humble and continually dependent on God.

When we rely on our own strength, resources, and knowledge, we assume we can handle life without any help from God. Our weaknesses are there to remind us of our need for God. We never will face anything that God's grace cannot empower us to handle. We serve a God who is more than enough, and His grace is more than enough, every time and in every situation. Anytime you feel weak, remember that when you rely on His grace, you are at your strongest. God's grace is sufficient because God is always enough.

God, I thank You for the sufficiency of Your grace. I thank You that Your grace empowers and equips me to deal with whatever I may be facing.

Jesus uses our weaknesses to lead us to rely on God's strength.

First Love

"Nevertheless, I have this against you, that you have left your first love." (Revelation 2:4)

No one suddenly wakes up and says they don't love Jesus anymore. It is a slow process that happens gradually over years. Unanswered prayers, unexplained hardships, unexpected loss, and unmet expectations all can lead to a loss of hope and a dwindling of our love for God. Sometimes our love for Jesus grows, and at other times it grows cold. When your love for God flounders, everything in your life flounders. When love grows cold, religion becomes ritual. It becomes mechanical and routine, and it becomes nothing more than going through the religious motions.

Sadly, that is what happened in Ephesus. The church there was a great church. They believed correctly, served continually, and defended the faith consistently. But over time their love began to grow cold. They had not walked away from Jesus; they were just more interested in their works *for* Jesus than in their relationship *with* Jesus. They were busy *for* Christ. but there was no closeness *with* Christ.

How can you tell if your love for Jesus is growing cold? It's growing cold when other things become more important to you than God, when life gets so overcrowded that it pushes fellowship with God to the side, when you seek the approval of others more than the approval of God, and when you become indifferent toward sin. If you find that you are drifting away from God and feel like your love for Jesus is not what it once was, then today is the day to start refreshing and rekindling the relationship.

God, You are my first love. I don't want anything to change that. Help me to never take You for granted but to always do those things that keep my love for You burning bright.

The works we do for Jesus will not be pleasing to Jesus unless they're done out of love for Him.

Rekindle the Flame

"Remember therefore from where you have fallen; repent and do the first works." (Revelation 2:5)

While it is true that married love deepens and grows richer over time, it is also true that it can lose the excitement and wonder of the honeymoon phase. When a husband and wife begin to take each other for granted and life becomes routine, then love is in danger of growing stale.

The honeymoon phase had ended at Ephesus. The dynamic love relationship with Jesus grew into spiritual apathy and indifference as they took their relationship with God for granted. The Ephesian church had become so busy serving that their work for God had diminished their love for God. They lost sight of what was most important in their relationship with God, which was their love for Him.

The good news is that Jesus tells us how to rekindle our love for Him (principles that also apply for rekindling the love in our marriage). The three-step process includes remembering, repenting, and returning. *Remember.* Remember how things were in the beginning? Remember the joy you had spending time with God? Remember how you used to pray, read, and worship? *Repent.* Let the conviction of remembering how things used to be lead you to make a commitment to turning things around. *Return.* Return to God by redoing those things you did in the beginning. Return to the loving habits of grace you once had, and follow them again. Whenever you feel your love fading, put these steps into practice and rekindle the flame.

God, revive the fire of my love. Inspire my mind, ignite my heart, and show me what I can do to keep my love for You from ever growing cold.

Your love for Jesus always can be rekindled.

Listening to God

"He who has an ear, let him hear what the Spirit says."
(Revelation 2:7)

God loves to speak to His people, and He speaks to us in a variety of ways. The question isn't whether God is speaking; the question is whether we're listening for His voice.

God primarily speaks to His people through *His Word*. His words show us truth, correct our mistakes, and train us to live God's way in this life (see 2 Timothy 3:16–17). The Bible is our handbook for life, and if we're not spending time reading the Bible, then we are tuning God out and silencing the main way He speaks into our lives.

God speaks to us through *Jesus*: "God, who at various times and in various ways spoke in time past to the fathers by the prophets, has in these last days spoken to us by His Son, whom He has appointed heir of all things" (Hebrews 1:1–2).

God speaks to us through our *circumstances*. When we are going through difficult situations, we must remember that God wants to speak to us in our pain. C. S. Lewis said, "God whispers to us in our pleasures, speaks in our conscience, but shouts in our pain."[14] In other words, God uses difficulties to grab our attention.

God also speaks to us through His Holy Spirit, through Creation, through other people, and through prayer. But when we're listening for God, we must make sure that it's His voice we are hearing and not our own thoughts or someone else's ideas. God's voice *never* will contradict His Word and *always* leads us into deeper fellowship with Him.

Father, I want to be still and listen for Your still, small voice. As You speak to me, I want listen with a prepared heart and a willing mind, ready to obey Your voice.

> **Jesus always will give us clear guidance if we are listening for His voice.**

Embracing God at Christmas

Then Mary said, "Behold the maidservant of the Lord! Let it be to me according to your word." (Luke 1:38)

Her name was Mary, and she was a young girl from a small village called Nazareth. We assume she was a girl just like any other girl from that area, living a simple life in a simple village.

But she also must have been a girl unlike any other girl, seeking the things of God and living out her faith as best as she knew how. Her dreams, like the dreams of most girls in her situation, would have been to be married and raise a family. When the time was right, she would be married to an upright man named Joseph. This is where the story gets interesting. An angel appeared to give Mary some news: "Mary, . . . you have found favor with God. And behold, you will conceive in your womb and bring forth a Son, and shall call His name Jesus" (Luke 1:30–31).

Mary didn't respond by saying, "Yeah, I'm not really interested" or "Ah, hold on a second. I think you have the wrong Mary." Although she asked, "How can this be?" (verse 34), the feeling that radiates from the pages of Scripture isn't one of disbelief as much as it is one of logistics. After the angel spoke of how God would use Mary, she didn't run from God's plans for her life. As challenging as it would be, as life-changing and even unsettling as it would be, she embraced and accepted her permanent role as part of what would be forever known as the Christmas story.

Mary's faith and willingness to embrace God's Word as it was told to her, along with her submission to God's will, exemplify to all of us of what God can do in the life of someone who is willing to embrace His will and surrender to His Word.

God, may I glory in Your presence and embrace Your Word as I worship You this Christmas.

> **Embrace Jesus and His Word, and watch how God can use you.**

Here I Am to Worship

"For we have seen His star in the East and have come to worship Him." (Matthew 2:2)

Although Christmas is a season that should be filled with peace and goodwill, it also can be a season filled with hectic hustling and bustling and nerve-racking credit card spending. The holidays can bring a flurry of heightened emotions that can occasionally result in an unhealthy level of stress that prevents us from engaging in worship and praising the One we are supposed to be celebrating.

This Christmas, and every Christmas for that matter, we need to remember that Jesus is the greatest gift, and worship is the only proper response. Worship is not just something we do; it is a lifestyle we choose to live. It is living out that which comes from deep within our hearts and souls. It is the expression of our intense love for God. The wise men knew how to worship, and they went to great lengths to be in the presence of Jesus. Their journey was an act of worship, their attitude was an expression of worship, and their gifts were a demonstration of their worship.

If we are going to properly worship Jesus during the holidays and beyond, we must begin by making the decision to express our love for God in everything we do. We must make the continual decision to bring ourselves into the fellowship of His presence. And sometimes during the holidays, that means we must go to greater lengths to make that happen. Our relationship and our worship grow when we bring ourselves to Jesus. Worshiping God is giving Him our best, because He gave us His best: Jesus.

Jesus, I choose to intentionally worship You during this Christmas season. Help me stay focused on You and Your goodness and not become distracted with holiday busyness.

Worshiping Jesus is the most important thing we can do, especially during Christmas.

God with Us

"Behold, the virgin shall be with child, and bear a Son, and they shall call His name Immanuel," which is translated, "God with us."
(Matthew 1:23)

The Incarnation did not happen merely to let us know that God exists. It happened so that God could be with us. God supernaturally worked during Jesus's arrival to draw near to us. What are you doing this Christmas to draw near to Him?

Having a personal relationship with Jesus requires that we spend time with Him when it is both easy on our schedules and difficult to manage. For most people, the Christmas season is one of those difficult-to-manage times because there is so much going on in our lives. That's all the more reason to take the time during this special season to communicate with God regularly and lovingly. That means more than "saying your prayers" before you go to bed. It means having the type of prayer life that leads to *real* communion with God, communion in which there is an intimate sense of His presence in your heart and life. Consider Psalm 63 as an example of what a heartfelt prayer life looks like. A personal relationship means allowing God to speak to you. It means coming to the Bible to read it, seeking to understand it, and spending time meditating on it so it can shape and transform the way you live out His Word. Take a look at Psalm 119 to see how God's Word can shape your life.

Christmas is when God moved heaven and earth to draw near to us. Make sure you move whatever you need to move in your life to draw near to Him during this holy season.

Dear God, show me how to draw closer to You and live in constant communion with You.

The unapproachable God became approachable when Jesus came near.

The Christmas Conflict

"Then Herod . . . sent forth and put to death all the male children who were in Bethlehem." (Matthew 2:16)

Christmas is supposed to be a time of joy and compassion, but it often can be filled with hostility and anger. As you go shopping, you inevitably will see fights break out over parking spots, people ruthlessly plowing over others to get that special sale item, kids yelling and screaming in stores, and a general lack of consideration among the shopping masses. Add to that the family squabbles that can arise and all the other holiday tensions and pressures. Christmas can be filled with more conflict than celebration.

As off-putting as these struggles can be, the conflict of the original Christmas was far more severe than the conflicts we experience today. Satan did not want there to be a first Christmas. In fact, he did everything in his power to stop Jesus from being born. He made various attempts in the Old Testament to wipe out the Jewish people, because he knew the Messiah was coming from them. When those attempts failed, he enlisted the help of King Herod, who ordered the death of all male children born in Bethlehem around the time of Jesus's birth. But God is greater than any opposition, and God will do what He sets out to do.

Conflict inevitably arises when we lose focus and take our eyes off Jesus. God wants us to live at peace with each other, but the enemy wants to cause conflict. When conflicts begin, let God calm your heart and refocus your thoughts on what really matters.

God, please bring Your peace into my Christmas. Wherever conflicts arise, help me look to You as the source for all my needs.

When tensions rise, let Jesus refocus your thoughts.

Christmas Music

"And suddenly there was with the angel a multitude of the heavenly host praising God." (Luke 2:13)

God loves music, and in the Bible, God's people often can be found singing and playing music (see Zephaniah 3:17; Mark 14:26). Scripture communicates the power and importance of music to us in many ways. The book of Psalms is filled with references to instruments and singing, indicating that music has an appropriate place in our worship of God. Music can move us, ease our minds, lift our spirits, bring us to tears, and bring us to our knees in worship.

Singing is an important part of who we are and who God created us to be. We all have different gifts, strengths, and favorite styles of music, but Scripture encourages all of us to find the music that allows our hearts to sing and connect to God. Music that honors God will cause our hearts to sing, and when our hearts sing to God, worship happens. God can use music to transform us from the inside out. Listening to music that glorifies God and speaks of God's nature and character can renew our minds, encourage our hearts, help us remember important Scriptures, and bring us into fellowship with Him.

Make the most of your Christmas singing this year and seek out songs that worship, praise, and give thanks to God. God doesn't care how you sound when you sing; He cares about the position of your heart. May your Christmas music bring joy to your heart, peace to your mind, and worship to your spirit.

Jesus, help me to have a lifestyle of worship, praising You in every situation. I believe there is power in worshiping You. May I offer You the sacrifice of praise this season.

Let's sing more songs that encourage our worship of Jesus.

Silent Night, Holy Night

"And she brought forth her firstborn Son, and wrapped Him in swaddling cloths, and laid Him in a manger, because there was no room for them in the inn." (Luke 2:7)

It was not so silent on the night Jesus was born. Unlike the picturesque Nativity scenes depicted on Christmas cards, the night of Jesus's birth would have been filled with restless animals and the painful sounds of childbirth. But even though the arrival of Jesus was not a silent night, it was a holy night.

The birth of Jesus wasn't an ordinary birth of an ordinary man. The birth of Jesus was the incarnation of God Himself. The unapproachable God became an approachable, accessible, knowable man. Jesus, who was born in a manger, fully represented God and His love, mercy, righteousness, compassion, glory, and holiness. God was perfectly represented in the humanity of Jesus.

It's no accident that the Christmas season is the noisiest, busiest, most materialistic, and most stressful time of year. If Satan can keep us from being silent and quieting our hearts before God, then he can distract us from listening to what God is saying to us and truly celebrating the holiness of Christmas. Whether it's the noise of the crowds at the mall or the shouts of excited children opening presents, Christmas is hardly silent. Yet, if we take time to retreat from the commotion and take time for communion with God as we consider what it meant for God to become man, we will begin to transform our not-so-silent days and nights into holy moments this season.

God, I choose not to be overwhelmed by circumstances but instead choose to sing of Your beauty and greatness. I choose to praise Your holy name.

Jesus wants to break through our busyness to remind us of His holiness.

The Awe of Christmas

"Do not be afraid, for behold, I bring you good tidings of great joy which will be to all people." (Luke 2:10)

What things cause you to become amazed? Is it visiting a majestic place like a mountaintop, gazing at a natural wonder, standing at some ancient historical site, or watching a child being born? The night Jesus was born was an amazing and awe-inspiring event as God sent His Son to Earth so that He could make a way for humanity to have eternal life. It was an event that caused the angels to reveal themselves and make their voices heard in song. Can you imagine how the shepherds must have felt at the sight and sounds of angels?

It seems like we tend to appreciate fewer awe-inspiring moments these days. Perhaps it's because technology has brought the world to our fingertips, or perhaps we have allowed ourselves to become too busy to slow down and let ourselves be amazed. Unfortunately, this can also mean that we are having fewer awe-inspiring moments with God. We can become too comfortable with God, and therefore those things that should awe and amaze us can go unnoticed or underappreciated.

Christmas should be a time when we attempt to have more awe-inspiring moments with God, not less. Today, find a way to rejoice like the angels did as God became man. Jesus should never cease to bring you to a place of absolute awe.

God, forgive me for all too often not coming to You with the proper sense of awe and admiration. I bow before You in awe of who You are. Help me to always live in reverence of You.

Our response to the miracle of Jesus' birth should be one of awe and wonder.

Hold On!

"Hold fast to My name." (Revelation 2:13)

Walking with God is not easy. When we choose to follow God with our whole hearts, things often get harder. But faith means that we keep going. We keep pressing on. We keep persevering. Persistence is part of living out our faith. God doesn't always take away our difficulties or struggles, but He has given us what we need to persevere, to bounce back, to keep going, and to hold fast.

Holding fast means not allowing anything to pull us away from total commitment to God and His Word. Holding fast involves obedience that leads to blessing. As Proverbs 4:4 says, "Let your heart hold fast my words; keep my commandments, and live" (ESV). Holding fast embodies our faithful commitment to, and confidence in, Jesus.

Life is full of experiences that test us, drain us, and wipe us out. When we are worn out, that's when we are tempted to say to God, "I can't do this anymore." But Jesus uses our struggles to develop our relationship with Him (see 1 Peter 1:6–9). True commitment to Jesus is demonstrated through persevering over the long haul, not just the short term. Every situation is an opportunity for perseverance to build us up and to trust God more. God has given us the ability to persevere, or to hold fast, by responding with a confidence that knows God has a good plan for our lives.

God is faithful, even when we have no idea how things will turn out, and it is during those times when it is most important to hang tight and hold fast to God and His Word.

Jesus, may I keep my mind fixed on You, because then my actions won't waiver.

> **Holding fast to Jesus and His Word has its rewards (see Revelation 3:11–12).**

Do You Make God Sick?

"Because you are lukewarm, and neither cold nor hot, I will vomit you out of My mouth." (Revelation 3:16)

Some people make God sick. It sounds harsh, but it's true. Either you are for God, or you are against Him, but indifference makes God's stomach turn. G. Campbell Morgan wrote, "There is more hope of the man outside the church in all . . . that coldness, . . . than for the man within the church who is near enough to its warmth not to appreciate it, and far enough away from its burning heat to be useless to God and man. [There is a] greater chance for the heathen who has not heard the Gospel than for the man who has become an evangelized heathen."[15]

North of Laodicea were the healing hot springs of Hierapolis, and to the south were the refreshing cold springs of Colossae. But by the time water made it to Laodicea from either location, it was lukewarm and repulsive, like the faith of those who lived there. The church in Laodicea had become compromising, conceited, and Christless, and Jesus told them their indifference made Him sick. But Jesus didn't leave them spiritually stranded. He provided them with guidance on how to change their terrible situation.

Jesus's cure for our poverty is His spiritual wealth. His cure for our spiritual nakedness is to clothe us with robes of His righteousness. His cure for spiritual blindness is spiritual truth (see Revelation 3:18–19). Jesus's cure is more of Himself. More of Jesus is the only way to rid yourself of a lukewarm faith (see Revelation 3:20).

Lord God, give me a heart that burns with love for You! Forgive me for the times I have been lukewarm. Jesus, I gladly open the door of my heart and welcome You to come in today.

The only way to avoid becoming lukewarm is to stay connected to Jesus.

Knock, Knock . . .

"I stand at the door and knock. If anyone hears my voice and opens the door, I will come in and eat with that person, and they with me." (Revelation 3:20 NIV)

Is Jesus standing outside your church looking in? Laodicea was a church of tireless activity and apparent success. They were confident and in need of nothing (see Revelation 3:17). They were a congregation with a five-star rating and offered something for everyone. The only problem was that Jesus was standing on the outside looking in. Can you imagine Jesus standing outside His church looking in? Can you imagine the head of the church, knocking at the door, waiting for someone to let Him in?

Jesus can be standing outside a church if is He is not central to the preaching. A church that focuses more on feel-good messages rather than on preaching and teaching Jesus consistently and principally will find Him standing outside. Any church that is trying to creatively redefine its mission into something other than Jesus's final commission to the church to go and make disciples, teaching them to obey all that He commanded (see Matthew 18:19–20), may find Him standing on the outside looking in. And any church that seeks to build community that "does life together" but doesn't keep Jesus in the center of that fellowship is in danger of Jesus standing on the outside looking in.

Jesus must be in the center of our personal spiritual lives, and He must be in the center of the spiritual life of any church, or we might just find Jesus standing on the outside looking in.

Jesus, I invite You in so that we can have close and personal communion together. The thought of sharing the fellowship of a meal is a wonderful picture of intimacy with You.

Jesus seeks intimate fellowship with His people.

Blessings from the Book

"Blessed is he who keeps the words of the prophecy of this book." (Revelation 22:7)

God knows the end from the beginning. The book of Revelation is a snapshot of things to come. It is a glimpse into the end of the world as we know it. Unfortunately, many Christians have kept their distance from this book because they fail to see how it applies to their everyday lives. But prophecy is important, and the prophecies in the book of Revelation come with a blessing for all who hear, understand, and hold to the words found in it.

Jesus often spoke about the future, and He often rebuked people who did not seem to be able to understand the significance of things happening around them (see Luke 12:56). Jesus knew that understanding prophecy would help protect us against deception. The world is filled with counterfeit ideologies and false religions, and the best way to protect against artificial truth is to know genuine truth, which only comes from God's Word. Revelation wasn't intended for us to overanalyze current events and be preoccupied with conspiracy theories about the end times. It is intended to give us peace and hope, because Jesus was, is, and always will be victorious. In short, we have hope because God wins!

The book of Revelation was written to seven churches who were struggling under persecution from the outside and conflict from within, churches that had real problems, faced real suffering, were confronted with real hostility, and had to combat real deception. The book of Revelation was written to provide real hope and confidence in the sure and sovereign hand of God.

Jesus, soften my heart and strengthen my will so I can live as this book calls me to live.

The Revelation of Jesus Christ gives us a heavenly perspective about the future.

Coming Soon

"Yes, I am coming soon." (Revelation 22:20 NIV)

Jesus is coming back! Unquestionably, the events revealed in the closing chapters of the Bible are some of the most reassuring promises in the Bible. We have a description of the eternal city of Jerusalem coming down from heaven and a promise that righteousness will reign on Earth. God has pledged to make a new heaven and a new earth for His people with the Tree of Life and its healing river returning from a paradise that was lost when Adam sinned. Not only is all this good news, but it should affect the way we live today.

The promise of Jesus's return is intended to give God's people hope, but Jesus made it clear that it should do more than that. The primary importance surrounding Jesus's return is that people need to be ready for it. We demonstrate our readiness for the return of Jesus by taking the time to clean up our lives and take out the trash as we confess our sins and ask God for help removing it all. We demonstrate our readiness by staying close to Jesus and keeping our fellowship and intimacy with God a priority. We demonstrate our readiness for His return by loving others. Nothing proves that God's love has changed us more than when we love others as God has loved us. The more we understand and anticipate the soon return of Jesus, the more motivated we will be to act and live rightly today.

Jesus, I eagerly await Your return, but in the meantime, help me to live in a spiritual state of readiness. Strengthen me and give me the wisdom I need to be found serving You when You return.

Jesus is coming soon, and that should cause us to live for Him today.

Jesus in the New Year

"The life which I now live in the flesh I live by faith in the Son of God." (Galatians 2:20)

God is preparing you for eternity. This life is all about Jesus and what He wants to do in and through your life as He also prepares you for an eternity with Him. For many, a new year brings reflection on a year gone by and preparation for the year to come. A new year also brings the chance to turn the page and start fresh. Whatever your new year contemplations include, new year plans should not be made without Jesus. But just seeking to sprinkle a little more Jesus in your life is not enough.

As you look ahead to the new year, one of the primary resolutions Christians should make is to obey Jesus better and more completely. Obedience to Jesus's Word always brings fulfillment in life, so when Jesus gives us instructions, we need to obey immediately. If we wait until everything makes perfect sense before we obey, we might never obey. Sometimes understanding won't come until after we have obeyed. Faith is not demonstrated by what we believe, it is demonstrated by how we live considering what we believe. Too many Christians want just enough Jesus to get into heaven and enough of the world to get what they want here on Earth.

As you have spent the past year listening to the words of Jesus, it should have become painfully obvious that our faith should produce obedience to Jesus and obedience to His words bring blessing, and disobedience to Jesus and His words brings only trouble. For a new year filled with blessing and joy, let your faith motivate you to seek Jesus, serve Jesus, trust Jesus, wait on Jesus, and obey Jesus in everything.

Jesus, help me day by day to grow in the grace and in the knowledge of You until I can say, "It is no longer I who live, but Christ lives in me." (Galatians 2:20)

Obedience to Jesus is the key to spiritual insight and blessing.

ABOUT THE AUTHOR

Mike Lutz loves writing inspirational, memorable, and life-changing words. Having two non-fiction books published (*Discovering God's Will for Your Life, God Everyday: 365 Life Application Devotions*), Mike also has written an end times thriller, *The Armageddon Initiative*, the first book in the Jack Bishop series. Mike's most recent book, *Beyond the Gang*, is an amazing story of redemption and hope based on the life of former gang member Gabriel Nieves.

Mike lives in Southern California with his wife, Colette, where he works, writes, and serves in his local church. In Mike's spare time (what little there is of it), he enjoys reading, surfing, traveling, playing guitar, trying new food creations, and taking walks with his beagle.

For more information about Mike and his writing, go to www. MikeLutz.org.

ENDNOTES

1. N. T Wright, *Simply Christian: Why Christianity Makes Sense*, (New York: HarperCollins, 2006), 148.

2. Charles Swindoll, Insight for Today: "A Promise for Those Who Mourn," July 18, 2018, Insight for Living, https://www.insight.org/resources/daily-devotional/individual/a-promise-for-quot-those-who-mourn-quot.

3. Charles Swindoll, "A Promise for Those Who Mourn."

4. Martin Luther King, Jr. address at Syracuse University, Syracuse, New York, 1961, http://dailyorange.com/2019/01/syracuse-dr-martin-luther-king-jr-s-messages-resonate-half-century-later/.

5. Paraphrase of the maxim attributed to Ralph Waldo Emerson: "Sow a thought and you reap an action; sow an act and you reap a habit; sow a habit and you reap a character; sow a character and you reap a destiny.

6. St. John of the Cross, *The Collected Works of St. John of the Cross*, trans. Kieran Kavanaugh and Otilio Rodriguez (Washington, D.C.: ICS Publications, 1991), Kindle.

7. Quoted in E. M. Bounds, *Purpose in Prayer* (Racine, WI: Treasures Media, 2007), 7.

8. Jonathan Gottschall, *The Storytelling Animal: How Stories Make Us Human.*

9. John Calvin, *Commentary on a Harmony of the Evangelists, Matthew, Mark, and Luke*, vol. II (Edinburgh: The Calvin Translation Society, 1845), 131.

10. C. S. Lewis, *Mere Christianity* (New York: Macmillan, 1952), 40–41.

11. A. W. Tozer, *Man: The Dwelling Place of God* (Chicago: Moody, 2008), Kindle.

12. Martin H. Manser, ed., *The Westminster Collection of Christian Quotations,* (Louisville, KY: Westminster John Knox Press, 2001), 206.

13. Quoted in George R. Night, *The Cross of Christ: God's Work for Us* (Hagerstown, MD: Review and Herald, 2008), 62.

14. C. S. Lewis, *The Problem of Pain* (San Francisco: HarperCollins, 2001), 91.

15. George Campbell Morgan, *A First Century Message to Twentieth Century Christians* (New York: Fleming H. Revell, 1902), [203].

ALSO AVAILABLE FROM MIKE LUTZ

ALSO AVAILABLE FROM MIKE LUTZ

DISCOVERING GOD'S WILL FOR YOUR LIFE:
YOUR JOURNEY WITH GOD

MIKE LUTZ

"If you are looking for practical information relating to God's will for your life, this is the book for you."
—Levi Lusko
Pastor, Fresh Life Church

ALSO AVAILABLE FROM MIKE LUTZ

BEYOND THE GANG

"The events in this book are true and a real part of many youngster's lives today. I believe that lives will be touched by Gabriel's story!"

—Ernest " Kilroy " Roybal
Ex-Founder of The Mexican Mafia and
founder of Homiez 4 Christ Ministries

GABRIEL NIEVES & MIKE LUTZ

Made in the USA
Middletown, DE
03 December 2022

16860770R00230